The *Scalawag Scholar*'s Notes on Virginia 2012:

A Skeptical Commentary on the Frauds and Fables of the Virginia Gentleman

By Larry Lamar Yates

Published by
Social Justice Connections LLC
P.O. Box 2061
Winchester VA 22604
www.scalawagscholar.com

Copyright © 2012 by Larry Lamar Yates
All rights reserved. No part of this book may be reproduced in any form or by any means, electronic or mechanical, including photocopying, recording or by information storage and retrieval systems, without written permission from the publisher, except by a reviewer who may quote passages in a review.

Library of Congress Control Number:
2012913973
ISBN: 978-0-9819471-1-2

SOCIAL JUSTICE CONNECTIONS

"You have come here," said Powhatan bluntly to Smith in 1609, "not to trade, but to invade my people, and possess my country." (Philip Alexander Bruce, The Virginia Plutarch)

This Book's Origins

I came to the Commonwealth of Virginia in 1964 as a skeptical but eager to do good 14 year old world-traveled white teen liberal. Since then, being a do-gooder skeptic has been very good to me.

I have tended to distrust what conventional voices told me about where to go, who to talk to, and what to believe. Unconventional paths I foilowed instead have led me to hundreds of Virginians and hundreds of places in Virginia that I love and respect. My love and respect is what drives me to expose the FFV – the Frauds and Fables of Virginia – in this book.

These Frauds and Fables aren't just pretty stories. They are the central part of a 400 year old scam – a scam run by a cast of unsavory characters operating as "The Virginia Gentleman." And that scam is hurting real people today.

The Virginia Gentleman's scam deludes people with a phony history that undermines our will to take action, and with bogus "facts" that lead us astray. It frees an element of respectable criminals from responsibility for their quite amazing wrongdoing –

wrongdoing done in plain sight, yet invisible when looked at with myth-blurred eyes.

Thomas Jefferson wrote his Notes on the State of Virginia in 1781, responding to questions about Virginia posed to him by “a Foreigner of Distinction, then residing among us.” The information Jefferson painstakingly gathered about rivers, minerals, and so on is easily available to us today.

What’s harder to find is the truth about how our society is run, and how it got this way. So that’s what these Notes on Virginia seek to provide.

Today’s Virginia is not the idyllic republic of white rural yeomen that Jefferson envisaged – which is not all bad. But instead, it’s the center of an arrogant global empire. And it’s governed by a bitter and hard-hearted conservatism with roots going back to 1607.

It’s a place Jefferson would never recognize, and Pocahontas and her people couldn’t have imagined. But most of us Virginians still look at what’s around us, and see it through a soft lens of Frauds and Fables as the land of Pocahontas and Jefferson.

In the 1940s, James Branch Cabell, an heir to Jefferson's Virginia and by any measure a Virginia Gentleman, made a good start at debunking Virginia's Frauds and Fables. His book Let Me Lie was a satirical review of Virginia's fictitious history of itself. But Cabell believed the Virginia Gentleman was a dying species, and he was writing a sardonic obituary to his own kind.

Cabell's mockery of Virginia's "authorized version" taught me a lot, and is still a good read. But the Virginia Gentleman doesn't die. Like a B-movie monster, he just shows up in the next sequel in a new form. The post-Civil War Virginia Gentleman that Cabell knew, like the slave-owner or the adventurers of Jamestown, is gone. But the position of Virginia Gentleman has always found a new claimant. Today it's the Republican heirs to Jim Crow, who benefit from a suburban constituency that can be told pretty much anything is "Old Dominion tradition."

In this book, you will find information you already know, but looked at a little differently. And I think everyone will come away with some new and astonishing facts. But my main hope, dear reader, is that these Notes will strengthen your own healthy skepticism, while giving you a little more confidence in your ability to do good. Armed with those strengths of the mind and heart, I hope you will take your own less traveled paths in the real world behind the curtain of the Frauds and Fables.

What's Wrong With Fables, Anyway?

...Virginia,
Earth's only paradise,

Where nature hath in store
Fowl, venison, and fish,
  And the fruitful'st soil
  Without your toil
Three harvests more,
All greater than your wish.

And the ambitious vine
Crowns with his purple mass,
  The cedar reaching high
  To kiss the sky,
The cypress, pine,
And useful sassafras.
    from Michael Drayton's "To the Virginian Voyage," 1619

Like me, perhaps you enjoy Virginia's wily landscape –mountains that are hills, an ocean that is a bay, always underneath us the long rolling rise towards the west, everywhere streams born to run pure, baring the soil down to native rock.

And Virginia's native flora -- the grotesquerie of pokeweed, the subtle red hidden in fields of broomsedge, the pretty foolscap flowers of the jewelweed along streams marked by great sycamores.

And its fauna – the foolish white-tailed deer, the tireless turkey buzzards overhead, the night madness of the tiny screech owl, the delightful blue flash of the skink's tail.

But of course all of this – and much more -- was here long before anyone ever spoke the word "Virginia."

The Virginia Gentleman's fables take full advantage of the natural beauty around us. But what they really are is very focused propaganda supporting a certain kind of society.

In his 1887 translation of Aesop's Fables, George Townsend wrote that a fable "will necessarily seek to inculcate some moral maxim, social duty, or political truth." Aesop's Fables, though, each teach a different truth. Sometimes they even contradict one another.

But for Virginia Gentlemen, there is only one "truth," told over and over since 1607. All of their fables are of fine knightly men who take care of others in need and act nobly and efficiently in every situation.

James Branch Cabell described "the official history of Virginia as a work of art, 'in the more freely interpretative form of fiction.'"

This is no secret. I found most of the countervailing facts in this book either during my own Virginia wanderings or on my own somewhat overloaded bookshelves, with some help from the local library and the World Wide Web.

Of course, I never would have found these facts if I'd stayed on the Interstates, breathed only the treated air of the malls and fast food chains, if I'd stayed in the house come evening when Vanna White begins to turn The Wheel. I wanted to know about this place and who actually lives in it. Apparently you do too.

I also want to respect and support the folks who are being lied about – the priests and the prisoners, the artists and abolitionists, the welfare workers and the scholars, the martyrs and the mockers.

Readers will find that in this book African-Americans have a special place.

That's largely because they are at the center of Virginia history. African-Americans were much more pro-active and effective than most of us are encouraged to think, and I show that. They also were the group of people that the Virginia Gentleman was most obsessed with – at least, besides himself.

I am a white person, by which I mean mainly I have never had the experience of being treated as Black. So I of course do not speak for African-Americans. What I do try to do is to think and write about African-Americans as human beings, who have the same intelligence, emotional capacity and ability to change the world as anyone else. Given what I have read from "respectable" white sources while reading this book, I see that is not typical. Also, in my life I have been less prone to avoiding contact with African-Americans than most white people, so I am aware personally of some African-American people, practices and organizations that most white people are not.

I've picked up what I know about Virginians of all kinds at the meetings of neighborhood associations and cooperatives, in public housing and in communal group homes, participating in parades and funerals. I have been at election victories and community defeats, in the halls of the General Assembly and in the jury box, behind the fast food counter and speaking to a university graduation.

I have learned from homeopaths and housing counselors, hip hop radicals and homeless people, working class heroes and Richmond Main Street bankers, carpetbagger peaceniks and community-rooted African elders. And always from the poor, who are at home exactly where they are, despite all that the wealthy have stolen from them.

Yes, I have read from one end of the library to the other, and have found books with remarkable lessons in thrift stores and book stores and libraries across the Commonwealth. I still own far too many of them.

So I have the privilege of being able to poke a few holes in the Frauds and Fables of the Virginia Gentleman. And I think perhaps I have a duty to do so also. While Virginia is far from eternal, it will outlive me. And after I'm gone, this information will still be needed, at least until the Virginia Gentleman finally is only a joke.

Who is Telling These Fraudulent and Fabulous Tales?

There is a core group of men who know quite well that they have enormous power in Virginia, and who think of themselves as Virginia Gentleman. This group has no defined boundaries or membership. And they certainly do not have – or need -- an organized process for telling lies about themselves. There is no Virginia Gentleman Ministry of Propaganda.

An essential element of really good propaganda is that it seems to come from nowhere, or even better, from the depths of your own mind.

The Virginia Gentlemen – the real human variations on that theme – have more than four hundred years of self-serving deception and political and economic power behind them. With that history, hints and references are enough. Over the centuries, outright lies can become "common sense."

All of the Frauds and Fables here are documented, and are shown to have real impacts on the real world of blood and breath. We can see who they benefit. Exactly how and when we were deceived is not as important as not getting fooled again.

Why Scalawag?

A scalawag, according to Webster's Online Dictionary, was "a Southern white who joined the Republican party in the ex-Confederate South during Reconstruction."

A Ku Klux Klan supporter in 1868 had a more fervent description, printed under a not very subtle political cartoon showing two men hanging from a tree:

> **"Words are wanting to do full justice to the genus scallawag. He is a cur with a contracted head, downward look, slinking and uneasy gait; sleeps in the woods, like old Crossland, at the bare idea of a Ku-Klux raid.**
>
> **Our scallawag is the local leper of the community. Unlike the carpet-bagger, he is native, which is so much the worse. Once he was respected in his circle; his head was level, and he would look his neighbor in the face. Now, possessed of the itch of office and the salt rheum of Radicalism, he is a mangy**

dog, slinking through the alleys..." (Lester)

A scalawag takes a political stance contrary to that of the slave-owners and their heirs. A lot of people see scalawags, like carpetbaggers, in a negative light. But then terms like "liberal" and "social justice" have become cusswords to some.

The day of the true scalawag is long gone. But I have allied for more than 45 years of adult life in many ways with African-Americans in Virginia. And though I was very aware my father is a Southerner with ancestors who fought for the Confederacy, and though I was born in and have lived almost entirely in the South, my first political decision, made at the age of nine or ten, was to join with the Union side of a boys' war game.

I certainly expect that some of those who hear about this book – and perhaps even a few that read it – will call me worse than "cur," "leper," and "mangy dog." Hey, otherwise, I just haven't done my job.

I am actually stealing a gimmick from a book the brilliant political commentator Dick Gregory published in 1964. The title was the "N word," and in it he wrote to his deceased mother, "Dear

Momma -- Wherever you are, if ever you hear the word "n*****" again, remember they are advertising my book."

Scalawag will never be as common or as hurtful a word. But perhaps I can help bring the word "scalawag" back into public discussion. Perhaps I can remind my fellow pale-skinned Southerners that not every one of "us" really is "one of us."

Reader's Note

This book responds to each of 21 Frauds and Fables of the Virginia Gentleman in order, as listed on the next pages. At the end of the book there is a bibliography, in which I have tried to list all the sources of quotes I have used, as well as of any information that is not common knowledge. In the text I have made a note of the particular source for the information there in (parentheses). I hope you will find yourself drawn to read some of these books. Some of them are amazing, and I hope in the text I have made clear how much I owe those who told so much of the truth before I started this work.

Twenty-One Frauds and Fables of the Virginia Gentleman

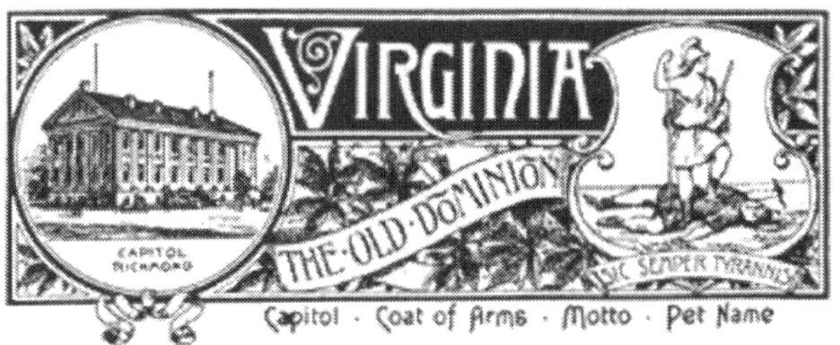

Capitol · Coat of Arms · Motto · Pet Name

POKEWEED
Natural Virginia's Ragged but Glamorous Botanical Retort To The Lawns of the Virginia Gentleman

Fraud and Fable Number One: Virginians Have Inherited A Rational And Gracious Society

Purpose: To distract us from looking at the facts right in front of us by having us believe we live in a fantasy.

Virginia, though lovely in so many ways, grew from bitter roots, and they have borne poisonous fruits. Virginia is not Hell, but there certainly is Hell in Virginia.

Some of the fruits that lie rotten along our highways today:

- Virginia's only rival for per capita executions in the world is the tiny family-owned dictatorship of Singapore.
- Virginia does less to welcome its ex-prisoners to full citizenship than any U.S. state but Kentucky.
- Virginia's economy is deeply tied to the continued toxic and climate-changing use of coal.
- Despite the rhetoric about government close to the people, Virginia's towns, counties and cities have less power over local issues than those of almost every other state. State government in Richmond determines whether localities can regulate spreading toxic sludge, or protect job rights of gay people, or require contractors to pay a living wage.

•

> **Charles played around the plantation 'big house' until he reached the age of five, then his play days ended... he was carried to the field to pull the grass from the young cotton... Now he went to his task daily; from early in the morning until late in the evening..... The long toilsome days completely exhausted the youngster. Often he would fall asleep before reaching home, and spend a good portion of the night on the bare ground. Awakening, he would find it quite a problem to locate his home in the darkness of night.**
> From 1937 interview of Charles Grandy born 1842, enslaved in what is now the City of Chesapeake. (Library of Congress)

- Virginia is more dependent, economically and politically, on military action than any region on earth. The preponderance of military power in the whole world  is directed from Virginia. Nor is this a new thing, nor just an accident of geography.

In 1839, the Virginia Military Institute was established; it was the first state military college in the U.S. Richmond was a major producer of military hardware during the nineteenth century, especially for the Confederacy, with the first arms manufacturing in the area dating back to 1797. War and preparation for war have always been on Virginia's policy agenda.

> **"It is ... beyond my understanding how the Europeans could have accepted the help, the food, the know-how of survival in this (for the Europeans) strange land; then they turned on the Indian Samaritans and wrested everything from them. They even attempted to wrest our very heritage from us. Greed is a very real disease. It can eat the very heart right out of man as it did to those Europeans."** Rev. Phyllis Branham Hicks (Whitlock)

- Virginia law protects landlords and property-owners even when that protection harms their neighbors and tenants– unless the property-owners are poor and Black.

- Virginia rulers are deeply resentful of independent women. A proposal to use an unnecessary medical process to sexually violate and humiliate women seeking abortions would have passed the General Assembly in 2012, until powerful and well-organized protests brought it to light. Back in 1746, an enslaved woman who had tried to poison her master was burned alive. Her name was Eve.

- Virginia's laws limiting the rights of lesbian, gay, bisexual, transgender and queer people are as harsh as those as any other state. One of Colonial Virginia's first executions was of a "sodomite."

- Virginia does almost nothing to protect its environment that it is not forced to by federal law.

- In Virginia, the poor are despised and the newcomer is repressed.

- Virginia has one of the most regressive state tax systems in the nation.

- Virginia has a per capita income higher than that of 41 states (just above Alaska and California), but its Southside and Southwest regions have a higher percentage of people in poverty than do those in any state but Mississippi.

What are the roots of this unkindness in such a beautiful and generally prosperous state?

Its roots are in the choices made by a small group of men in the 1600s, and by the generations of those who inherited their power. At every turn, they made choices that enriched themselves, increased the misery of others, concentrated power in a few hands, and harmed the soil and waters.

In the earliest years, their fear and greed led them to betray promises to their native allies, and to turn a business venture into an invasion, and then to turn the invasion into genocide, setting a pattern that was carried across a continent.

> **"We believe that the English colonists did not want Pocahontas to return to her homeland....Greed in combination with a surge of newly found power overrode efforts of the British Crown to work respectfully and peacefully with the Powhatan Nation. Some men who had not held elite status in England carved out enormous power for themselves in the English settlement."**(Custalow)

In Virginia's first century, wealthy and powerful Virginians divided their workers into "black" and "white," setting in motion the second great machinery of sin peculiar to the United States of America.

Conquest, slavery and fear of the other were not new to the world in the 1600s. But whiteness, as a political and social status, was invented here in Virginia.

The attachment to owning other human beings grew among Virginia's leaders. In 1861, it led them to participate in a military coup against the nation they had helped to create.

> **"In 1707 'King' Carter [the wealthiest man of his Virginia] requested court permission to chop off the toes of 'two incorrigible negroes.. named Barbara Harry & Dinah. County officials readily granted him 'full power to dismember,' a penalty applied to white men only for the most heinous crimes."** (Berlin)

They launched a fratricidal war fought to defend a despicable system of human exploitation.

In 1902, Virginia's rich and powerful consolidated their power in a harshly racist constitution that limited the power of all non-wealthy Virginians.

In the 1920s, this consolidated power came into the hands of one of the most powerful political bosses in U.S. history – Harry Flood Byrd – who stayed in power until his death in 1965, attacking progressive reforms for everyone in the nation from his solid Virginia base of "polite" white supremacy.

> **"When asked whether [a certain constitutional] clause might lead to discrimination, delegate Carter Glass replied: 'Discrimination! Why, that is exactly what we propose; that, exactly, is what this convention was elected for."**
> (Alexander, Ann)

In the 1950s, inspired by James J. Kilpatrick, a journalist with delusions of political grandeur, and under Byrd's leadership, Virginia led the South in opposing full human rights for the descendants of its slaves, working to undermine the Supreme Court's order for school integration.

In the 1960s, racism and attachment to power led men whose tradition had been in the Democratic Party for generations to move precipitously to the Republican Party and remake it in their image.

> **"[After quoting Kilpatrick's attack on the Supreme Court for the Brown v. Board of Education decision] My friends, if I should make such a vicious attack upon the**

> **Supreme Court of the United States because I did not agree with one of its decisions I would be branded as a loud-mouthed crackpot and raving radical."**
> Speaking From Byrdland, by Howard W. Carwile, whose cover blurb states that 'Carwile, as a 'white' Virginian, has rocked all Byrdland...'

Here in Virginia, the U.S. wars in Indochina and Iraq were planned; the arming of fundamentalist Afghanis and Saudis was dreamed up; the overthrowing of democratic governments from Guatemala to Iran to the Congo was coordinated.

Today, the heirs – in style if not in fact -- of the original group of settlers and legal bandits are still in power. These heirs, the Virginia Gentlemen, still believe they can do no wrong, and that the inferior classes and groups can do no right without their guidance. They still believe that whatever enriches them is proper.

> **"The [Virginia] oligarchy's 'velvet glove' approach to both the lower- and middle-class white population and to the entire black population has**

> **always been shaped by a code of 'gentlemanly' behavior that was almost 'royalist' in tone and appearance. This leadership has cared no more for the vast white population than it has for the collective black population since its perception of its role, in addition to being oligarchical, has been aristocratic."**
> (Moeser)

True, they see all around them the natural glory of the Commonwealth, which they could never have created.

They see on their own state flag the promise of the people's overthrow and destruction of all tyrants.

They hear, on Sunday mornings, the words of the rabbi who long ago put the poor and wounded first and condemned the accumulation of wealth and those who glory in it.

They know those words spoken by the man who is the greatest embodiment and the greatest nemesis of the Virginia Gentleman, Thomas Jefferson --"I tremble for my country when I reflect that God is just."

But they still continue, unable to imagine the failure of their schemes in their fog of Fraud and Fable.

Virginia Fraud and Fable Number Two: The Virginia Gentleman is Defined by Breeding and Character

Purpose: To encourage us to believe that Virginia's élite are by nature supposed to be in charge.

"In the seventeenth century, all the work of a public character was done by the foremost men in the community; whether it was to choose the site of a new town, or to pass on a new bridge, the county court almost invariably selected the commissioners from among the wealthiest and most prominent citizens. In naming these officers in the order appointing them, the court never failed to designate them as 'gentlemen'..."
(Bruce, 1907)

"...in any society self-made men will imitate those for whom greatness is a birthright. This explains the tremendous pressure to conform to the gentleman type..... The gentleman ... is heir to the aristocratic knowledge that he owes his

place to the structure of society, and not to anything that he can do especially well." (Weaver)

The history of a word can tell us a lot that is otherwise hidden.

Today, the left and the right, liberals and conservatives, are playing keepaway with the word "eugenics." Conservatives connect supporters of women's reproductive freedom back to early 20th century activist Margaret Sanger, who supported eugenic means of "improving the race." Liberals can as quickly point to the Nazi-like eugenics of racists like Virginia's own Walter Ashby Plecker (More on him in **Fable and Fraud Number 13, Virginia's Native People Vanished Long Ago, Replaced by Whites and Blacks**.) Everyone agrees – at least for now – that eugenics is bad stuff.

The word "gentleman," on the other hand, doesn't excite anyone these days. It shows up on public toilet doors, or to

GENTLEMEN

indicate that an establishment is one where women are unwelcome unless young and undressed.

But 'eugenics' and 'gentleman' both come from the same Latin source -- the word "gens," meaning race or ancestral line. Originally, being defined as a gentleman had nothing to do with how you acted, and everything to do with who your ancestors were (or were believed to be.) As Richard Weaver put it in the quote above, the gentleman was defined by the existing "structure of society," not by any personal actions or qualities.

It is not true, then, as many of us believe, that a gentleman is a man who is gentle. Gentle or genteel are adjectives that came along later, and are supposed to mean "like a gentleman." Similarly, today we might even call a dog "noble," but originally using the word for anyone not of noble (and human) descent would have been a serious criminal offense.

Philip Alexander Bruce, a chronicler of the Virginia Gentleman, wrote "the line of social separation between the gentleman and the common laborer was even sharper than that between the military officer and the ordinary soldier ... because, under the influence of inherited feeling and habit, and by the force of actual law, all Englishmen recognized and acted upon differences in social rank."

It is hard for us now to grasp that the Englishmen who founded Virginia believed sincerely that gentlemen were quite distinct from other humans in their heredity – that gentlemen belonged to a different “gens.”

Today, a family coat of arms is a silly thing we put next to the bowling trophies. When Virginia was settled, only the chosen few were allowed by law to have a coat of arms.

And the people with these silly shields on their mantelpiece were – or at least believed they should be -- Virginia’s early rulers precisely because they had them.

Bruce was a big fan of the silly system he described. Brent Tarter, in his 2007 article “Making History in Virginia,” writes that Bruce “was an influential voice among the southerners who were conspiring to unravel as much as possible of the social, economic, and democratic political changes that had been forced on the South as a consequence of its loss of the Civil War. It was the same old tune: ‘Carry Me Back.’” (Tarter, Making History)

Conservatives like Bruce or Weaver, of course, can’t or won’t see that society’s structure changes all the time, under all systems. Certainly Virginia has had a succession of bosses and political machinery. Almost all of them have claimed the Virginia Gentleman title, though, and that has been enough for conservatives to delude themselves that they are actually honoring a genuine tradition.

Throughout Virginia history, the Virginia Gentleman has been defined by heredity, or more often, by imagined heredity. We still hear today of “good families” and “good stock.” And those ideas are still as absurd as they were in the 1600s.

In a 1954 publication of the Virginia State Bar, attorney John Randolph Tucker was eulogized, with much attention paid to his ancestry, and the fact that from his great-grandfather on, each of his direct paternal ancestors was a member of the Virginia Bar. The eulogist was Eppa Hunton IV, himself the grandson of a Confederate officer who was also a U.S. Senator, and the son of the founder of Hunton and Williams, still one of Virginia's most powerful law firms. Hunton noted that "the career at bar of these five Tuckers covers the entire life span of our country and aggregates 264 years. Happily the tradition is being carried on in the sixth generation in direct line, John Randolph Tucker Jr. ...." (Muse) This sixth scion, however, was only briefly a Delegate to the General Assembly, and then served as a Richmond Circuit Court judge, not a very distinguished position. And the representative of the seventh generation, John Randolph Tucker III, was "merely" a police officer in Henrico County. Worse, after his retirement, this seventh scion was convicted of having struck and almost killed a highway construction worker while driving under the influence of alcohol. (Mckelway)

Still, the six generations of notable Tuckers seem to demonstrate the kind of pedigree that rationalizes the Virginia Gentleman myth.

But all we really learn from the story of succeeding Tuckers is that the sons of wealthy and successful men have a substantial head start in life, and also that these fortunate sons take care of each other. Such pedigrees certainly do not demonstrate that the next generation of the series will naturally be worthy to govern.

The laws of statistics teach us that there is only one situation where it makes sense to expect the next throw of the dice to be the same as the last six throws. That situation? When the dice are loaded.

The Virginia Gentlemen have always had to struggle to impose on others their belief that they are deserving of power from birth. People have a frustrating tendency not to submit to their betters, even in Virginia.

Modern historian Kathleen Brown describes a more insecure gentry than Bruce portrays. She suggests that Virginia Gentlemen "could boast land, wives and servants that other men lacked; but these did not necessarily make them great men in the eyes of their neighbors and tenants." So they passed laws that limited the wearing of gold and silk to the highest ranking Virginia Gentlemen, and brutally punished those who disrespected authority. As "colonials whose dependent and marginal relationship to

London diminished their status," Virginia Gentlemen "could never achieve enough success to reassure themselves that the foundation of their identity would not collapse." (Brown)

By 1907, Bruce's own generation of Virginia Gentlemen were engaged in a struggle to shore up the foundation of their identity. The myths of past Virginia Gentlemen could only help.

Shortly before Bruce wrote, a British observer of Virginia, Arthur Granville Bradley, published a book of memoirs, Other Days, Recollections Of Rural England And Old Virginia, 1860-1880. He came from the land where gentlemen were invented. His book mocked "the aristocratic ancestor which

Virginians, in sheer naïveté and harmless vanity, have established in a shadowy way to their own satisfaction."

Writing about the family lines leading back to Jamestown that Bruce extolled, Bradley teased that "The ladies knew all their second cousins twice-removed throughout the State, and who their respective fathers and mothers, possibly even grandfathers and grandmothers, had married. But when they got further back they became, for the most part, vague, decorative, and fanciful."

As supercilious and snobbish as Bradley was, it seems he accurately captured the essence of the Virginia Gentleman – a self-serving hoax.

On the other hand, though the aristocratic claims of the earliest Gentlemen were a bit dubious, they were far from being rough-hewn entrepreneurs or skilled pioneers.

The Virginia colony began as a government-subsidized business operation, and everyone who started out with a substantial amount of land had it to some extent because of his government connections.

As the colony grew and diversified, it helped immensely to "know somebody," or as we would say, to "network." Then ever more than now, élite networks were networks of white men.

> **"One of the most common features in the background of successful slaveholders was a generous patron who provided the contacts, the education and often the capital to get the incipient planter going... Devereux Jarratt lost out on his inheritance when both parents died without leaving a will. By hiring himself out as a teacher to a succession of wealthy planters, however, Jarratt established the contacts that secured him the private funding for a religious education in England. He returned to office as an Episcopal minister in Bath Parish, Virginia. From that office, he built up a comfortable estate that in 1782 included twenty-four slaves, eleven horses, and twenty-six cattle."**(Oakes)

And as time went on, certain families and their friends got a solid hold on the levers of power.

> **"Virginia saw the rise of families of gentry who**

intermarried for generations and built up a landed aristocracy....Relationship was noted to a degree that made the term 'Virginia cousin' a symbol for remote [*and perhaps mythical? – Yates]* **kinship. A strong caste spirit grew up... from 1670 to 1691 every official position in Henrico County was filled by a member of the Randolph family or of two other families...Thus colonial Virginia developed a privileged hereditary bureaucracy so that offices were handed from father to son and the social system became fossilized with the impedimenta of lineage."** (Calhoun)

Of course, all of these practices survived into our day. After all, we are still living with the remnants of the Byrd Machine, which carried successful Virginia Gentlemen into the last third of the twentieth century.

Virginia Gentlemen as Masters

To Philip Alexander Bruce, "Such men as William Byrd, Richard Lee, Adam Thoroughgood, and the elder Nathaniel Bacon, men who owned many slaves and thousands of acres of land, [who] besides filling the principal political offices, occupied in their respective parts of Virginia the same position of influence as that occupied by the largest landowners in the English shires." Bradley, with no system to defend, and with a basis for comparison of the two "aristocracies," scorned such comparisons. (Bruce, 1907)

But there was another critical difference between the English and Virginia Gentleman, besides the relative paltriness of the Virginia "aristocracy."

In England, only one kind of "gens," of ancestral line mattered. Either you could claim ancestors from the gentry, or you were one of the common folk, who were oddly described as having "no ancestors." In Virginia, by the end of its first century, there was another kind of ancestral line that mattered the most of all – the line of the "one drop of blood" that could "pollute" any family with African-ness.

This radical difference from English society is what sustained the Virginia Gentleman, at least as a myth. As time went on, whites here in North America showed little interest in maintaining the old English class divisions. In fact, one hears that some of them supported the revolutionary idea that they were "equal" to their gentlemen betters, and even wanted a so-called "Constitution," "Bill of Rights," and various other arrangements that tended to undermine the supremacy of the well-born.

Slavery and Revival of The Gentleman

> **…. the presence of the indentured servant and slave….as we have seen, had such an important effect in maintaining the class differences inherited from England.** (Bruce, 1907)

The master-slave relationship gave Virginia's rulers a new way to believe in their God-given superiority and authority, and the specialness of their "gens." The Virginia Gentlemen were particularly delighted that, as they saw it, the African "gens" was so complementary to theirs. Obviously, to them, they had been born to be slave-masters – and the African, of course, had been born to be enslaved.

By the 1830s, this myth was full-fledged, up to and including some defensiveness about the North and its selfish mongrel people.

> **"Our northern *brethren*, as you call them," said B--, "never can take this view of it. They have not the qualities which would enable them to comprehend the negro character. Their calculating selfishness can never understand his disinterested devotion. Their artificial benevolence is no interpreter**

of the affections of the unsophisticated heart. They think our friend Jack here to be even such as themselves, and cannot, therefore, conceive that he is not ready to cut his master's throat, if there is any thing to be got by it. They know no more of the feelings of our slaves, than their fathers could comprehend of the loyalty of the gallant cavaliers from whom we spring; and for the same reason. The generous and self-renouncing must ever be a riddle to the selfish."
(Tucker)

This masterpiece of self-deception is from The Partisan Leader, a novel by a law professor at the College of William and Mary, and, yes, a relative of all those other Tuckers. It prefigured the Confederacy and the Civil War, and was as much political propaganda as literary fiction. It had a plot about divided brothers, an honorable man protecting his kinswoman, and various other romantic themes. But its main focus was on making the case for Southern secession. It assumed the birthright superiority of Southern white men.

In fact, the God-given symbiosis of white master and black slave was seen as natural and perfect even after "the war" by the Virginia Gentleman. Thomas Nelson Page, an extremely popular postwar novelist of the Lost Cause myth and of a prewar Virginia Golden Age, used fictional ex-slaves to tell his stories of the good ol' days. According to an online project of the University of Alabama Library "The South's upper class embraced [Page's] 'Marse Chan' as the defining description of their antebellum civilization .." This 'Tale of Old Virginia,' which includes duels, heroism, and a Juliet and Romeo romance ending in appropriately romantic deaths, is told to us in the supposed voice of a still deeply loyal ex-slave after the white protagonists are all dead. It is written as if a mortal peasant with his crude broken speech were telling a story about gods.

It is hard enough to believe that readers could stomach Page's white characters, with their exaggerated virtues. But Page's African-American characters, who remained servile decades after Marse had been killed in The War and freedom had come, were as far from real humanity as any creature Edgar Allen Poe imagined.

Brent Tarter sums up "the Virginia Novel tradition" as "glorifying the past as if all the slaves had been happy, all the planters genteel, and no one else there." (Tarter, Making History)

Virginia Gentlemen and Their Ladies

But of course, there were others there – including the Virginia white lady. As a matter of mundane biology, after all, without her there could be no more Virginia Gentlemen. But in the Virginia Gentleman's ideology, she had other seemingly more important (and certainly more mentionable) functions.

As the word "gentle" evolved over the centuries towards its current usage, it first meant "noble, generous, courteous, polite." At a later stage, it came to mean "soft" or "tender" or "mild," words we would consider more likely synonyms today. (Oxford)

These earlier words imply condescension. They describe qualities people in power may choose to show towards others with less power. The Virginia lady was believed to have been created to be, along with the slave, a person to be condescended to in a kind and protective way.

Protection of women – being a lady's champion – had always been one aspect

of knightly chivalry. But though seventeenth century England was not a peaceful place, it lacked the opportunities for derring-do of King Arthur's days. In Virginia, however, there were real and very alien enemies. First there were the "savages" – the native people -- and then there were the enslaved, a permanent potential enemy right in their own homes and workplaces. Virginia Gentlemen were always at the ready, many of them serving in local militias. That they were violent, but could curtail their violence where it concerned the ladies – that was their claim to nobility.

As with the supposed mutual affection between the master and slave, there is no evidence that this chivalrous attitude towards women actually existed. Did white male Southerners abuse or rape or disrespect "their" women less than other men? More likely, as Stuckey writes. "behind the mythology of the southern gentlemen and southern belles were, in the overwhelming majority of cases, the coarse people and coarse culture that one might suspect ... in a society so dependent on force..."

Another sometime Virginian, Edgar Allen Poe, in one of his macabre tales, describes a moment that may more accurately portray what lay behind chivalry.

In the story "The Fall of the House of Usher," the heir of the House, the victim of a "constitutional and family evil," has buried his twin sister, and then, in a moment of terrible insight, realized he has buried her alive, and that she is returning for him.

> **".. then without those doors there did stand the lofty and enshrouded figure of the lady Madeline of Usher.... For a moment she remained**

> **trembling and reeling to and fro up on the threshold – then, with a low moaning cry, fell heavily inward upon the person of her brother, and in her horrible and now final death-agonies, bore him to the floor a corpse, and a victim to the terrors he had dreaded."**

Could Poe, who in his intoxicated genius saw so much, have drawn here a powerful truth behind the gracious façade of male-female relations among the Southern gentry? Was the Southern lady, having been buried alive by her beloved gentleman, yearning to bring about his death also?

Hundley's Social Relations

In 1860, just before the Civil War began, Virginia-born Daniel Hundley published his Social Relations in the Southern States. The book is one of the more subtle defenses of the slavery South. He mocks other Southern whites (mostly wannabe "Southern gentlemen)," and assures his supposed Northern readers that no society is perfect, neither North nor South.

Still, Hundley spares no cliché in assuring us that almost all slaves are happy, as demonstrated by their cheerful songs and banjo-picking back in the quarters. And he is just as sure that the daughters and wives of the slave-owners are happy with their excellent lot:

> **And if in nothing else, in this at least is the Southern Gentleman to be commended--*he educates his daughters at home.* Hence the well-bred and well-educated daughters of the Summer Land, are the model women of the age in which we live ... Ah! thou true-hearted daughter of the sunny South, simple and unaffected in thy manners, pure in speech as thou art in soul, and ever blessed with an inborn grace and gentleness of spirit lovely to look upon, fitly art thou named:**
>
> **"A perfect woman, nobly planned,**
> **To warm, to comfort, and command;**
> **And yet a spirit still, and bright**
> **With something of angelic light."**
>
> **Such a woman can well-leave to the strong-minded of her sex all political twaddle and senseless disputes about the "Rights of Woman," alienable**

or inalienable: for she will always be loved and admired the wide world over."
(Hundley)

Like the Africans he holds in slavery, the women "of" the Virginia Gentleman are born to be, conveniently enough, exactly what he needs. And like the slaves, they are delighted to be what their nature determines they must be.

The most famous expression of the "political twaddle" that Hundley scorned was, of course, the Declaration of Sentiments of the Seneca Falls Women's Rights Convention in 1848. And perhaps that Declaration's most powerful overarching statement was that man "has usurped the prerogative of Jehovah himself, claiming it as his right to assign for her a sphere of action, when that belongs to her conscience and to her God." The sophisticated Harvard grad Hundley found it easy to mock Northern abolitionists, and even the recently executed John Brown. But he does not mention this devastating feminist critique, though he must have known about it.

However, in a book that flaunts its cynicism and hardly mentions religion, Hundley does turn to the Bible and the authority of Saint Paul to justify the Southern Gentleman's control of "his" women:

> **"...when the Apostle commanded that women should not be suffered to speak in public, but on the contrary to content themselves with their humble household duties, he not only spoke as the inspired servant of God, but also as a man possessed of uncommon common-sense. For since to the family belongs the education and gradual elevation of the race, it is most important that mothers should be pure, peaceable, gentle, long-suffering and godly--which they never can be, if permitted or inclined to enter the lists and compete with selfish and lustful man for the prizes of place and public emolument."**(Hundley)

Attacking Feminism Before Attacking Feminism Was Cool

William R. Taylor's critique of the Southern white myth, Cavalier and Yankee, was published in 1961, before the Second Wave of feminism. But Taylor was nevertheless acute enough to see that the "plantation fiction" of Southern white male writers was a response not only to militant abolition, but to "the first stirrings of the movement for woman's rights..." He suggested not only that the male writers were seriously alarmed by feminist ideas, but that "Southern women were in a certain sense being bought off, offered half the loaf in the hope they would not demand more."

Taylor quotes South Carolinian Mary Boykin Chesnut on some of the anxieties of the wives and daughters of slave-owners. One was the fear of insurrection or even just plain murder. Chesnut wrote, after a neighbor was killed by slaves, "I am sure I shall never sleep again without this nightmare of horror haunting me." The blatant fact of white men's slave children was another; Chesnut wrote that a man's "wife and daughters ... are supposed never to dream of what is as plain before their eyes as the sunlight."

Of course, as troubled and subordinate as Chesnut's life was, she was still a wealthy woman with slaves to meet many of her daily needs.

The Virginia Gentleman's chivalry did not extend, even in theory, to enslaved women. They were simply seen as animals, as property, as whatever the white man chose to see them as. Rape and violence were merely the harshest expression of a total disrespect. This touching story is about one of the subtle aspects of this disrespect.

A woman was nursing her child and observing the Union troops entering her part of Virginia, when one officer patted her child on the head and asked her child's name. She said the child was Charlie, like his father; the officer asked what the father's name was, and she told him "Charlie Sparks." The soldier took his leave with "Goodbye, Mrs. Sparks," treating her as a married woman with a respectable place in society. Of course, she had never before in her life been addressed with that kind of respect by a white person, and she never forgot the moment. (Sterling)

All white women, on the other hand, were in theory equally deserving of the Virginia Gentleman's gallant respect. But the less wealthy majority of white women were no fainting flowers of gentility. They were hard-working rural women, though they were still supposed to follow all the rules that applied to upper-class women. Their version of the "humble household duties" that Hundley assigned them to was carried out not in a mansion, but in a rough cabin far from any amenities, in a society without free public education, public health measures, with little access to divorce or any legal protection, and with few respectable opportunities for women's economic independence.

Hundley's book divides Southern whites into several classes, one of which is "Poor White Trash." He suggests this is a small group, and he describes them as the descendants of "outcasts and paupers, picked up in the back slums and cellars of London, and transported at the public charge to Virginia, and there sold in the market-house to the highest bidder.." As so often, the Virginia Gentleman's theories are theories of breeding. These "Trash" are not poor by circumstance, or because of individual failings or family dysfunction. To Hundley, they are doomed by their heredity, just as surely as the Gentleman is blessed by his.

Most non-slaveholding white Southerners, however, were struggling not with their flawed heredity, but with harsh socio-economic realities.

> **".. about three-quarters of all white families owned no slaves.. they ranged in status from yeomen famers, who together with their wives and children worked with a hired slave or two during .. to tenants ... [working] either on their own holdings or hired out to neighbors... to squatters and transients..."**
> "Black and White Hands in a Slaveholders' Republic" from American Work by Jacqueline Jones.

All of this work took place in an agricultural economy based on tobacco or cotton. Both commodities were traded globally and subject to regular booms and busts far beyond the control of small farmers.

Of course, women were never completely powerless, despite the Virginia Gentleman's machinations. Some of the successful struggles of women in Virginia are discussed in another Note.

“Let Women and Negroes Alone”

In yet another novel of the South, the title character, George Balcombe, responds to the idea of educating women –“Let women and negroes alone ... Leave them in their humility, their grateful affection, their self-renouncing loyalty, their subordination of the heart ...”

Edgar Allen Poe is not often counted among the true Virginia Gentlemen. But he lived in their world, and accepted its standards, at least at a superficial level. Swallow Barn, a popular novel of that world by John Pendleton Kennedy received his praise in a review: “We have not yet forgotten, nor is it likely we shall very soon forget, the rich simplicity of diction -- the manliness of tone -- the admirable traits of Virginian manners, and the striking pictures of still life, to be found in Swallow Barn.”

In that book so praised by Poe, we find this portrait of Frank Meriwether, a Virginia Gentleman.

"....it is very pleasant to see Frank's kind and considerate bearing towards his servants and dependents. His slaves appreciate this, and hold him in most affectionate reverence, and, therefore, are not only contented, but happy under his dominion...

It is refreshing to behold how affectionately vain [his wife] is of Frank, and what deference she shows to him in all matters, except those that belong to the home department; for there she is confessedly and without appeal, the paramount power. It seems to be a dogma with her, that he is the very "first man in Virginia," an expression which in this region has grown into an emphatic provincialism. Frank, in return, is a devout admirer of her accomplishments, and although he does not pretend to have an ear for music, he is in raptures at her skill on the harpsichord, when she plays at night for the children to dance ...On these occasions, he stands by the instrument, and nods his head, as if he

comprehended the airs.”
(Kennedy)

He takes everything, gives nothing, and condescends even to his wife. As Shakespeare’s Hamlet observed, “one may smile, and smile, and be a villain.” Indeed. One may smile and be courtly and polite and always do what he believes is best for you – and be a villain. And if you are fortunate, and you live in Virginia, your life will be recorded as exemplary – and you will be remembered as a Virginia Gentleman.

Fraud and Fable Number Three: The Virginia Gentleman is Frank and Decent

Purpose: To distract us from the constant con game that the Virginia Gentleman is always running on us and the ways that he so effectively manipulates us.

> **“To begin with his pedigree, then, we may say, the Southern Gentleman comes of a good stock. Indeed, to state the matter fairly, he comes usually of aristocratic parentage; for family pride prevails to a greater extent in the South than in the North. In Virginia, the ancestors of the Southern Gentleman were chiefly English cavaliers, after whom succeeded the French Huguenots and Scotch Jacobites.”**(Hundley)

> **“.. around about the whole mansion and domain [of Usher] there hung an atmosphere peculiar to themselves … an atmosphere which had no affinity with the air of heaven, but which has reeked up from the decayed trees, and the gray walls, and the silent tarn, in the form of an inelastic vapor or gas – dull, sluggish, faintly discernible, and leaden-hued.”** (Poe)

For those who believe in human pedigrees, that we are each mainly an expression of our ancestry, the only reasonable explanation of the Virginia Gentleman is a literally monstrous one.

As in Poe's tale of the family and the mansion of Usher, there must be some inherent biological defect which makes the Virginia Gentleman cruel, deceptive and vainglorious.

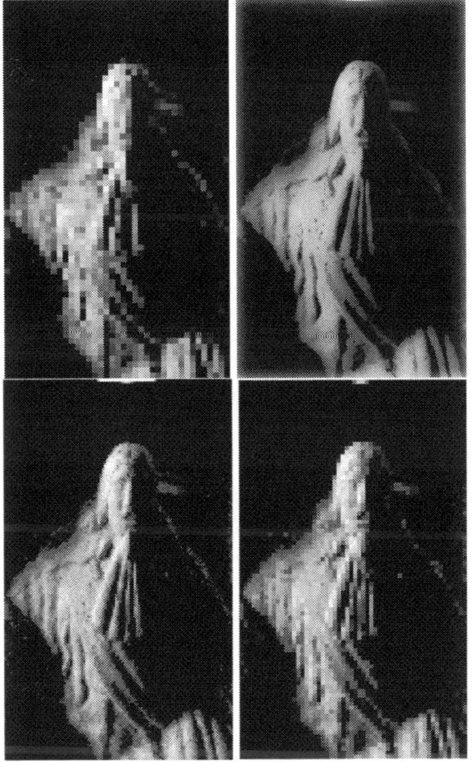

Luckily, we live in an age where we can pretty much dismiss human pedigrees as determining character. We can also dismiss the idea that the Virginia Gentleman (or his English ancestors) really come from one strain of humanity, Cavalier or otherwise. They are as much mongrels as the rest of us here in the U.S. of A.

So the Virginia Gentleman is not biologically distinct from the rest of us. Yes, he is different from us. He is abnormal. But it's a difference in behavior, not heredity.

The history of the Virginia Gentleman is like the process of ethnic succession in organized crime. We know that the Mafia succeeded Irish gangs, and then sometimes was in turn succeeded by Asian or African-American organized crime – and yet the basic goals and practices of organized crime stayed pretty much the same. The main difference is that our urban syndicates have a much shorter, and much less impressive, criminal history than does the Virginia Gentleman.

Working the Race Scam

The skill that most defines the Virginia Gentleman is the skill of deception.

Those of us who are amateurs at deception tend to think it involves grandiose lies and incessantly pounding propaganda into your victim's brain. But the true art of Virginia Gentlemanly deception is so subtle that you may never know you have been deceived. It's a nod and a wink, a slightly hushed tone of voice, perhaps a reference to "them." When the best of the Virginia Gentlemen fool you, you not only don't think you been fooled, you think you've been let in on the inside story.

The Virginia Gentleman is not only the master of, but the inventor of, the biggest scam in modern history, and perhaps in all history – the scam of race. Even today, tens of millions of people in this country still don't know it's a scam.

Some of the facts of the history of race are beginning to creep into public knowledge, but just in case you missed them:

1) *There is no biological basis for dividing humanity into "races," since all human beings are in the*

same species, and since there are probably no genetically pure groups of humans, and certainly none outside of Africa.

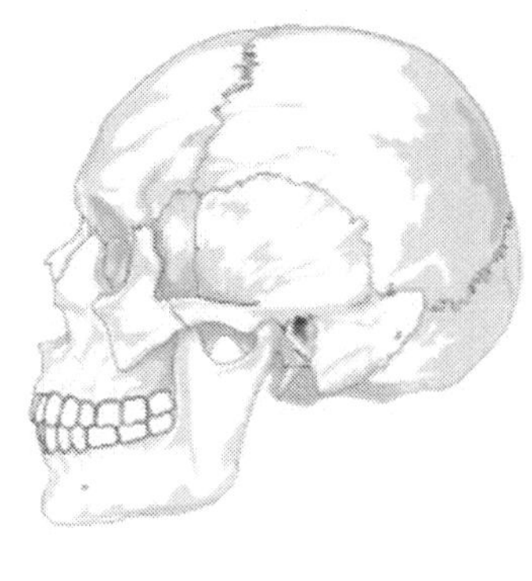

2) *In addition, culture and ancestry are entirely separate. Just because a person has light skin and blue eyes does not make her or him culturally European, any more than squinting your eyes makes you able to speak Chinese.*

3) *In medieval Europe, many people really believed that the aristocracy were of a different "race" or line of descent from the common people. Since this was obviously easy to disprove, it shows that some people will believe pretty much anything about their ancestry that strengthens their claim to high status.*

4) *Being, or not being, of African descent became critically important in seventeenth century Virginia, and soon in other*

British colonies, and then elsewhere, when people of African descent were defined as slaves for life and for generations to come, with no legal rights.

5) *Then anthropology (a discipline that, in the words of one anthropologist "emerged along with the expansion of Europe and the colonization of the non-Western world")(Lewis, Diane), provided scientific cover for the various racial divisions that had been invented.*

6) *In a kind of intellectual feedback process, the work of race scientists then was used as justification by defenders of slavery and subsequently by defenders of discrimination against people of color, up to and including contemporary racist books like The Bell Curve.*

If any of these points sound wrong to you, you need to do a little studying. If any of it really makes you mad, you might want to look into why a few generally accepted facts upset you so much.

Anyway, in the late 1600s, Virginia introduced the race scam in its earliest form. Here is a somewhat technical explanation of what happened, from the pen of Ted Allen, one of the most important theoreticians of race in our time, a largely self-taught revolutionary writer who spent long hours in various archives in Virginia.

> **A new social status was to be contrived that would be a birthright of not only Anglos, but of every Euro-American, a "white" identity designed not only to set them "at a distance" from the African-American bond-laborerers, but at the same time to enlist European-**
> **Americans of every class as active, or at least passive, supporters of capitalist agriculture based on chattel bond-labor. The introduction of this counterfeit of social mobility was an act of "social engineering," the essence of which was to reissue long-established common law rights, "incident to every free**

man," but in the form of "white" privileges: the presumption of liberty, the right to get married, the right to carry a gun, the right to read and write, the right to testify in legal proceedings, the right of self-directed physical mobility, and the enjoyment of male prerogatives over women. The successful societal function of this status required that not only African-American bond-laborers, but most emphatically, free African-Americans be excluded from it... (Allen)

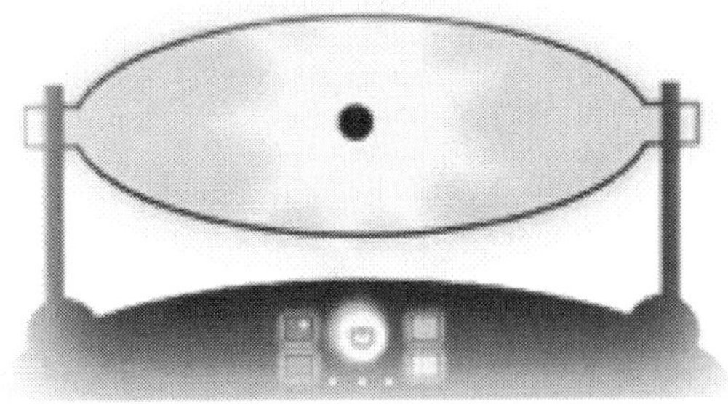

To us today, this may sound as if Allen is saying the early Virginia Gentleman was involved in some kind of global conspiracy.

But today white supremacy has become one of the most powerful institutions on the planet. In the 1600s, that wasn't even imaginable.

The early Virginia Gentlemen were ambitious, but they hardly guessed they were laying the groundwork for a new world order. They just wanted to ensure an obedient work force for their tobacco plantations, one that would have no reliable allies if they rebelled.

This is hardly an unusual tactic for bosses, who today set blue collar against white collar, women against men, younger workers against older ones, and so on, all the time. Of course, the bosses of seventeenth century Virginia were not just employers; they were also the government (as bosses often are), and to a large extent, they were even the church. So they could pass laws like this one, condemning millions of people to be born into lifelong servitude:

> **It is enacted that all servants. . . which shall be imported into this country either by sea or by land, whether Negroes, Moors, mulattoes or Indians who and whose parentage and native countries are not Christian at the time of their first purchase by some Christian. . . and all Indians, which shall be sold by our neighboring Indians, or any other trafficking with us for slaves, are hereby adjudged, deemed and taken to be slaves to all intents and purposes any law, usage, or custom to the contrary notwithstanding.** (Virginia General Assembly, 1682)

And, of course, the rewards those bosses stood to gain were far beyond any a midlevel corporate manager could imagine today.

> **"Having enslaved black people and confined the remaining white servants to a subordinate place in Chesapeake society, the grandees knit themselves**

together through strategic marriages, carefully crafted business dealing and elaborate rituals... By midcentury, the great planters had forged an interlocking directorate ... From their new place atop Chesapeake society, planters began to spin out a vision of social relations that emphasized deference and authority. The creation of the plantation regime transformed patronage into paternalism and a new sense of mastership emerged." (Berlin)

The first Virginia Gentlemen did not know their race scam would keep them, or others like them, in power for centuries to come. While satisfying their own greed, they laid a foundation that the succeeding generations of Virginia Gentlemen, and the master class across the South and beyond, could build on.

Racism: A Family Tradition

Over the centuries, Virginia Gentlemen and their various colleagues have created a variety of elaborate racial ideologies that have changed as society has changed. They ranged from imagining that Africans needed less oxygen than whites to explaining racial disparity as resulting from different family structures. But in every case, the theories presented the greedy, ignorant and careless Virginia Gentlemen as the rational leaders of society, protecting the rest of us from flawed people of African descent.

Meanwhile, the people of African descent did far more than their share of the most unpleasant work and the work that needed the most planning and thinking.

Deceiving other people is easier if you fool yourself. The Virginia Gentleman has always had an elaborate machinery of self-deception, from fine universities to fantastic and formulaic fiction to ceremonies of the governing classes in praise of themselves – to, the grandest of all, their ludicrous rewriting of history.

Using People With "Benevolence"

The second crucial skill of the Virginia Gentleman is the skill of using personal relationships, especially with his perceived inferiors, in a way that appears to be benevolent.

In other words, the Virginia Gentle man always strives to be a patron, a patriarch, patronizing, and providing (or appearing to provide) patronage – following in the sacred footsteps of the Virginia Gentleman who was the Father of our Country.

Rhys Isaac's Pulitzer Prize-winning The Transformation of Virginia 1740-1790 is a social history of the changes that undermined the position of the plantation gentry by 1790.

There have been several such transitions, with "The Virginia Gentleman" of the day being overthrown by a new power structure, which then claims the title for itself. The Virginia Gentleman, after all, is above all a fraud. He claims to be the heir of a direct line running through the gentry of the 1600s to the plantation owners of the 1850s, and so on. Politically and organizationally, this "direct line" is phony. Power in Virginia, as everywhere else, has followed economic shifts and demographic changes. Today's Virginia Gentleman probably wouldn't know a tobacco plant if if bit him, nor would he be much good at brutally managing child labor in coal mines and industrial plants. Nevertheless, this imaginary heritage has a very real impact, like the imaginary concept of race, to this day, on how power is exercised in Virginia.

Isaac shows us how the plantation gentry operated to maintain power. They used deceptive behaviors the Virginia Gentleman has used often since.

In eighteenth century Virginia, elections were completely public events, and Virginia Gentlemen both dominated the process and won all the offices. As Isaac wrote, "Elections provided for the endorsement of the most eminent of gentlemen to attend the legislature at the center of the province as custodians and revisers of the body of laws itself." The whole election process "clearly showed the paternalistic dominance of the gentry," as the wealthy and eminent bought rum for all those voting and graciously acknowledged each vote they received as a tribute from their lessers.

By the time of Harry Byrd, despite apparently radical changes like the secret ballot and supposedly universal manhood suffrage, the process was little changed. Byrd's "organization," as his friends preferred it be called, or "machine," as critics named it, was built on cronyism and patronage – a system he had literally been born into. You don't need to watch people vote if your myths have been in their brains since childhood – and if the "wrong" people are blocked from voting.

In the biography Harry Byrd of Virginia, Ronald Heinemann refers to Byrd's "vast number of friends across the state," who included "courthouse politicians," "General Assembly cronies," and "associates in the business world." "Many of them," Heinemann notes, " had been friends of his father," and he returned their favors of support and information with "patronage, support for legislation, and a box of apples at Christmas time." The relationshipsHeinemann describes as Byrd's "two great friendships" are with his two closest political associates. And of course from these "friends" of Byrd's, his organization's reach extended into the local governments and business that he helped, and that helped him, and on to the clients that those local men patronized.

Undoubtedly, Harry Byrd believed that these relationships, or many of them, were genuine friendships. But what sustained them all was preserving power and privilege. Heinemann describes Byrd as having an "obsession with his personal integrity," and says tellingly that "like the plantation owners of the antebellum South, Byrd lived the code of the gentleman...."

Of course all of us, as humans seeking to be honest and humane, should be concerned with our personal integrity.

But what Heinemann calls "integrity" is what I would call pride. Byrd was suspicious of those with ideas or proposals he had not endorsed, and responded bitterly to personal attacks. His so-called "integrity" did not include having the integrity to question his own beliefs and actions.

Such a man is no-one's real friend. Harry Byrd's life was consumed with political calculation. He was a master of relationships – but not relationships of depth or value. He was a true Virginia Gentleman to the (empty) core.

Political Opportunism

The Virginia Gentleman, of course, claims he consistently follows in the conservative and traditional ideological footsteps of his forefathers.

This is sheer horsefeathers. In fact, he is a skilled opportunist, who has changed his alliances to meet his needs over and over.

- ✓ 1607-1775: Loyalty to the King of England (with occasional detours like Bacon's Rebellion and the confusion around the English Civil War)
- ✓ 1775-1861: Loyalty to the United States of America
- ✓ 1861-1865: Loyalty to the Confederacy
- ✓ 1865-1973: Loyalty to the Democratic Party
- ✓ 1973-?: Loyalty to the Republican Party

Every time, of course, the Virginia Gentleman swore oaths and assured everyone his loyalty was permanent and unchanging.

Yes, this country we live in has had a complicated history. But still, no group other than Southern whites has a political history this checkered.

After all, these were not minor shifts in loyalty. We all, as United States loyalists, understand the shift from George III to George Washington. But the willingness of some Virginians, whose state gave so many leaders to the Revolution, to try to

destroy the United States from 1861 to 1865 is hard to understand or justify.

After the Civil War, the Virginia Gentleman and his Southern comrades became Democrats. As such, they supported Andrew Jackson's style of imperial democracy. They voted and campaigned against the Wall Street and railroad wealth of the Republicans, standing up for the (white) "common man." Though the Virginia Gentlemen were certainly shaky Democrats by the 1920s, they stayed with the Party through the New Deal (which was massively popular among working-class Southern whites.)

Then the Democrats started including African-Americans in their constituency. The Republican Party, meanwhile, had moved on from its anti-racist Radical Republican past. Whee! The Virginia Gentleman and his counterparts jumped ship again, joining the traditional party of corporate wealth that they had supposedly hated since the 1860s.

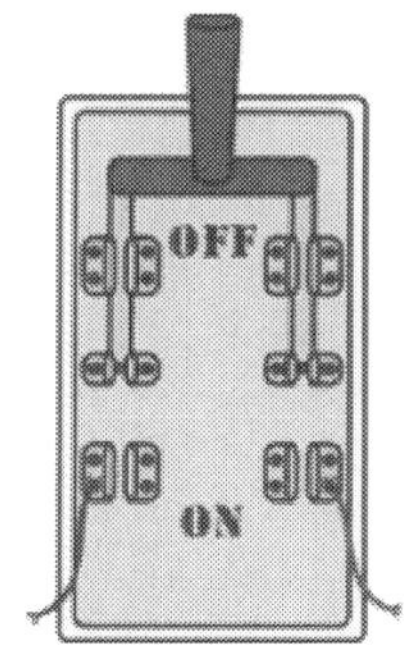

Of course, there is one common thread to all these decisions. In each case, Southern white elites were choosing their best prospect for maintaining their power over African-Americans and their other traditionally subordinate constituencies. Every other value was up for grabs, from oaths to the King to those to a Constitution, from commitment to the interests of working people to commitment to their "Confederate nation."

In fact, the political credo of the Virginia Gentlemen and their ilk could be well be this distortion of words from Jack Kennedy's inaugural address:

" Let every nation know, whether it wishes us well or ill, that we shall pay any price, bear any burden, meet any hardship, support any friend, oppose any foe, in order to assure the survival and the success of something as close to enslavement of African-Americans as we can get."

Fraud and Fable Number Four: Virginia's Agrarian Tradition Has Always Meant Respect For The Environment

Purpose: To conceal the Virginia Gentleman's devastation of the environment, and take credit for the beauty that still remains.

Environmental Destruction – An Old Dominion Tradition

"The swarthy population of [Powhatan's] kingdom had always been so widely dispersed and had possessed weapons of destruction so imperfect, that in spite of the passage of centuries they had been unable to check the incalculable increase in the multitudes of birds and animals haunting those aboriginal woods and waters." (Bruce, The Virginia Plutarch.)

It was the land, above all else, that set Virginia apart from the urban North. Thus the apologists paid particular attention to the supposedly arcadian rural environment of Old Virginia. Such descriptions always included the home, whose inhabitants were imagined to enjoy the bounty of a healthy farm economy.(Virginia Historical Society, Old Virginia)

Don't complain that the South is dirty and polluted. None of OUR lakes or rivers have caught fire recently. If you

whine about OUR scenic beauty, we'll kick your ass all the way back to Boston Harbor. (Monk)

Even today, Virginia still keeps its “arcadian rural” image. The image is hardly accurate. Modern Virginia, according to the Census Bureau, has only 32.1% of its land in farm use, and is 26th in the nation – right at median position among the states in the share of land devoted to farming. (U.S. Census, Farms)

More important than scenery, though, is the profound environmental destruction, at home and far beyond that the Virginia Gentleman is and has been responsible for.

Unlike the “weapons of destruction” of Powhatan’s people, modern Virginia’s “weapons of destruction” are very effective – both those built as weapons and those that destroy as a side effect of their operations. The seductive message of the Virginia Gentleman focuses on his supposed role as the guardian of green meadows and blue hills. In fact, he has consistently been the destroyer of Virginia’s natural gifts from his arrival, and has welcomed every opportunity to make money at nature’s expense.

Virginia is economically dependent on coal, a major contributor to global warming as well as the devastation of the Appalachian landscape.

Virginia is no longer a major coal producer, but continues to produce some coal. Trains carry Appalachian coal the width of the state, and it is shipped from the Hampton Roads ports. As a financial center, Richmond is one of the places where decisions about coal are made, and to which money made from coal flows. As a result, most of Virginia's Congressional delegation strongly supports the use of coal. ExxonMobil, the world's largest petroleum company, is also headquartered in Virginia. It's no coincidence that Virginia's current state leaders aggressively attack global climate science, repeating the lies of fossil fuel industries at the expense of our future.

Virginia's major industry today is the U.S. military, which is directed from Arlington, Virginia and dominates the state's two largest population centers, the Washington suburbs and Hampton Roads.

In 2003, Project Censored named "The U.S. Military's War on the Earth" as one of the year's top censored stories. Project Censored noted that the US military “generates 750,000 tons of toxic waste material annually, more than the five largest chemical companies in the U.S. combined.” Those were peacetime figures, from before the second Iraq War began.

In modern war, the massive, insidious and long-lasting environmental impacts are not even measured. Environmental harm is particularly associated with air war, overwhelming use of firepower, and vast fleets of motorized vehicles – all trademarks of U.S. military power since it gained global dominance.

In support of a bill to put the US military under the same environmental regulations as the rest of us, in 2009 a number of grassroots environmental groups sent a letter to the White House that included these words:

> **"Unregulated military projects have placed countless communities, workers, soldiers, and families at increased risk for cancer and other deadly disease from exposure to military toxins - the hidden casualties here at home. Even as we write this letter, contamination caused by munitions production, testing, and disposal is poisoning our drinking water**

wells, contaminating the air we breathe, destroying our lakes, rivers, and fisheries, and polluting our soils and farmlands." (Citizens)

The U.S. military spreads its pollution across the United States, and in fact all over the planet – including back in its Virginia home base.

According to a Norfolk Virginian-Pilot article from November 2, 2010, "Virginia is chock-full of military bases on the Superfund list. At least 14 are on the list today, 11 of which are in Hampton Roads." (Harper) (The Superfund list names the contaminated sites in the U.S. most urgently in need of cleanup.)

Then there are the various industrial facilities in Virginia that, even in a not very industrial state, have contaminated our streams with mercury, PCBs, and the like. Virginia's Department of Environmental Quality found in 2008 that two-thirds of the stream miles on which they had data were "impaired" or "threatened" by pollution. (And DEQ had data on only 31 per cent of Virginia's streams.) Gentle treatment by a bipartisan pro-business state government ensures that the corporations involved suffer at best minor fines and restrictions.

A small and mostly not very aggressive Virginia environmental movement struggles just to keep things from getting worse, and to get the existing grossly inadequate rules enforced.

Tobacco and Wandering Cattle

> **Those who labor in the earth are the chosen people of God, if ever he had a chosen people, whose breasts He has made his peculiar deposit for substantial and genuine virtue. It is the focus in which He keeps alive that sacred fire, which otherwise might escape from the face of the earth.**
> Thomas Jefferson, Notes on the State of Virginia

But back in the day of the first colonists, Virginia was a land of happy farms and fields, carefully tended by Jefferson's "chosen people," right?

Sorry. The colonists who settled Virginia worked for a corporation, after all. And that corporation's investors, and later Virginia landowners, were seeking a profit, not a paradise.

As Professor Virginia Anderson shows in her fascinating book, <u>Creatures of Empire</u>, the farming model that English colonists in Virginia knew back home – a balance of livestock, grains, and other products in an integrated and relatively sustainable system based on local markets – did not cross the Atlantic to Tidewater Virginia, the coastal area that was the home of the original colony. (Later, this kind of agriculture did emerge, though based more on German and Scotch-Irish roots, in the Valley of Virginia – but that was more than a century after Virginia began, and it was never the typical pattern for Virginia.)

Virginian colonists originally hoped to get wealth the same way the conquistadors did farther south in the Americas – by stealing gold and silver, and then making others mine what was still below ground. But "No gold, no silver and no precious metal slept in [Virginia's] bowels." Of course, Philip Alexander Bruce, telling us John Smith's story, notes, "its lands were fertile, its woods full of valuable timber, and its waters teeming with fish…" Unfortunately, though, these riches could not be simply stolen and put on a ship. (Bruce, 1929)

Tobacco, though, was the next best thing to gold. It did require work, but once white Virginians understood how to grow and cure it, tobacco became easy to convert into money.

Tobacco drove Virginia's economy. The currency for trade and payment of debts was tobacco. Tobacco was what made Virginia possible.

Tobacco was also a crop that exhausted the soil and required new fields after a few years, encouraging a constant "churning" of land from forest to field to wasteland.

This all happened with the active support of the colonial and post-Independence governments of Virginia, which after 1730 ran a tobacco inspection system that controlled both the quantity and the quality of the crop to maximize the overall income from tobacco. Such a system, of course, like most government regulation of economic activity, generally benefits the wealthiest and most politically powerful. (Unknown Author)

The overgrown wastelands that tobacco created would look pretty much like untouched forest to us modern folk. But the two are far from the same thing to native plants and animals. In fact, the wildflowers and weeds and birds that most of us are used to are invasive species that came over with European colonists.

> **The wild turkeys frequenting the woods were of remarkable weight and afforded a popular repast. The clouds of wild pigeons arriving at certain seasons in incredible numbers, were killed by the tens of thousands, and for many weeks furnished an additional dish for the planter's table. So vast were the flocks of wild ducks and geese in the rivers and bays during the greater part of the year, that they were looked on as the least expensive portion of the food which the Virginians had to procure for the support of their families.** (Bruce, 1907)

Also, livestock, as Creatures of Empire shows, had an entirely different role in Virginia than in England. In a country with plenty of land and little labor, and with its enormous profitability keeping the focus on tobacco, Virginian colonists did not put their time and work into caring for livestock.

Instead of fencing in cattle and pigs and feeding them, Virginians fenced them out of the tobacco and other fields and left them to fend for themselves. This, of course, meant these large alien animals required much more space to feed themselves, especially in forested areas. It also meant that they directly competed with wildlife. Animals that the English thought they "owned" were roaming in traditional hunting grounds, nourished by the plants and soil and streams that had always been there.

These European animals were an unprecedented threat to the staple foods of the native people, both the cultivated corn, squash and beans, and the "wild fruits, berries, acorns, hickory nuts and walnuts ... the gathering of these foods fell to the women... [and] the work of women was more essential to the material welfare of their people." (Virginia Women's Cultural History Project.)

In other words, the Virginia colonists sent out emissaries of destruction into woodlands and gardens that their human and animal neighbors needed for their own survival. Then they expected the native people to leave these edible intruders alone, respecting "private property."

Virginia's first colonists probably could not have come up with a plan more destructive to the local animal and plant life. Following the profit motive and the corporate mandate that brought them across the ocean, their path led directly to the transformation of the country they had come to, and to the undermining of its human, plant and animal inhabitants.

> **What was known as "wolf-driving" was, in many counties where this kind of animal still prowled about freely, one of the most popular forms of sport ; it was**

> **the annual custom in Northumberland, for instance, as late as 1691, for the county court to make public arrangements within regularly appointed limits for the thorough scouring of the forests for these hated vermin.**
> (Bruce, 1907)

Anderson captures the arrogance of the colonists with these words – "Colonists looked forward to the day ... when Indians acknowledged the superiority of English culture and adopted it as their own." This was the attitude of people who had lived in what they called Virginia for less than a century, whose survival depended on crops they had gotten and learned about from the Indians, and whose lives were dominated by tobacco, also obtained from the Indians.

But after all, the Indians were, according to John Smith's Generall

Historie of Virginia, "an idle, improvident, scattered people, ignorant of the knowledge of gold, or silver, or any commodities..." Not only did these Englishmen not see the ecological web around them, they didn't even value the efficient and sustainable use of corn, beans, squash and wild foods, though this would continue to be the key to survival for all Virginians for the next few centuries. Only the use and exchange of commodities with money value was truly meaningful to them, and so tobacco dominated agriculture and all uses of land.

The heirs of these colonists continued in much the same way, abetted by the institution of enslavement of Africans, into the 1700s, during and after the Revolution. Historian Theodore Whitfield described their status in the early 1800s with these words: "Slaves multiplied; plantations stretched themselves across wide acres.... and the weary soil pointed the poor and industrious whites to the mountains." (Whitfield)

Over the Blue Ridge

In and over those mountains, which were a barrier to the plantation system, a different Virginia did form, more egalitarian, more based on small farms and a diversity of products and not as much on the intensive labor of enslaved people.

During the early nineteenth century, the political struggle between these two regions dominated Virginia politics. We do not generally think of this as an environmental debate. But if we look at where Virginia's scenic beauty is found today, and where its agriculture for food production has been, we see it mostly west of the Blue Ridge. If that element of Virginia had become dominant, as Tidewater Virginia feared it would, we might see a different Virginia today.

Of course, during the Civil War the larger part of western Virginia left the state and formed the new state of West Virginia. Pressing to get back their lost land never became a major issue for the Virginia Gentleman.

Not So New South

During the economically depressed years after the Civil War, fields returned to wasteland in much of rural Virginia, but not, of course, to what they were when the English came. For example, key predators, especially wolves, were largely wiped out by this time. (Virginia's bounty payments for killing wolves began in 1632.) And Virginia industrialization began to expand beyond the longstanding tobacco and other factories of Richmond and the ironworks in the west. As Edward Ayers notes in his book The Promise of the New South, "Beginning in the 1880s... the key Southern industries began to take shape." In Virginia, these included sawmills, turpentine camps and phosphate mines, as well as coal fields.

During this period, the propaganda of the Lost Cause and of the wonders of pre-war plantation life became popular. One writer noted "the white-columned porticoes of the favorite colonial architecture now mouldering in decay," just as these various porticoes became symbols in the propaganda that would culminate in the novel and movie Gone With the Wind decades later. (Ayers)

The cities the planters' descendants were fleeing to included phenomena like Roanoke, which, thanks to railroad development, Ayers tells us, grew from 400 to 25,000 residents between 1881 and 1892. But this urban growth was not an indication of a general boom; Virginian writer Lewis Harvie Blair said it indicated "a declining or decaying state, with agriculture on the wane and the social order disturbed ..." and that people moved to the cities especially for "more security." (Ayers)

The economic base for these cities, railroads and other developments was very different from that of the industrialized North. Ayers reports that "most Southern industrial workers labored in forests and mines rather than factories," and in rural areas rather than in cities. Southern industry was largely extractive, dependent more on wood or coal than water for energy, and developing relatively few skilled mechanical or clerical jobs. (Ayers)

Coal Miner Blues

In Virginia's southwest and throughout Appalachia, coal seemed to bring about a social transformation during this period. However, as with tobacco, coal itself did not drive social change and environmental destruction.

Ayers notes that coal mining was hardly new to Appalachia. Coal had long been mined in Appalachia, but mostly from small mines for local use. "Farmers," Ayers wrote, "dug the coal when other work on their farms allowed."

The changes blamed on the product "coal" were the results of political decisions that put a few people in positions to become wealthy from the product. In the case of Appalachia, in Virginia's coalfields and elsewhere, the people that became wealthy were outsiders, armed first with legal tricks and then, when organized resistance increased, backed up by public and private law enforcement. Ultimately, of course, literal pitched battles were fought between those who worked the mines and the mine-owners.

Some of this history was still visible in 1989 when I visited southwest Virginia's coalfields during the Pittston Coal strike. I saw a community profoundly united against the coal owners, their strikebreakers, and the state police protecting those strikebreakers. What I remember most is a sign outside a small convenience store which stated "State police not welcome for the duration of the strike." This sign on that kind of store made it very clear that the coalfields were still occupied territory.

Friendly Neighborhood Toxic Sites

Some years ago, I worked for the Center for Health, Environment and Justice, founded by Love Canal leader Lois Gibbs. My main job was talking to grassroots people all over the U.S. who wanted to stop local environmental abuses.

In the north, these conversations frequently involved industrial sites and waste dumps – impacts of large scale industry and urban development. These major industrial sites in the North usually have a legal and commercial history that provides some limited information on their risks.

On the back roads and in the stream valleys of the South, there are probably hundreds of polluted sites that today are completely unknown to any living person, never had any permits or licenses, and do not show up in any government records. Of course, many of these are located near traditionally African-American communities, the homes of people whose protests were least likely to be listened to. Examples include buried pesticides, power substations with transformers leaking PCBs, sewage sludge contaminating rural wells, and sites where creosote and then other toxics were used to coat telephone poles. In some cases, this was "mom and pop" small-scale waste disposal. In other cases, as with sewage sludge, urban interests were sending their toxic liabilities "away."

So-called Superfund sites are the best documented and protected toxic sites. That doesn't mean barbed wire fences, spotlights and guards 24-7 though.

One example of a smaller Virginia Superfund site is Culpeper Wood Preservers. At this site, water contaminated with highly toxic chromated copper arsenate, formerly used in pressure-treated lumber, was released into the environment.

The U.S. Environmental Protection Agency, with its usual “happy talk” language, understates the risks, for example stating it was “determined in 1986 that homeowner wells were not contaminated. However, ground water sampling in 2007 and 2008 confirmed that the contamination has now reached the drinking water wells of three homes in the vicinity of the Site.” In plain English, an underground toxic plume is clearly spreading over time from the site. Most likely, more wells will be contaminated in the future, and “An unnamed tributary ... [of] Jonas Run potentially could be contaminated.” (U.S. Environmental Protection Agency) Culpeper is a growing community, halfway between Charlottesville and the D.C. suburbs. Will its development and this toxic material intersect?

Fredericksburg is a larger Virginia city, located on the I-95 highway midway between the D.C. suburbs and Richmond. Nearby is the L.A. Clarke and Son Superfund site, where creosote was used to coat railroad ties. The aquifer there is contaminated to some degree. (U.S. Environmental Protection Agency) Roughly half of Virginia’s drinking water is groundwater, either from wells or as the supply for a public system. (Yates calculations from data in (Kenny)) This generally means water from underground aquifers, which are invisible and often hard to test or even to accurately describe.

"Cleaning up" contaminated sites like the two above usually just means moving the toxic materials to another location. So after one company makes its money while contaminating a site, another makes more money removing and storing the still toxic material. (There are sometimes safe ways to convert material to a non-toxic form, but they are rarely cheap or simple.)

The more informal and fluid organization of the South's industries, and their location in rural communities, made the South a natural place to dispose of waste, when waste disposal became a profitable industry in the twentieth century. Robert Bullard, the intellectual leader of the African-American environmental justice movement, brought this out in his book Dumping in Dixie: Race, Class, and Environmental Quality, which also focused on another key Southern characteristic – a large and subordinated African-American population.

Even today's ordinary waste is much more complex and dangerous than ordinary waste in the nineteenth century. And truly hazardous waste is produced in massively greater quantities than ever before. The majority of this hazardous waste in the United States sent to civilian landfills goes to the South. Bullard has determined that one third of the landfills in the U.S. that take the most hazardous waste are in five Southern states, and that those nine landfills have 60 per cent of the national capacity.

None of these especially dangerous landfills are in Virginia, but Virginia has been a major waste importer in recent decades. In 2010, 28 per cent of the solid waste landfilled in Virginia came from out of state, with 7.5 per cent coming from New York alone (Virginia Department of Environmental Quality.)

A Virginia Landfill Community

Where does this waste go? A lot of it goes to Charles City County, located between Richmond and Williamsburg.

The 2010 census found that about 41 per cent of Charles City County residents were white. About seven per cent were native people, mostly from the Chickahominy, a state-recognized tribe. Most of the rest were African-American. Though Charles City County Courthouse is only about thirty

miles drive from Richmond, the county's average household income was three quarters of the state average. Its per capita annual retail sales barely exceeded fifteen hundred dollars; clearly residents spend most of what money they have outside the county. Only eleven per cent of its residents had college degrees, though about one third of all Virginians did. (U.S. Census Bureau, Charles City County)

In the midst of this poverty, Charles City County's website lists nine historic plantations within the county. They include Westover, home of the Byrd Family, and Shirley, which describes itself as being "the oldest family-owned business in North America," operating

since 1638. Even though these plantations still exist as tourist attractions, clearly their significance as economic powerhouses is long gone. The legacy of Virginia's once great families is of little value to their neighbors today. (Of course, those great families provided little benefit to their neighbors back in the day.) (Charles City County)

But in the early 1990s, Charles City found a new economic powerhouse – a private landfill operated by Waste Management, one of the nation's largest solid waste handlers. The result, according to a pro-waste industry article -- "The landfill made possible a tax cut on real estate from $1.29 to 70 cents per $100 of assessed value. In 1994, Charles City was also able to replace the run down school buildings with a $22 million school complex, the debt on which the county will use future landfill fees to pay. In 1998, the landfill brought in $3.7 million – one-fourth of the county budget…" (Logomasini)

Ms. Logomasini, writing for the Competitive Enterprise Institute, considers this a positive outcome for Charles City County. Others might not be so sure the tradeoff is worth it. It seems pretty clear that Charles City County's future is pretty much limited by its decision to become a waste recipient community.

As with tobacco, and as with coal, waste does not spontaneously come to dominate an entire community's economy.

Moving waste from one place to another for profit is a relatively new idea. It arose as waste disposal began to become more regulated, and waste became more complex. In 1978, in *Philadelphia v. New Jersey,* the U.S. Supreme Court ruled that trade in waste was protected interstate commerce. (Brickwedde) States and communities lost their power to block "foreign" trash, and most urban areas felt much less pressure to find solutions like reduction of waste and recycling close to home.

Instead, our laws and our people of wealth have created a waste industry. And the rest of us have mostly accepted this new entity as almost a natural force, just as most colonial Virginians experienced the tobacco economy as irresistible and invisible, as a condition of life. The garbage of wealthy cities flows to poor rural areas, and thanks to our system of laws and privileges, it seems as inevitable as water flowing downhill.

Our economy is a human creation, mostly built for the benefit of specific people. If we put the economy's rules first, "the environment" is no longer the whole ecosystem that sustains life. It's just whatever is left to enjoy after the economy's rulers take what they want and damage what they will. Under those rules, we will never achieve again what our predecessors took for granted – a Virginia where not a single stream or river is "impaired."

Virginia's Disaster Centuries

In a few short centuries, a temperate place with a wealth of water, flora, and fauna, and with a well-developed human lifestyle for enjoying that wealth, has been utterly transformed, to an extent we don't yet fully understand.

The Virginia Gentleman has moved carelessly from one form of exploitation to the next.

There have always been people resisting, trying to protect the natural legacy that the Virginia Gentlemen continually attack. The first resisters were the native people, whose source of life was threatened.

The book The True Story of Pocahontas: The Other Side of History, by Dr. Linwood "Little Bear" Custalow and Angela L. Daniel "Silver Star," tells a remarkable story. But almost as remarkable is the reason it was published now. In its Foreword, Chief of the Mattaponi Tribe Carl "Lone Eagle" Custalow explains why part of the oral history of the Mattaponi is being shared after having "lain secret for almost 400 years."

The reason for the book's revelations is the fight of the Mattaponi people against the proposed King William Reservoir. The reservoir would have destroyed the river and wetlands that have sustained them. But the Mattaponi did not fight alone. As the book states, "for the first time, through mutual respect, people have become emotionally, if not physically, invested in our survival." (The Mattaponi received substantial support from the Sierra Club, the Chesapeake Bay

Foundation, the Southern Environmental Law Center, and other groups.)

In September 2009, the Norfolk Virginian-Pilot newspaper reported, “after 22 years, millions of dollars and repeated court dates,” the City of Newport News dropped the Reservoir project, recognizing they could not overcome the opposition to it, and also that water consumption had not increased in their city along with population increases.

As we enter Virginia’s fifth century, the continuing stewardship, and the continuing moral and political power, of native people, as well as the growing awareness of the emergency that environmental exploitation has created globally, can change how this place we live in is treated. We will see if it changes enough to matter, and what the continuing cost of the damage already done will be.

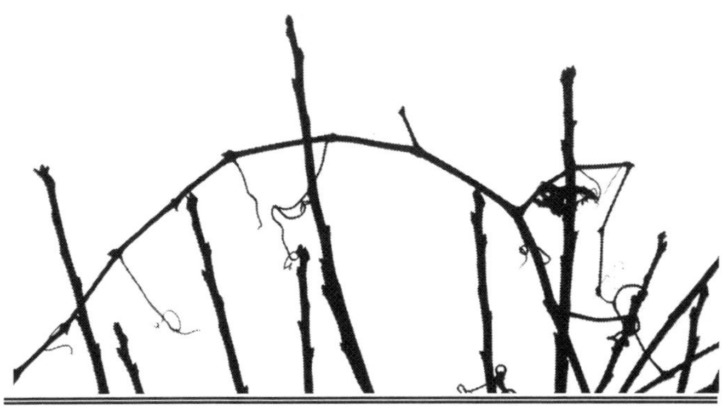

A Final Note: Whenever a writer dares to praise the environmental practices of indigenous people, certain "contrarians" are eager to point out flaws in the picture. So let me cut that off right now. I would be shocked if the Powhatan Confederacy had no "bad" environmental practices. But I dare anyone to even suggest that the Powhatan nation had such terrible practices that they needed to be smashed by foreign invasion, or that tobacco agriculture was an improvement. To put it differently, give me a freakin' break and *just don't bother*.

Fraud and Fable Number Five: The First Virginia Gentlemen Were Skilled Masters Of Theirs And Others' Destinies

---

Purpose: To suggest that the Virginia Gentleman of today comes from a long tradition of competence and natural mastery.

Subtitled: The First Defeat of the Virginia Gentleman

It is critical to the myth of the Virginia Gentleman that he always seem successful. After all, he can hardly be an aristocrat and a natural leader if he is constantly seen getting his butt kicked. Nor does it suit his legend for us to see that the Virginia Gentlemen's only real victories are in nasty business and political deals, while he almost always loses in valiant combat.

The one great defeat at Appomattox, of course, is undeniable. That defeat has required the Virginia Gentleman to do a Herculean job of turning a crushing defeat into some kind of redeeming event. The work of Jubal Early and others to inflict the Lost Cause fantasy on us is described in **Fraud and Fable Number 10, White Virginia Rightfully Cherished a Noble Lost Cause**.

What we do know is that the Virginia Gentleman did defeat the native people who were here, and specifically Powhatan's Confederacy. Obviously. Right?

Well, yes, obviously, since Virginia has been, well, Virginia and not Powhatan territory for centuries. But as far as the qualities one associates with Virginia Gentlemen – military genius, gallantry, and chivalry – well, on all those grounds, the Virginia Gentleman lost to his first foe. As Helen Rountree writes in her 2005 book Pocahontas, Powhatan, Opechancanough: Three Indian Lives Changed by Jamestown, the Powhatan Confederacy lost because "the outlanders came from a country with a huge population compared to the Powhatan one, and they had a cash crop that could entice plenty of replacements for those who had died."

Ironically, what actually happened to the Powhatan Confederacy is a lot like the typical Confederate Fable of the outcome of the Civil War. The native people had the best generals, fought the most chivalrous fight, and won the battles – but there were just too damn many English colonists.

The Truth About Pocahontas?

The True Story of Pocahontas, mentioned in **Fraud and Fable Number 4, Virginia's Agrarian Tradition Has Always Meant Respect for the Environment**, is among the few books that have been written about the history of a specific native North American people by that people. It is essentially an official history from a people who were defeated, and seemingly erased, some 350 years ago.

The book's authors, Dr. Linwood "Little Bear" Custalow and Angela L. Daniel "Silver Star," tell us they are sharing information that the Mattaponi people have had for all that time, and have now chosen to disclose.

Pocahontas has long been a white folks' icon, first for upper class Virginians, and now for Disney. So the book's most obviously shocking assertion is that Pocahontas was murdered by the English.

This would seem to put a dark shadow over that great Virgina story, the Pocahontas/John Smith romance. But that story, of course, is complete fiction.

Pocahontas was a small child when John Smith visited her people. And John Smith had told exactly the same story before, about being rescued from execution by a young lady, except in that story, she was a Turkish princess.

Cabell's Let Me Lie hilariously debunks the whole story, establishing that the Pocahontas/Smith story was "either invented or else borrowed" by John Smith. Cabell then goes on, tongue firmly in cheek, to state that this does not change "the unshakable position of Pocahontas in the official history of Virginia."

Lost Cause historian Philip Alexander Bruce refers to the Pocahontas story as "the most exquisite idyll in the course of American history.." (Bruce, 1929) His choice of words is unconsciously appropriate; the first idylls, by the ancient Greek poet Theocritus, were short poems about the antics of mythical creatures in the woods and fields.

Even Guy Friddell's 1973 The Virginia Way, a picture and text book of praise for the Commonwealth found on coffee tables and library shelves all over Virginia, repeats Smith's fabrication as truth.

Of course, all these predated Disney's even more preposterous version, in which the pre-pubescent Pocahontas, child of a traditional non-European culture, becomes a shapely young woman well versed in the language of Western romantic love.

> **"No, you have to go back," Pocahontas answered. "No matter what happens, I will always be with you. Forever." Then Pocahontas leaned down and the two gently shared their last kiss.** (Disney)

Custalow and Daniel state that John Rolfe, the Englishman who originated tobacco as a commercial crop, learned how to cure tobacco from his native neighbors (though he used non-local tobacco). This makes sense; his neighbors had been growing tobacco for centuries. But they say that Rolfe learned specifically from the priests of the Powhatan Confederacy. Tobacco, after all, was a ritual substance, not a recreational drug, to the native people. And, the authors state, Rolfe married Pocahontas, daughter of the Powhatan Confederacy's leader, in order to gain the relationship with the priests that would give him access to this information.

The origin story of Virginia tobacco, as the Mattaponi tell it, is pretty sordid. It's a story of deception, and of "industrial espionage," as well as of murder.

The Failure Years

Tobacco was such an amazingly successful crop that it ensured not only the survival of the Virginia colony, but its prosperity.

It saved Virginia from what had looked like complete failure. Before tobacco, this whining complaint had pretty much summed up how the colonist felt about where they had ended up:

> **"It was the Spaniards good hap to happen in those parts where there infinite numbers of people, whoe had manured the ground with that providence that it afforded victual at all times; and time had brought them to that perfection [that] they had the use of gold and silver .... so that what the Spaniard got was only the spoile and pillage of those countrie people, and not the labours of their own hands.**
> **But had those fruitfull Countries beene as salvage, as barbarous, as ill-peopled ... as Virginia, their proper labours ... would have produced as small profit as ours."** (Smith)

In other words, "we English wish that we had colonized a place where somebody else has already done the work for us, like the Spanish did."

It is hard to overestimate the lack of preparedness of the Jamestown gang. In Virginia, hunting was critical to survival. But in England, few people hunted, mostly wealthy people for whom it was a hobby. Back home, the people who hunted from necessity were considered poachers – thieves of someone else's game in the eyes of the law. Not only were most of the colonists ignorant of hunting when they came to Virginia, they found it strange that the Indian men spent so much time engaged in what to them looked like sport. (Weatherford)

Jamestown had a hard history. The colony would not have survived even one winter without aid from the Powhatan Confederacy (and also without stealing food at gunpoint from native people.)

In fact, in 1610, the colonists made the decision to give up Virginia, as recorded by William Strachey, secretary to the colony:

> **It soone then appeared most fit, by a generall approbation, that to preserve and save all from starving, there could be no readier course thought on,**

then to abandon the Country, and accommodating themselves the best that they might, in the present Pinnaces then in the road,... with all speede convenient to make for the New found Land, where (being the fishing time) they might meete with many English Ships into which happily they might disperse most of the Company.

A true reportory of the wracke, and redemption of Sir Thomas Gates Knight, by William Strachey, as quoted in the Encyclopedia Virginia

The colonists had actually abandoned Jamestown when they encountered the ship of the new Governor sent from England. Whether emboldened or embarrassed by him and the reinforcements he brought with him, they returned to Jamestown to try again.

Nevertheless, Virginia went from this misery to the splendor of Williamsburg in a century, and, as Jack Weatherford notes in Native Roots: How the Indians Enriched America, "all of this prosperity came from the highly profitable sales of one single Indian crop – tobacco." He adds "By the time of the American Revolution, tobacco accounted for approximately a sixth of the combined exports of all thirteen colonies." (Weatherford)

The greed of tobacco growers led to the development of a cruel system of slavery. Taxes on slaves also became a source of wealth for the colonial government, as shown by this fragment of a letter from the Governor of Virginia in 1700:

> **"I am in hopes that this year, please God, there will come in a good many negroes so that there may be money enough in a year or two to build a house for his Majesty's Governor, as also the Capitol."**
> Francis Nicholson, Governor of Virginia, writing to the Council of Trade and Plantations in London, June 1700 (Pope-Hennessy)

Indian Fighters

But wait, there was fighting, wasn't there? Didn't the English defeat the Powhatan Confederacy with their superior weapons and military knowledge? Well, not so much.

As late as 1622, Powhatan's brother, Opechancanough, who had succeeded him as leader, led a coordinated attack against the English that killed almost one out of three of the colonists. In response, Rountree writes, the devastated colonists formed what she calls "an English reservation." Without the lure of tobacco wealth, that huge military and psychological defeat would probably have been the end of the Virginia colony – sort of the "Tet Offensive" of the Powhatan Confederacy's war against their invaders.

Corporate Mission

In the days of Jamestown, corporations did not have lives of their own, as they do today. Every corporation was chartered for a set term by the government, in order to meet a specific purpose. To justify their enterprise to their masters, in 1610 the Virginia colony's English leaders published <u>A True and Sincere Declaration of the</u>

Purpose and Ends of the Plantation Begun in Virginia. In this document, they stated three purposes:

> **"first to preach and baptize into Christian religion .. a number of poore and miserable souls...**
> **Second ... transplanting ... the multitude of increase of our people ... as a Bulwarke of defense, in a place of advantage, against a stranger enemy..**
> **Lastly ... by ... possessing to themselves a fruitful land, whence they may furnish and provide this Kingdome, with all such necessities and defects .. under which we labor, and are now enforced to buy .. at the curtesie of other princes..."**

By the "Christian religion," the English of course meant their own brand of Protestantism. The second point suggested the Virginia colony would give relief from Britain's overpopulation by bringing British people to America to expand English power. The third point suggested that Virginia would provide goods to England that the mother country would otherwise have to buy from foreign nations.

Patrick Buchanan in his Decline of the West cites the first point as showing that the U.S. has roots as a Christian nation. However, Buchanan fails to mention any signs of serious attempts to convert the native people, or even any signs of substantial piety among the colonists. The Jamestown colonists made the obligatory statement of a religious reason for the invasion of the Powhatan Confederacy because their society required it, just as U.S. incursions into Guatemala or Vietnam or Iraq have always been accompanied by statements about freedom and democracy.

Empty rhetoric aside, the goals of the Jamestown colony were to project the power of England across the ocean, strengthening its military position and its economy as well as the power of its Anglican ideology. As ugly as these goals were, in the end they all became secondary to making money on tobacco.

Corporate Incompetents

To summarize, Virginia was founded by an essentially incompetent corporate expedition, which only survived, and eventually prospered, by sponging off the native people, and by accidentally finding a lucrative product for sale.

Militarily and organizationally, they were a pathetic joke.

I have a copy of Magill's First Book of Virginia History, published in 1908 as a revision of an 1897 book. This children's book made much of Lee's "quiet dignity," and Stonewall's "splendid career." (Magill) (By 1897, Ms. Magill had been in the habit of defending the Confederacy for a long time. In 1863, she was exiled from Winchester, Virginia, where I live, by the Union administration under General Robert Milroy, because of her habit of writing letters harshly criticizing Federal officials. (Quarles)) But when it came to the first Jamestown settlers, Ms. Magill apparently ran out of loyalty to traditional Virginia icons:

"...although James was King of England, he was not a very wise man; so

he chose for his colony broken-down gentlemen who, through extravagance and indolence, had lost their fortunes, and hoped to grow rich in the New World by digging away a little earth and picking up gold." (Magill)

The Jamestown episode is often described as "heroic." To see a failure of planning by a corporation resulting in a poorly organized invasion of another people's country, as heroic is downright bizarre. This has to rival the Lost Cause idea as one of the great achievements of propaganda. But then, that's what the Virginia Gentleman really is – an imaginary creature of propaganda, the illusion of a bold Cavalier intended to disguise the avarice, arrogance and incompetence that dominates Virginia's real history.

Fraud and Fable Number Six: Washington, Jefferson, And Their Generation Were Unique Leaders In The History Of Democracy And Liberty

Purpose: To claim a spot for Virginia with the high points of so-called Western Civilization, thereby ennobling, or at least excusing, the ugly parts of Virginia history.

Since this legend is especially deeply rooted in our minds, I have invented a Questioner to bring up some of the thoughts that may occur to my readers.

Questioner: Wait a minute! Some of these so-called disgusting Virginia Gentlemen of yours were the Founders of our Nation!

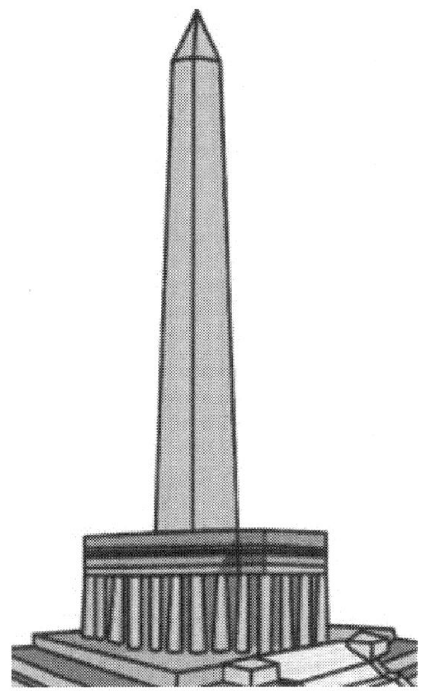

Well, yeah. And?

Questioner: So how can you say that they were merely greedy frauds? Look at this amazing task they performed? No one has ever done anything like it in human history!

So, how do you know that? What are you comparing them to? After all, Jefferson wrote this about our first founding document, the Declaration of Independence:

> **This was the object of the Declaration of Independence. Not to find out new principles, or new arguments, never before thought of, not merely to say things which had never been said before; but to place before mankind the common sense of the subject....**
> Letter to Henry Lee, May 8, 1825

Questioner: Well...

We imagine that the Founders are just plain better than anyone in history at what they did. But what kind of sense does that make? Were these the first people in the world to establish a republic, to fight a revolution?

Questioner: No, but...

In fact, hardly any USAn knows enough history to have any idea whether our Founders are particularly unusual, let alone unique in all history.

A few of us have heard that the Iroquois League – or to use the name they use, the Haudenosaunee system -- was probably a model for the United States. Most of us are unaware that their confederacy has existed for perhaps four times the lifetime of the United States.

But for every one hundred of us that know about the Haudenosaunee, there may be one or two that know about the political structures of the Kikuyu or Balante. Both were stateless societies, active grassroots democracies – the Kikuyu in Kenya, and the Balante in Guiné-Bissau.

The Balante were described by revolutionary leader and theoretician Amilcar Cabral in these words:

> **"a society without any social stratification: there is just a council of elders in each village or group of villages who decide on the day to day problems. In the Balante group property and land are considered to belong to the village but each family receives the amount of land needed to ensure subsistence for itself, and the means of production, or rather the**

instruments of production, are not collective but are owned by families or individuals. Among the Balantes women participate in production but they own what they produce and this gives Balante women a position which we consider privileged, as they are fairly free." (Cabral)

Just as the Balante were a key constituency in the Guiné-Bissau independence struggle, the Kikuyu were the core of the struggle in Kenya. And like the Balante, their democratic way of life contributed to the revolutionary process.

"...the traditional Kikuyu political structure was decentralized and inherently democratic, with effective decision making and enforcement powers resting

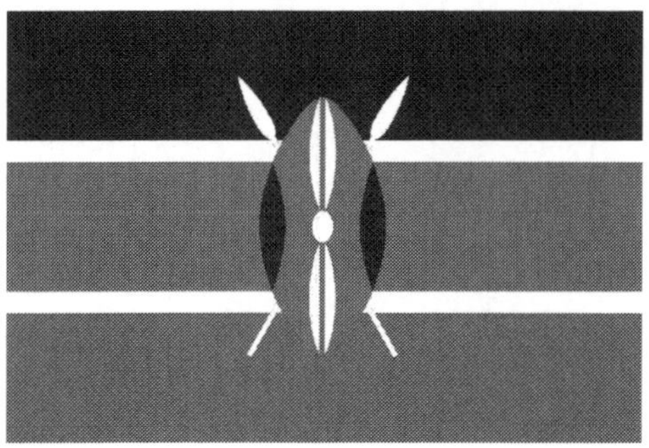

for the most part in numerous local hierarchies of councils within each sub-tribe. We have noted, with respect to this kiama or council system, that: (1) councils were convened as the occasion demanded and reached decisions on the principle of discussion until unanimity was achieved; (2) the particular council convened (sub-clan, village, neighborhood, etc.) was determined in each case by the scope and nature of the question or dispute at issue; (3) composition was based on the principle of lower-level representation on higher-level councils,' with the latter owing their authority to the

former; (4) the spokesman or muthamaki of a given council, whether that of the village or the ridge -- which represented the largest fixed administrative unit -- was responsible to and acted in the name and with the approval of the entire body; and (5) positions of leadership were achieved, within a system of age-grades or ranks, rather than ascribed and were limited in duration by the periodic accession to political authority of junior generation-sets."(Barnett)

Of course, the Balante, the Kikuyu and the Haudenosaunee did not just fall into their systems of government. They are, after all, human beings with the same mental and moral equipment that we have. They figured out these systems.

Questioner: Okay, so these primitive societies had something like our Republic....

There is no such thing as a "primitive society." Every human being has the same depth of history behind her, and the society she lives in reflects a lot of thought – as well as some greed, cowardice, lust for power, and various ugly characteristics.

Questioner: Yes, but they didn't have the depth of our constitution – the protections, the Bill of Rights...

That's a good point. They didn't. They didn't have explicit language to prevent torture, home invasions, forcing one's religion on other groups, and so on. But that's because they did not come out of several centuries of brutal religious wars and battles over kingship and lordship over others. Let's face it. Europe was an ugly mess in the centuries before the U.S. Revolution.

A lot of the offenses that the Bill of Rights protects us from are things that normal human beings wouldn't even think of, let alone practice. Sure, the rest of the world is no paradise, but Europe was in the midst of some real horrors in the years before 1787. Most societies have rules against cannibalism, but they wouldn't put them in their constitution or basic law because every child knows not to do that. The same goes, in many societies, for injustices like locking people up for saying things, or breaking up families by selling the different family members. These things just are not done.

Questioner: None of these societies have accomplished what the U.S. has.

And you are referring to genocide of our native neighbors, slavery diminishing only slightly into racism, and the building of the greatest empire in history with the most powerful weapons?

Questioner: No, I'm talking about freedom – about votes for women, civil rights, environmental action, free speech, now even gay rights...

Now you are talking about rights that the Founders didn't give us. In fact, rights that people had to fight and die to get **despite** the original system. Again, people in many "primitive" societies have these as a birthright.

Certainly the Constitution got some things right. Above all, it has provided a framework for including, or at least starting to include, the vast majority of the population that were effectively non-citizens when our nation began. But just in the exclusion of women from power (which actually got worse after the

Revolution) and our acceptance of hereditary slavery, our nation started out way behind the political systems of the Haudenosaunee, the Balante, the Kikuyu, and many other peoples.

Questioner: I don't care what you say! I'm an American!

That's right. You like your system because it's yours – it's all you know. You are like someone defending the

virtues of a Chevrolet as the best car in the world when you've never even seen a Ford, let alone a Lamborghini or a Prius. To paraphrase an ugly comment from back in the day, you have no opinions on this issue which any reasonable person is bound to respect.

Come back and tell me about the Founders after you have studied some of their competition, and we can talk.

Questioner: Wait! What about Jefferson?

OK. I was wondering when you would get to T.J.

Yes, he was a Virginia Gentlemen, complete with slaves, a plantation, and a mother who was a Randolph.

And yes, he took some radical positions on some issues. But on the big issue of slavery, the one that would decide the future of the nation, he was at best conflicted.

Historian William Freehling describes Jefferson's approach to the issue: "Jefferson blasted slavery only in *private* correspondence and in his published Notes on Virginia – published anonymously, characteristically, 'lest it produce an irritation.' When Jefferson was asked to endorse an antislavery poem publicly, he refused lest he lose his influence." (Freehling, 1990.)

These days, the general attitude towards Jefferson is to pity him for being so divided in his mind and heart. However, I recently read Garry Wills' <u>Negro President: Jefferson and the Slave Power</u>, and am feeling somewhat less inclined to pity. (Wills)

Wills' title is not one of praise, like Bill Clinton's title "the first Black President." Jefferson earned that then insulting name from Northerners, because the votes available to the South due to the three-fifths rule helped elect him in 1800. That rule gave slave states three-fifths of a vote for every slave, even though slaves did not vote.

Wills goes to describe Jefferson's many actions, particularly as President, as "a protector and extender of the slave system." These include his reversal of John Adams' Administration's support of the Haïtian Revolution and his acquisition of Louisiana and Florida as areas open to slavery.

Only a few years after the delicate balance of the Constitution was achieved between New England and the South, Jefferson was perceived as "allied with enemies of New England's way of life," and this "feeling was widely echoed through town meetings and legislative gatherings in the North."

The Jefferson we imagine today seems to live in an era unrelated to the Civil War. In fact, as President of the United States at a crucial moment, he was undeniably part of the process of strengthening the slave power and moving the nation towards war.

Questioner: Slavery really isn't the point. Jefferson made the Revolution.

Jefferson was mostly a man of words, and mostly written words used by other political leaders. He never fired up a crowd like Patrick Henry, and he never wrote pamphlets that moved thousands of ordinary colonists to action like Thomas Paine. He certainly never led troops in battle like Washington.

There was a real American Revolution that involved people being persuaded to take action and then winning a war (with their French allies.) But Jefferson contributed little directly to that contest of political power.

I am a fast writer with some skill at finding the right way to express what others are trying to say. I don't claim to be the elegant writer that Jefferson was, but I know what he was doing when he rolled out those pages of the Declaration.

That writing was a very important task, which he rightly claimed as one of his three major life accomplishments. But many of the failed revolutions in human history probably had manifestoes as eloquent as ours. Actually winning took mobilization, where Paine excelled, and military leadership, Washington's strength.

Questioner: Oh darn you! What about religious freedom?

There, I think you have hit upon Jefferson's greatest political accomplishment. He cared deeply about this issue. But then so did the majority of voters, that is to say white male Virginians with property.

Norman Cousins' book In God We Trust: The Religious Beliefs and Ideas of the American Founding Fathers was published in 1958, before the current onslaught of propaganda on this issue. He quotes Jefferson in his Autobiography – "by the time of the revolution, a majority of [Virginia's] inhabitants had become dissenters from the established church, but were still obliged to pay contributions to support the pastors of the minority."

Most white Virginians were Baptists, Methodists and Presbyterians, not deists like Jefferson, but they had the common experience of having a religious system imposed on them by law.

Jefferson, as a cosmopolitan intellectual, did understand that Virginia's Statute of Religious Freedom included "within the mantle of its protection, the Jew and Gentile, the Christian and the Mohometan, the Hindoo, and Infidel of every denomination." (Jefferson, Autobiography)_But the majority of the people, whatever their opinions about Hindoos and Infidels, supported this popular statute. Jefferson wrote in his Notes that the "spirit" of Virginia's non-Anglican dissenters "had risen to a degree of determination which commanded respect." (Jefferson, Notes) In other words, the dissenters had visible political power they could use to get what they wanted.

It was probably inevitable that Jefferson would win his battle for, as he wrote, "demolition of the church establishment." He was not just on the side of the good guys and of history; he was on the side of a majority seeking to carry out an obvious goal of the Revolution they had just won. But it is still undeniable that he did fight the fight, that he added eloquence and learning to it, and that he certainly helped to open the way for truly universal religious tolerance.

So, I will give Jefferson lots of points on that one. But he still totally ducked slavery. Historian John

Chester Miller devotes an entire book to Jefferson and slavery, but in the last chapter concludes “Jefferson asked to be judged by his acts rather than by his words. But on the issue of slavery he emerges with greater luster if he is judged by his words rather than his acts.” That’s a harsh – but fair – judgment. (Miller)

And that finally compromises his every claim to be a freedom fighter. Let’s compare his freedom-fighting status that of just one anonymous African-American couple. The wife was hit by her mistress, and she struck back. The enslaved woman was told that the next day she would get a serious beating – and of course the master had the authority to kill. With her husband’s help, she hid in a cave for seven years – until the end of slavery. (Sterling)

This is only one story, of course, of thousands we have and tens of thousands that are lost. But who was the greater freedom fighter, Jefferson or those nameless heroes?

Questioner: Heck, I give up.

‘Bye. It’s always more fun to argue with someone you made up.

Nevertheless, the people refused to obey the voice of Samuel; and they said,

Nay, but we will have a king over us.
That we also may be like all the nations;
and that our king may judge us, and
go out before us, and fight our battles.
I Samuel, 9:19–20.

upstream from this place in Eisenhower
Valley
earthmovers and bulldozers
are preparing the ground of an old military
base
for new development
they have cleaned up the site
which means that
only a few spent shells and chemical spills
only one or two or ten forgotten fifty gallon
drums
slowly ease poisons
a few molecules at a time
to confound the tiny creatures
that feed the fish

that feed this kingfisher
that chatters bitterly at me as I walk by
on this the last Veterans' Day of the
1900s

in classical Greece
the kingfisher
was named Halcyon
and was ascribed the power to calm
the waves
for long enough to raise young
in nests that rode on the sea
according to the story
healthful and peaceful waters
gleamed in the sun
on those halcyon days
and life was nurtured there

> *... this assault has blotted out the*
> *whole pattern of democratic life in an*
> *appalling number of independent*
> *nations, great and small. And the*
> *assailants*
> *are still on the march..*
> *Franklin Delano Roosevelt, January 6,*
> *1941*

this stream is dark from fallen leaves
under a clouded sky and
runs shallow on a riprap–channeled
course

there where the broken concrete
creates
a tiny cataract

an egret stands below
stationed for prey

since my mother died
in the spring
where I once saw great blue herons
I often now see egrets
clothed in their mournful white grace

beyond the expected daughterly devotions
my mother nurtured one particular person's
memory
that person was her father's stepmother
a woman of enterprising kindness
today is an appropriate day
to keep that memory fed
for that woman's closest claim to fame
(made more than once in the local paper)
was that she kept correspondence
with hundreds of American soldiers
during Hitler's war

giving each of them in some small way
her powerful civic comfort

that still warmed my mother
wars and decades later

> *... As I watched it circle overhead ....*
> *flinging indiscriminate bolts of death*
> *earthward, I could visualize the scene*
> *below. Men, women, children and*
> *animals, caught like rats in a flood.*
> *A Quaker in Quang Ngai, Vietnam, 1969.*

my war was a different war.
It was one to avoid,
in order that one could later be President or
Vice–President, and
it was a war to regret or defend in decades
of arguments not yet ended, and
it was a war to refuse,
as I did thirty years ago
when I wrote my personal letter to the chief
soldiers
telling them I would only enter their ranks
with public intention to divide them
and to blunt their effort

having chosen to undermine that military
enterprise,
how can I then honor those earnest letters
of half a century ago that my mother
cherished?

I never knew their writer
but I don't think those letters urged
that corporate schemers rework
permutations of radar and the B–29
to the edge of doomsday
or that the blood–purchased Four Freedoms
were intended only for Exxon or Bechtel
and not for brown–skinned villagers

my guess is that she urged those young men
to do their duty
to beat Hitler and his allies
and then to come home to those that loved
and supported them
to come home and

experience
something like
halcyon days

*veteran, from Latin veteranus, from veter,
vetus— old. An old soldier; an
experienced or aged person*

it is eleven o'clock.
I remove my cap
and stand still
choosing to give honor even when
honor is a complicated matter
startled, gulls on the stream
rise all together
and hanging together
flap and soar upstream
in their long collective experience
they have learned the wisdom of fleeing
the immense danger in any sharp gesture

here, there, I see
a single bird
with all the beauty
of the very finest weapons
jets, missiles, unknown flying objects
magic in the air

while in their whole flock
the birds embody panic
rushing on without pause
like the flights from Paris, Kosovo, Pnomh
Penh,
from Nagasaki

or perhaps tomorrow
from Moscow and Beijing and Washington

my father rode a bomber over Germany
was probably cursed by people helpless on
the earth
was certainly forced into
a long fall in the chilly vulnerable darkness
when shells shattered the plane

a distant cousin of mine
lived in Honolulu in 1941
when the forces of the Empire attacked —
the civilians there were the last people in
the world
to know what had happened
they waited a long day to find out
whether they were captives, hostages,
targets
or, as it happened, safe this time

we can be the weapon–bearer or the target
we are old and experienced
we are veterans
at both parts

when we accept the will of one single
potency
clean lined, well aimed,
eventually
we come to threaten every possible route
that life could take

to the green, to the light
to the sustaining ocean

as a flock, though,
we flee, disordered,
clumsily
desperate for the end of the danger
aching to reach
all together and in the long run
halcyon days

> *It is for us the living, rather, to be dedicated*
> *here to the unfinished work*
> *which they who fought here have thus far so*
> *nobly advanced.*
> *Abraham Lincoln at Gettysburg.*

and so this Veterans' Day
I add my letter to the many already written
that praise those
who bravely accept the hardest civic tasks
and when I assert that
today's responsibility is not the same as
yesterday's
I do not dishonor either one

ending Hitler's power was a necessity
but it was not done
so that this nation could then replicate that
feat
in a thousand more victories
each one meaner and more mechanized than
the last

nor was it done for Eisenhowers or for
monuments

it was not done for the ambitions of any faction

it was done to destroy empires, not to build one

my father's and mother's generation fought that war
in the still–surviving hope
that each one of us could rest
settled again on the waters
with the great fearsome flurry finally over
neither weapon nor target
doing the best we can
as the creatures we happen to be
to nurture life
on peaceful pure waters
in sun
in shadow
in damaged streams
still finding their way
to the sea

Fraud and Fable Number Seven: Slavery In Virginia Was The Good Kind of Slavery

Purpose: To establish that even when it was at its worst, Virginia was still enlightened, or at least special.

> **"… all the colonies had slaves. This was not bad for the slaves. In their own country, they were cannibals, or man-eaters, and very degraded in every way. They were much better off in this country, where they were taught to know about God and about other things which were very good for them."** (Magill)

> **"Out of the natural reverence for intellect and virtue there arises an impulse to segregation, which broadly results in coarser natures, that is, those of duller mental and moral sensibility, being lodged at the bottom and those of more refined at the top."** (Weaver)

Slave-owners have, naturally, preferred to believe absurdities about those they held in slavery. The first quote immediately above is from a history book for children; the second quote is from an academic book by an author called "one of the founders of the traditionalist wing of the post World War 11 conservative movement." (Scotchie) Both distort reality to defend slavery.

Weaver's comment, of course, assumes

first the more intelligent are also always the most moral, which is not only inaccurate but very un-Christian. He also states as a fact that there is a natural process that puts the better people at the top. Apparently that natural process involves going to other people's countries, kidnapping people there, and forcing them to do your heavy labor.

TIMBUKTU

Justifying slavery requires the creation of a fantasy world, where the scholars of Timbuktu and the builders of Zimbabwe become subhuman cannibals, and society orders itself automatically from best people to worst.

These lies generally translate to one Big Lie, one we still hear, that "they were better off."

People who know they are "better off," of course, do not risk their lives in rebellion.

I think that what whites believe about insurrection by enslaved African-Americans is one of the best tests of their ability to grasp the humanity of those enslaved people. After all, few white people haven't said at some point "Well, if anyone did that to me, I would rebel..." And in fact, much of the popular white rhetoric of the Revolution, the Confederacy and even World War II was about unwillingness to be "enslaved."

In one of the first known statement against enslavement of Africans by white North Americans, agreed on by a worship meeting in Germantown, Maryland, in 1688 by Mennonites and Friends, the authors explicitly asked whites to imagine slaves taking up arms for their freedom, as any white would:

> **"There is a saying, that we should do to all men like as we will be done ourselves; making no difference of what generation, descent, or color they are... If once these slaves... should join themselves -- fight for their freedom ... will these masters and mistresses take the sword at hand and war against these poor slaves. Or, have the poor negers not as much right to**

fight for their freedom, as you have to keep them slaves?" (Hendericks)

In the decades after slavery of Africans began in Virginia, there were no illusions about the ability or desire of people of African descent to rise up in insurrection just like "all men."

In 1680, the Council of Virginia received a report "of the Discovery of a Negro Plott, formed in the Northern Neck for the Distroying and killing his Majusteies Subjects ... with a designe of Carrying it through the whole Collony of Virginia..." The rebels were described as "Evill and Wichked." But the report does not mention ingratitude, nor suggest that any whites had duped them into rebelling, two themes that would appear in later years after such plans were identified. The main recommendation of the report was "not to permit [Negro Slaves] to hold or to make any Solemnity or Funeralls for any deceased Negroes." In other words, the slave-owners' only concern was to impose whatever brutal conditions their economic interests required to keep these people in slavery. Insurrection was an expected cost of doing business, in an era when real liberty was the privilege of a few. (Council)

No Longer Business as Usual

One hundred and fifty years of slavery later, insurrection by slaves was a source of more complex emotions and ideas. Questions of "all men being created equal," as well as the moral concerns of Quakers, Methodists, and others, had resulted in challenges to slavery, and therefore in slave-holders coming up with elaborate self-deceptions. One of the biggest was that African-Americans would only revolt if a Yankee taught them to.

The insurrection led by Nat Turner in 1831 was probably the most widely reported and discussed of them all. Henry Tragle's book, <u>The Southampton Slave Revolt of 1831</u>, is a storehouse of contemporary material on this event. It includes newspaper reports that demonstrate the lack of any human feeling towards the rebels. The Richmond Compiler stated, before much was even known about the revolt,

"The wretches who have conceived this thing are mad – infatuated – deceived by some artful knaves, or stimulated by their own miscalculating passions. The ruin must return on their own heads..." The Richmond Enquirer wrote about "the horrible ferocity of these monsters.." and said of Nat Turner, "he was artful, impudent and vindictive, without any cause or provocation..."

Virginia Governor Floyd had much of the responsibility for responding to the insurrection, including ultimately analyzing its cause. In a November 1831 letter, he shared the basic analysis of the contemporary newspapers, without their passion but with little more respect for the rebels. His finding was that "the spirit of insubordination which has, and still manifests itself in Virginia, had its origins among .. the Yankee population." He went on to blame "Northern incendiaries, tracts, Sunday Schools, religion, and reading and writing...," essentially dismissing the idea that enslaved African-Americans could decide to rebel on their own. Floyd did however, grant one shred of dignity to the rebels, noting that "all died bravely indicating no reluctance to lose their lives in such a cause." (Tragle)

AFRICAN-AMERICANS HEADED FOR THE UNION LINES

The Largest Slave Insurrection

We do not often think of the Civil War as an insurrection of the enslaved African-Americans – but of course it was the largest one, as well as the last one. There was no single violent uprising of the enslaved, as many had thought there might be. As activist and historian Vincent Harding points out, such an uprising, especially at the beginning of the war, might have alienated the North. So, "instead of mass insurrection, the Civil War created the context for a vast broadening and intensifying of the self-liberating black movement which had developed before the war." (Harding, <u>There is a River</u>)

By the end of the war, hundreds of thousands of enslaved peoples had left Confederate control, and about 200,000 of them belonged to a force in armed combat against the slavocrats. These men were in uniform, and bearing arms issued by the Union Army. But white Virginians saw them as not much different than Nat Turner or Gabriel Prosser.

Two white women in Winchester, Virginia, recorded their thoughts during the War, including the first time they saw African-American troops. These two women's diaries were interpolated into one book, Winchester Divided, by historian Michael Mahon.

Linda Lee, a Confederate sympathizer, described her first sight of these troops as "a most revolting spectacle ... [with] such rambling, shambling, tumbling .... such grinning and grimacing..." She saw it as showing "the madness and folly of the Yankee government," and certainly not as demonstrating any inherent desire for freedom by these human beings.

Lee's fellow Winchester resident, Julia Chase, was a Union sympathizer. But she was no abolitionist, and described the African-American troops as "as a sight .. that I never expected to see." She understood that the troops' goals was "to conscript all the able bodied Negroes ... in the county." Even though this was action in support of her beloved Union, her immediate concern was "we ... shall have no one to do anything for us in the way of cutting wood, tilling the ground, & c." Far from being inspired by this new and courageous addition to the Union armies, she was mostly concerned with the inconvenience she would face as slavery collapsed around her.

So Few Insurrections

Eventually, a time came when slavery was more than a generation in the past, and could be studied as history – of course, as white history.

John Fiske's Old Virginia and Her Neighbors, published in 1897, stated that "It is one of the remarkable facts in American history that there have been so few insurrections of negroes." Fiske then went on to cite plots and conspiracies in 1687 and 1710, and then to describe the punishments for runaways, the legal impunity of masters who killed slaves, and restrictions on even the use of medicines (potential poisons) by enslaved people. Fiske also noted approvingly that the punishment of mutilation existed to "protect white women against the horrible crime which then as now he [the African-American man] was prone to commit." (By this, of course, he referred to rape of white women.)

Fiske also writes about Billy, a man who had escaped from slavery and was "lying out and lurking in obscure places," and "devouring and destroying stocks and crops" and robbing houses. Billy, who seems to have conducted his own one-man guerrilla war, had a reward put on his head of one thousand pounds of tobacco by the 1701 Virginia General Assembly.

Fiske never made clear why even these few rebellious acts he mentioned occurred, since he claimed that 'the treatment of slaves by their master was mild and humane," and referred in particular to "slavery in its mild Virginia form." In fact, the aspect of slavery that seemed to trouble the Victorian Fiske most was the existence of "illicit sexual relations." Fiske suggested that "in many a southern home there were earnest hearts that deplored" slavery for this reason. But it does not seem to have occurred to Fiske that the rape of enslaved women might have itself been a motivation for rebellion.

For all their cruelty, the Council of Virginia two centuries before had a much more realistic view than Fiske. They saw the humanity of their slaves, and consciously chose to be cruel. Fiske and others invented an imaginary slavery without brutality.

"Cherished as Loving if Lowly Friends"

A more "modern" approach was that of historian Ulrich Phillips, who wrote during the harshest days of the Jim Crow system. Phillips was one of the first historians to look into the detailed records of plantations in order to come to his conclusions. But, as his 1929 Life and Labor in the Old South shows, he accepted most of what masters wrote, while seeing people of African descent as inherently inferior.

He believed the propaganda of his day, and falsely described the Africans who became enslaved as having "lived naked, observed fetish, been bound by tribal law, and [practicing] primitive crafts."

Life and Labor only mentions

insurrection three times, and mainly as something that happened elsewhere, Haïti for example, and that "brought as fruit of apprehension a new crop of statutes to make assurance increasingly sure that the South should continue to be 'a white man's country."

Slavery was, in Phillips eyes, a relatively benign business system, in which slaves were "cherished not only as property of high value but as loving if lowly friends." Insurrection was not common, he claimed, nor was its threat all that important. Thus he dressed white supremacist fantasy in the clothing of hard research.

> **Will Ann Rogers relates a story told by her mother about what happened when she was auctioned in Richmond, Virginia:**
> **. . . When they sold her, her mother fainted or drapped dead, she never knowed which. She wanted to go see her mother lying over there on the ground and the man what bought her wouldn't let her. He just took her on. Drove her off like cattle, I recken. The man what bought her was Ephram Hester. That the last she ever knowed of**

any of her folks. (Library of Congress)

Beyond the Colossal Myth

In 1943, American Negro Slave Revolts was published. Its author, Herbert Aptheker, was a member of the Communist Party then, and a leading member and theoretician of the Party for most of his life. As a Communist, Aptheker was unable to ever get a tenured position teaching history, though he continued to do scholarly work throughout his life. And as a Communist, he had made a commitment to seeing every human as equal, and to supporting struggle, violent if necessary, by the "lower" classes.

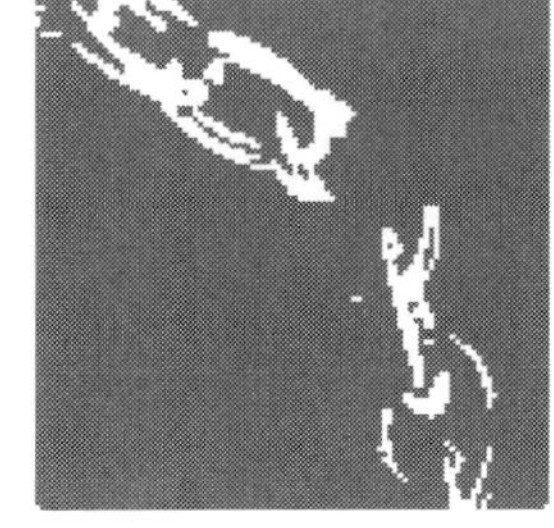

Aptheker described his book at its close as an attempt at "depicting in realistic terms the response of the American Negro to his bondage." Part of his realism was his recognition that "the colossal myth of the sub-humanity of the Negro ... [was] basic to the entire social order.."

Neither Fiske nor Phillips could see

beyond this "colossal myth" to the human beings that were enduring slavery. When Aptheker broke through this myth, even with the limitations of 1940s scholarship, he was able to write more than 350 pages about a wide range of insurrections and rebellions by enslaved African-Americans. Since then, information on more rebellions has come to light. Yet we know that some of the rebellions against slavery have been as absolutely lost to history as the rebellions of victims of other totalitarian systems.

How these writers see the insurrections against slavery shows us far more about them than it does about people of African descent. No slaveholder, of course, supports a right to rebel. But the slaveholders of 1680 recognized that the human beings they held in bondage would rebel, given the chance. However, as time passed, slaveholders and those who were sympathetic to slavery were less and less able to see why slaves would and did rebel.

In 1843, in a speech calling on those enslaved in the South to rise up in insurrection, Rev. Henry Highland Garnet said "In every man's mind the good seeds of liberty are planted." It is a truth that illuminates slavery – and the white response to it -- in an instant.

Listening for Gabriel – 1987

(The name Gabriel here refers both to the angel who traditionally sounds the last trumpet and to Gabriel Prosser, a Black Richmonder who led a well-planned but unsuccessful rebellion in 1800. I lived in Richmond in 1987.)

As I write in this Virginia summer night,
While the cicadas repeat their ancient rhythm
In tiny voices sharp as steel,
While leaves rustle in the hot winds of drought
From Southampton County to Harper's Ferry,
I listen for Gabriel.

I cannot stop listening for Gabriel.

I cannot stop listening for the trumpet.

Not long ago, I stopped to rest
By a lake scented with water lilies,
Ringing with birdsong,
My back at ease against a tree.
But the peace was broken
By the dull shudder of engines overhead.
I remembered that each person that I loved
Stood naked to the deadly sky.

I cannot stop listening for Gabriel.

And I cannot stop listening for another Gabriel,
Who lived in the same city I live in,
Who walked Richmond's streets,
Who shopped in Richmond's markets
And listened to talk about
Respected gentlemen exercising power,
And who spoke so clearly about that power
That many others,
Like him held in captivity,
Listened to Gabriel,
Listened for his call,
And on a rainy night
Followed him into insurrection.

Though the slave-owners hanged Gabriel Prosser,
This land still rings with his challenge.
This place is no inheritance
from a pale English lady monarch;
It is the birthright of dark children
Whose parents' sweat made it bear fruit.

And all of us who share this land

Are still listening
For Gabriel.

And for Gabriel.

After slavery was wrestled to the ground,
Freedmanstown was built on vacant land
below the Custis Mansion in Arlington
for those that had outlasted slavery.
Forty years ago, their heirs were relocated,
(Perhaps to a subsidized Bantustan)
And five walls were built to house
The planning of the final war.

As I drive past the Pentagon,
I remember the many that have come
To declare peace,
The women that circled this Virginia soil with ribbons,
The man who gave his body up to fire,
The chants of twenty years;
And I still listen
For the final single note.

I listen for Gabriel.

And I listen for Gabriel,
As Dred Scott is once again told
He has no rights a white man need
respect,
Only this time the judge speaks
Afrikaans,
While lunatic visions of a past that
never was
Once again cloud the mind of an old
man
In a white house across the Potomac,
As they did Tyler's mind
Before he helped fashion the
Confederacy.

And I listen for Gabriel,
In this dark night of a summer,
When Virginia is impoverished by more
than drought,
Though the gray ships crowd Hampton
Roads
And the poor of Pittsylvania
Are promised
Treasures of uranium;

And the gentle hills of Fairfax
Are lost in an arrogance of dazzling walls and windows.

I don't know whether I listen in hope or in fear,
But I know I listen
With faith in certain ancient truths.

"I will bring you out of the affliction of Egypt....",

"Woe to them that devise iniquity!"

I am
Listening for

I am listening for

Gabriel.

Slavery Didn't "Happen," It Was Chosen

Chattel slavery of people of African descent is often treated as something that grew naturally, rather than being instituted consciously by human beings.

The Virginia Farm Bureau Story, a public relations effort with no claim to being an ideological history, provides a modern example of this thinking. The author tells us that "Tobacco and slavery grew together," that "The plantation system grew with tobacco," and that "Tobacco dictated the location and routing of roads in the Piedmont." The author writes as if slavery spontaneously emerged from amidst the tobacco leaves.

Tobacco had been cultivated and used in what became Virginia for centuries, if not millennia. In all those years, it grew leaves and roots and flowers, but never grew hereditary chattel slavery, huge plantations, or even a system of roads. The responsibility for these changes is on wealthy white colonial Virginians who wanted to make the maximum amount of money from tobacco export.

The African-American scholar-activist W.E.B. DuBois wrote "There was never a time in the history of America when the [slavery] system had a slighter economic, political and moral justification than in 1787. And yet with ... this growing evil before their eyes, a bargain largely of dollars and cents was allowed to open the highway that led straight to the Civil War." (DuBois, 1896) 1787, of course, was when the Constitution of the United States was proposed.

DuBois continued ".. there began, with 1787, that system of bargaining, truckling and compromising with a moral, political and economic monstrosity..."

Virginians, including Washington, Jefferson and Madison, were at the center of that "bargaining" and "truckling." From the writings of the latter two, we know that at least some of the time they could see that the future of the U.S. with slavery was extremely ugly. But they never chose to act. They let "tobacco and slavery grow together," and then other leaders welcomed "cotton and slavery," and then "cotton and Jim Crow..."

People of African descent experienced the insidious growth of race-based oppression into every part of life. A field worker of the Virginia Writer's Project recorded a folk tale that shows this vividly. In the story, a cruel mistress was beating a young slave girl for not obeying a command quickly enough. Suddenly, "an ole horn snake" came out of the bushes and chased "ole missus" up a cherry tree. The snake "stuck his horn in de tree." The white mistress just sat up in the tree eating cherries. Then she fell out of the tree, dead. The snake's poison "had run all though dat tree an' into de cherries..." (Barden)

By the time of Uncle Tom's Cabin, this poison had permeated more generations of whites. Later, in the 1950s, Jim Crow was justified as "the

Southern way of life." Indeed it was, but that only came about choice by choice by choice – choices made by white people and their leaders.

Yet, refusing to recognize their own choices, "most white people saw the source of the racial problem in Black people, not in themselves and their institutions." (Stuckey) A common phrase in the 1950s to describe white supremacy was "the Negro Problem."

(This is why the 1966 issue of Ebony Magazine that highlighted "The White Problem" on the cover was so illuminating to my teenage consciousness.)

White guilt is a vastly overrated problem. I personally think Robert E. Lee may have been the only person who ever died from it. But avoiding white guilt is a very popular excuse for also avoiding white responsibility.

The facts show that slavery was chosen by the slave-owners, that they could have made changes.

Today, the institution of racism takes a different form. But the majority of us still perpetuate it every day. And we do it with less serious attention that we give to selecting our choice for

America’s Best Home Video of Falling Kittens.

Fraud and Fable Number Eight: Virginia's Whites Stood Together For The Southern Way Of Life.

Purpose: We are told that all whites went along with slavery, the Confederacy and Jim Crow. In reality, white people have, and had, choices, and a few did make the hard ones.

Some Virginia Race Traitors

> **"Why, I remember when a man was prosecuted here in this very county for havin' a seditious book – one about slavery, you know – in his possession, and lendin' it to a friend; and people were almost afraid to speak to him, or go bail for him. You Northern people don't know anything about what we call public opinion here."**
> (Tourgée)

"Race traitor" is a term used today by Noel Ignatiev and other members of the New Abolitionist Society. The New Abolitionists argue that "The key to solving the social problems of our age is to abolish the white race -- in other words, to abolish the privileges of the white skin." (Ignatiev)

It is unlikely that the white Virginians I describe in this section had thought the issue through to that extent. But their actions were genuine challenges to the whiteness of their day, and I think they deserve the noble title of Race Traitor.

In 1816, according to the papers of the Governor of Virginia, a white man deeply dissatisfied with the society he lived in helped to organize a slave insurrection in Spottsylvania County, halfway between Richmond and Washington.

"George Boxley, the chief of the conspiracy in this neighborhood, is naturally a man of restless and aspiring mind; wild and visionary in his theories, and ardent in pursuit of his designs. At an early period in his life, without any necessary qualifications, and with great respectability of character, he offered his services to represent the County in the Legislature .... During the late war with Great Britain ... he solicited the appointment of adjutant to the regiment, but was foiled by a more successful candidate. .... these repeated disappointments seem to have embittered his mind. ... he has declared that the distinctions between the rich and the poor were too great; that offices were given to wealth rather than merit... For many years he had avowed his disapprobation of the slavery of the negroes, and wished that they were free.

During the latter end of last summer ..., according to

the testimony of the negroes, he began the conspiracy. To facilitate the means of carrying it out he kept a shop for selling whiskey.... under the pretense of purchasing these, great numbers of negroes were received at this house; and the horrible plot which has been detailed in our first communication was formed....." (Holladay)

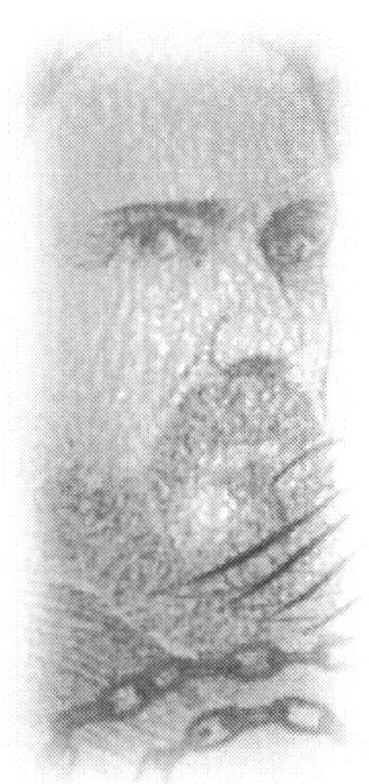

Boxley's story is not only Virginia history, but Indiana history, as he ended his life in that state. An online excerpt from A History of Hamilton County, Indiana, tells a rather different story, describing Boxley back in Virginia as a "wealthy and influential citizen" and veteran of the War of 1812, whose only crime was to help two enslaved people to escape

from Virginia. For this crime, the

Indiana account continues, he was sentenced to death, but escaped with the help of “a fine spring-saw [his wife] concealed in the hem of her skirt.” He fled to Ohio, was then spotted by some traveling Virginians who sought to capture him, and, after another escape, this time to Indiana, lived out his years with his family, serving as the local schoolteacher. (Sheridan County Historical Society)

Whatever the true story of George Boxley, whether he was an insurrectionist or merely a minor figure in the early days of the Underground Railroad, his case was taken seriously enough that two Virginia governors took action, first to have him punished and then to have him brought back from Ohio. Whatever he did, it was more than enough to have him seen as a traitor to white Virginia. This was, after all, a time when an honest handshake between a black and a white person would have been almost a revolutionary act.

Fifteen years after Boxley fled Virginia, another white man took what now looks like an even bolder step. He took as his teacher and spiritual adviser the African-American of the early nineteenth century who soon became the most hated and feared of all by white people -- the rebel leader Nat Turner. This almost unknown story seems as strange as an ordinary white guy becoming Malcolm X's golfing buddy, or the best man at Pancho Villa's wedding.

This is how Nat Turner told it in his comments to Thomas R. Gray while awaiting execution:

> **"for as the blood of Christ had been shed on this earth, and was now returning to earth again in the form of dew -- and as the leaves of the trees bore the impression of the figures I had seen in the heavens ... it was plain to me that ... the great day of judgment was at hand. About this time I told these things to a white man, (Etheldred T. Brantley) on whom it had a wonderful effect -- and he ceased from his wickedness and was attacked immediately with a subcutaneous eruption, and blood oozed from the pores of his skin, and after praying and fasting nine days, he was healed, and the Spirit**

appeared to me again, and said, as the Saviour had been baptized so should we be also -- and when the white people would not let us be baptized by the church, we went down into the water together, in the sight of many who reviled us, and were baptized by the Spirit ..."

from The Confessions of Nat Turner, The Leader of the Late Insurrection in Southampton County, published 1831.

Who was this white man, who was both saved and healed as the first ministerial act of Nat Turner? What were the truths of his life, and of the life of Southside Virginia in 1830, that led him to put his life in Nat's hands? Why did Nat heal and restore Brantley's life, only a few years before he led his comrades to take the lives of whites?

A book by Israeli historian Mechal Sobel about black and white people in 18th Century Virginia, The World They Made Together, makes a strong case that Africans and Europeans connected in surprising ways in Virginia. Like any good social history, it goes back to the reality of life, to the documents, to the nitty gritty.

I was astonished to find Sobel quoting from the documents of a racially integrated Baptist church in Southampton County, the county where Nat Turner lived -- a church founded in 1774 with an institutional conviction that slavery was unrighteous -- a church that in 1787 expelled a white couple for "using Barbarity toward their Slaves". I was also surprised to find that, a few counties away from Southampton, in the City of Portsmouth, the predominantly white Court Street Church had a pastor who was not only African-American, but an ex-slave. (Sobel) In 1787 and 1788, "Virginia Methodists reputedly freed more than a hundred slaves at one session of the Sussex County court." Enslaved people also served as ministers; one Northern Neck slave preached to congregations as large as four hundred. Baptist groups also bought the freedom of slave preachers. (Raboteau)

Etheldred Brantley was not as unusual as I thought; fifty years earlier, he wouldn't have been unusual at all. Sobel's book brought to life a brief period, when Baptists and Methodists first touched Virginia with their evangelism, when Christianity did indeed bring together the African and the European, and when many

Europeans apparently genuinely respected and learned from the spiritual experience of their fellow congregants with an African spiritual tradition.

Brantley, though, lived in a different time. Putting behind them the feelings of liberation brought on by the Revolution and the humble beginnings of evangelical sects, Southern whites had become more engrossed in the pursuit of easy wealth that the system of slavery encouraged.

After all, from the days of Nat Turner's rebellion, the Declaration of Independence was no farther back in the past than the launch of Sputnik or the accession of John XXIII to the Papacy are for us today.

Nat Turner certainly knew about the anti-slavery leanings of certain whites. He ordered those he led on his bloody rebellion to spare any Quakers, Methodists and Frenchmen they encountered. He assumed every other white person they would run into would be implicated in the slavery system. (Apparently he was right. Even those who denounce him as a vicious murderer have ever claimed that the whites he and his followers killed were anti-slavery.)

There was one more white man who was singled out for an encounter with Nat Turner, according to African-American writer William Wells Brown's account of the insurrection:

"Nat Turner ... foretold, that, at his death, the sun would refuse to shine, and that there would be signs of disapprobation given from Heaven. And it is true that the sun was darkened, a storm gathered and more boisterous weather had never appeared in Southampton County than on the day of Nat's execution. The sheriff, warned by the prisoner, refused to cut the cord that held the trap. No black man would touch the rope. A poor old white man, long besotted by drink, was brought forty miles to be the executioner." Clearly the whites of Southampton County had at least some grudging respect for Nat Turner as a prophet and a righteous man of God.

Nat Turner exercised enormous power, in life and in dying, even though by the law of his place and time he was only a beast of burden, not a human being. Because most whites, unlike Etheldred Brantley, could not face and accept Turner's power, he was left with only one way to use it – violent rebellion. Though he was seen by his white neighbors as sub-human, Nat Turner made history that shook the nation.

Brantley was not the last white Virginian to "betray his race." One white opponent of slavery went far beyond passing on pamphlets or freeing his own slaves.

> **"The case of James Allen, a [Virginia] Methodist, appears to offer the example of a white man who gave his life to make possible the escape of a slave. In this instance Holloway's Charles, with the aid of Allen, made his escape from his master. Allen was taken into the woods to be whipped until he revealed the location of the missing Negro. He refused to speak and the testimony sent to the governor reveals the harrowing details of his**

torture and death." (Johnston)

Another white American of slavery times did not die for her actions against the grain of racism, but she did go to jail. Mrs. Margaret Douglass, a white woman, was condemned by a judge in Norfolk, Virginia in 1853. She went to jail because she triggered the slave-owners' excessive, even absurd, fear of abolitionist propaganda getting to, and being read by, the people they enslaved. The judge's speech included this rant on these topics:

"There might have been no occasion for such enactments in Virginia, or elsewhere, on the subject of negro education, but as a matter of self-defense against the schemes of Northern incendiaries, and the outcry against holding our slaves in bondage. Many now living

well remember how, and when, and why, the anti-slavery fury began, and by what means its manifestations were made public. Our mails were clogged with abolition pamphlets and inflammatory documents, to be distributed among our Southern negroes to induce them to cut our throats. Sometimes, it may be, these libelous documents were distributed by Northern citizens professing Southern feelings, and at other times, by Southern people professing Northern feelings. These, however, were not the only means resorted to by the Northern fanatics to stir up insubordination among our slaves. They scattered far and near pocket handkerchiefs, and other similar articles, with frightful engravings, and printed over with anti-slavery nonsense, with the view to work upon the feeling and ignorance of our negroes, who otherwise would have remained comfortable and happy. Under such circumstances there was but one measure of protection for the South, and that was adopted. . . . ...the judgment of

the Court is, in addition to the proper fine and costs, that you be imprisoned for the period of one month in the jail of this city..." (Baker)

This frenzied language, coming from a judge, gives a sense of how irrational slave-owners became. Baker's description of an "anti-slavery fury" would have been news to abolitionists in the North, who when this legislation passed were struggling merely to maintain tiny organizations against widespread public opposition.

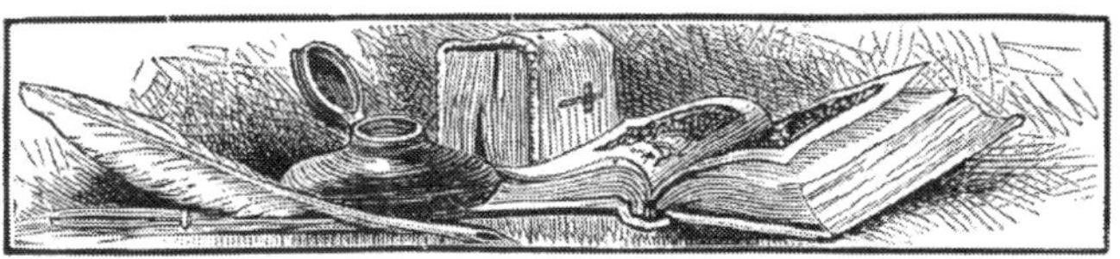

Wesleyan Heritage

Methodists, along with Baptists, had had a profound impact on Virginia during the American Revolution. Their struggle for legitimacy in the face of an established Anglican church put political clout behind the religious liberty ideas of Jefferson and others. The founder of Methodism, John Wesley, was a bitter opponent of slavery, and wrote about African people in his 1774 book Thoughts Upon Slavery:

> **"...the Negroes who inhabit the coast of Africa, from the river Senegal to the southern bounds of Angola, are ... remarkably sensible .... industrious to the highest degree ... fair, just, and honest in all their dealings .... far more mild, friendly, and kind to strangers than any of our forefathers were. Our forefathers! Where shall we find at this day, among the fair-faced natives of Europe, nations generally practicing the justice, mercy and truth, which are found among these poor Africans?"** (Wesley)

In 1789, The General Committee of Virginia Baptists adopted a resolution describing slavery as "a violent deprivation of the laws of nature," and urged Baptists to "make use of every legal measure to extirpate this horrid evil from the land." However, within four years, the Committee had dropped the issue under pressure from pro-slavery Baptists. (Raboteau)

As time went on, however, Southern white Methodists and Baptists increasingly disregarded the inconvenient beliefs in racial justice of some of their leaders. Eventually, of course, this led to a division of these denominations into Northern and Southern sections.

In 1843, a new church, the Wesleyans, was organized with Wesley's original abolitionist principles. (Coleson) In southwestern Virginia, central North Carolina and elsewhere, the mostly Midwestern members were in contact with white Southerners who shared these principles. The Wesleyans started sending missionaries to these groups in 1847, and these missionaries stood up for their beliefs publicly, as in this statement to a pro-slavery mob by Adam Crooks, a Wesleyan missionary in North Carolina:

> **"Nothing can be more certain than that slavery will prove fatal to the South if it is not peaceably abolished. The war between the antagonistic principles and interests of liberty and slavery, is bound to go on till one destroys the other. As well attempt to reconcile God and the devil, as**

to establish peace upon a permanent basis between liberty and slavery, and it is for every man to say which side he will take in the contest. Slavery will destroy the country if the country does not destroy slavery." (Crooks)

Their Virginia and North Carolina missionaries were indicted for inciting slaves to insurrection, even though their missionary work was directed at whites. None were imprisoned, but soon the slave-owners resorted to violence and mobs. In 1851, the three Wesleyan missionaries left the South. Jarvis C. Bacon, who served Grayson County, Virginia, died soon afterwards. The native Wesleyans also were arrested and mobbed, and many of them also left the South. (Crooks)

The Box Man of Richmond

Henry "Box" Brown was a well known abolitionist speaker. A book was published about him, and he developed a show, "Henry Box Brown's Mirror of Slavery," which he took on the road and New England and then in England for several years. His nickname came from his method of escape from slavery in Richmond. He was sealed into a box and shipped to Underground Railroad participants in Philadelphia. (Encyclopedia Virginia)

Brown was boxed up by a white man, Samuel Smith. Smith was later convicted of boxing up two other men to help them escape from slavery, and served six years in the Richmond penitentiary for the crime. While in prison, he suffered a murder attempt, and was refused a pardon by the Governor even though he was a model prisoner and the warden recommended his release. In 1856, when he had served his time and met with Underground Railroad representatives in Philadelphia, he told them he had helped many other African-Americans gain freedom from 1828 until his imprisonment in 1849. Smith was honored by Philadelphia African-American residents at a mass meeting with a resolution that welcomed him "as a martyr to the cause of freedom." (Still)

A Traitor to Whiteness Who Paid the Price

In the 1850s, John Kagi came from Ohio to Shenandoah County, Virginia, where his parents had been born and he had numerous kinfolk. He taught school there. He made his abolitionist feelings very clear to slaveholding Virginians, and was told to go back to Ohio and never return. Not long afterward, he wrote this in a letter to his family:

> **But I believe there are better times dawning, to my sight, at least. I can not now laboring and waiting without present reward, for myself alone, it is for a future reward for**

> **mankind and my dear father and sister. There can be no doubt of the reward in the end, or of the drawing very**

> **near of the success of a great cause which is to earn it. Few of my age have toiled harder or suffered more in this cause than I, and yet I regret nothing that I have done; nor am I in any [discouraged]** (sic) **at the future.** (Kagi)

In October of 1859, John Kagi did return to Virginia – to the town of Harper's Ferry, now in West Virginia, as part of John Brown's armed force attempting to seize the arsenal there. Kagi, already a veteran of anti-slavery combat in Kansas, was killed at Harper's Ferry.

I'm guessing that some pro-slavery Virginians were probably relieved that Kagi died in the fighting. It would have been profoundly embarrassing to try a man of Virginian stock – even of Swiss Virginia stock – for being John Brown's second in command, with the title of Secretary of War.

Confederate Cointelpro?

After John Brown's abolitionist incursion, "one of the worst witch-hunts in American history occurred as eccentrics and 'suspicious characters' of all kinds, many of them innocent strangers passing through, were mobbed, beaten and tarred and feathered in a vigilante effort to root out Yankees and potential Southern subversives." (Taylor) In Loudoun County, not far from Harpers Ferry, citizens "denounced and attempted to prohibit peddlers, book agents, travelers, and vendors of goods from traveling through the county," concerned that their intent "might be to incite slave insurrections." (Poland)

To put this in context, it's as if people today were crazy enough to think the clerk at the local 7-11 was responsible for 9/11.

Soon after the Harper's Ferry action, and driven partly by resentment of the popularity of John Brown in the North, the slavocracy took its most delusional step of all. It declared itself a "nation" and mustered an army. One particularly prophetic observer, South Carolina Governor Hammond, described the upsurge of "Southern patriotism" in December, 1860 as "very foolish," adding "It reminds me of the Japanese who when insulted rip open their own bowels."

White resisters to the slavery system were rare, and they paid a high price for their resistance. But these examples show that even in a slavery-dominated society, whiteness did not always trump the reality of common humanity.

October, After the Flood

the last time we talked to our neighbor

out on the Shenandoah river
he told us about the flood
that Hurricane Fran brought

an entire house
just upriver
had been washed off its foundation
he had seen it go

he said
if it had held
even an hour longer
that as the flood subsided
that house would still be standing
where it was built

instead it is a broken frame
in the silent trees
across the river from his house
and ours

he told us that story
that was the last time we ever saw him

we came to the bridge
after midnight on Friday
the deputy waved us down with his
flashlight
he said it wasn't safe to cross

the problem wasn't the river
it was running calm and shallow that night

he told us in the reticent and brutal
language of the law
there was an incident in progress
across the river

we had passed two ambulances
waiting by Zion Church
on the other side from the cemetery
on the other side of the Shenandoah

whatever those ambulances were waiting
for
was happening
when we returned an hour later

one of the ambulances passed us
lights flashing siren screaming
we found out later
he was in it

they told us
when we got back
it was all over
it was all right to cross

a deputy asked us which house we were
headed for
not the one with the lights on, he said
and we said no, next door

and another officer
came in and
checked our house with us quickly
to be sure the violence hadn't spread

into our home
and he told us
there had been
two shot
one stabbed

I went out in the moonlight tonight
to tell him goodbye
and wish him peace

he was a good neighbor to us
however his dying happened

I went down to the river
in the moonlight

I could see the stacked firewood on his land
remembered seeing him methodically
sawing logs
gifts from the flood
they will never warm him now

I don't know what happened
and maybe no one ever will exactly
there were
two men one woman
at least one gun
on a full moon Friday night

no one survived

the last time I saw him he told us
that if that house had held against the flood
even an hour longer
it would have made it

up on the ridge their house still stands
but it stands dark and empty
rage, jealousy, despair
like the roaring river
they all subside
in time

but a house may have a weakness
something simple snaps and
it cannot resist
the river
even for that one more hour
that would ensure survival

a man may
obtain
a gun
and when pain surges over the banks
of daily life
it's such a simple step to use it
so simple so quick
and so terribly wrong

he said
if it had held
even an hour longer
that house would still be standing

I stand in the moonlight
flood debris still caught in the branches
above me

some say that the flood may have happened
because so many of us

have made lawns
that run all the way down to the river
we have left no
brambles and roots
roots and limbs
in place
to slow the storm water

when the sky breaks open
it is as if, believing no flood could ever harm us,
we had prepared channels
to speed up the merging waters

it is as if we did not want
that hour
that minute
that we might gain

to be clear
to get a better grip
one that will last us until the flood has passed

up on the ridge
there is a dark and empty house
and there is the lighted one
where my heart's partner
goes about her business

by the unceasing river
I pray for the cool forgiving peace that the dead need
and I pray
for the time that the living need

to let the saplings leaf out
to let the guns rust
to let hearts learn more tender and more
subtle ways

and I start up the steep path towards home

Fraud and Fable Number Nine: African-Americans Were Bystanders During The Decades Of Increasing Sectional Division Leading to the Civil War.

Purpose: "Forgetting" the centuries of massive African-American efforts for their own liberation reinforces the belief that the Virginia Gentleman is the one and only one who makes history for Virginia, and is always in charge.

> **"It is in your power so to torment the God-cursed slaveholders that they will be glad to let you go free."** Rev. Henry Highland Garnet, "Address to the Slaves of the United States of America," National Convention of Negro Citizens in 1843. (Foner, 1972)

> **"Those slave-owners and slave traders said they were building a democracy. They didn't know anything about building a democracy... every generation since then has got to do the job they couldn't do, that they weren't qualified to do."** Thurgood Marshall, speaking to Vincent Harding (Harding, Sojourners)

We are often reminded, especially by Confederate apologists, that we cannot grasp the Civil War from a "presentist" 2012 viewpoint. It's quite true. But the Lost Cause viewpoint, a postwar propaganda tale idealizing Lee and Confederates and focusing on arcane arguments about states' rights, is just as removed from the war's reality as the corny vision of Lincoln the Emancipator leading an anti-racist crusade.

The real problem is that we are used to looking to the interactions of white élites to understand how our nation reached the point of civil war. We were raised hearing about the noble parade of Webster and Taney and Calhoun and the Lincoln-Douglas debates.

All that talk was a sideshow. The people that forced the great issue of slavery to the crisis point were neither white not élite, and they started the process long before there was even a United States of America, let alone before Congress started coming up with compromises to duck the issue.

Slavery Was the Issue

Slavery was the fundamental issue of the war. No one, especially in the South, contradicted this until after the war was over. At that point, when it was gone anyway, former Confederates realized how terrible their defense of slavery made them look. So they started working on their list of so-called "real reasons.” (For more on this, read below about Jubal Early and the Lost Cause propaganda in Fraud and Fable Number Ten “**White Virginia Rightfully Cherished a Noble Lost Cause**.”)

This 1861 statement by Alexander Stephens, Vice President of the “Confederate States of America” ought to settle the question. First, he specifically repudiated Jefferson and ideas of humans being “created equal,” and then he went on:

> **“Our new government is founded upon exactly the opposite ideas; its foundations are laid, its cornerstone rests, upon the great truth that the negro is not equal to the white man; that slavery, subordination to the superior race, is his natural and moral condition.”** (Thomas)

Not only slavery, but contemptible racism, was the “cornerstone” of the Confederate rebellion, according to its second highest-ranking official.

Of course, there was always, and especially after the war, a lot of discussion of the rights of sovereign states and the right of secession under the original Constitution. In The Southern Tradition At Bay, (Weaver) the major postwar advocates of these positions are reviewed sympathetically. And there is a lot of logic to their positions – but only if one accepts that people of African descent are not human beings.

If, on the other hand, people of African descent are and always were human, nothing the states and the national government as constituted in 1861 had agreed on in relation to them was valid.

If you kidnap me and keep me handcuffed in a basement while you sign my name to a lease, I am not obligated under law to honor that lease. All of the arguments for secession and for Southern states' rights are as invalid as that lease would be – at least for any person of African descent.

The Real Abolitionists

O.K. The Civil War was about the situation African-Americans had been put in. And it was the abolitionists who kept raising it until war finally came, right?

Of course, most of us have heard the story that Lincoln greeted Harriet

Beecher Stowe, author of the anti-slavery best-seller Uncle Tom's Cabin, with "So you're the little lady that started this great big war." Is that the answer? Obviously one little lady didn't do it all. But did "abolitionists," long the bugaboo of the South, force the issues that led to war?

I would say that the answer is "yes," but I would add that our view of abolitionists need some serious adjusting. The popular view of "abolitionism" is expressed by this language from an advertising-driven website on U.S. history:

> **"The abolitionist movement called for the end of the institution of slavery and had existed in one form or another since colonial times; the early case had been stated most consistently by the Quakers. Most Northern states abolished the institution after the War for Independence, reacting to moral concerns and economic unfeasibility."**
> (U.S.History.com)

The description continues with Garrison and so on; but already there is something major missing from this description. Let's see... What could it be? “I know, I know...” waving hand wildly. “Black people!”

In this moving passage, historian, activist and preacher Vincent Harding describes the actual first people to oppose enslavement of Africans for the Atlantic trade:

> **“...in those early precincts of despair, beginning in baracoons and oceanside forts, under multilayered surfaces of European domination and African betrayal, the struggle for black freedom was breaking out.... At that moment in our history, as the ominous shadows hovered near the coasts, we fought to remain in our homeland, to continue in the experience and tradition our peoples had created... we denied the European right to hold us, to rule our lives, to control our destiny. We affirmed our own freedom, our own being.”** (Harding, There is a River)

The struggle against slavery began when human beings were first stolen from the Motherland, not in 1652 or 1831 or 1861. And from the beginning the people who led that struggle, who fought hardest, who came up with the most creative and powerful ideas, and who made the most difference, were the people who were enslaved.

Many whites cared deeply about the issue of slavery. For a few, like John Woolman or Benjamin Lundy or William Lloyd Garrison, it was their major preoccupation. But hundreds of thousands of people of African descent thought about slavery every day -- for centuries. And they didn't have to agonize about whether they were against it, or how they should interact with their friends who were for it, as white people did.

By the time of the first white North American legislation against slavery, in Rhode Island in 1652, (Earle), people of African descent had been resisting the Atlantic slave trade for two centuries.

By the time John Woolman, the first widely effective white anti-slavery activist, began to persuade his fellow Quakers to renounce slavery in the 1740s, people of African descent had been organizing insurrections against North American chattel slavery for more than a century. Before William Lloyd Garrison was born, Haïtians had demolished slavery in their nation, as well as the colonial armies that defended it.

As a white anti-racist activist, I have a soft spot in my heart for the Woolmans and Garrisons and such, who showed me a path I have tried to follow. But as an organizer and a student of history, I have to recognize that changes are made by those who have the power and will to do so, not by those who, gosh, sure would like to see change.

> **".. I have never been able to understand how the slaves throughout the South, completely ignorant as were the masses so far as books or newspapers were concerned, were able to keep themselves so accurately**

and completely informed about the great National questions that were agitating the country. From the time that Garrison, Lovejoy and others began to agitate for freedom, the slaves throughout the South kept in close touch with the progress of the movement."

From Up From Slavery, by Booker T. Washington, writing about his Virginia childhood

In part, this awareness by the enslaved had came from having learned to understand what white people had to say. According to one study of "education in the slave quarter community," Africans enslaved in America educated themselves and their children to "be sensitive to the nuances of white behavior: to detect shifting moods, to anticipate anger, to play on fear, and to sense by a word or expression the fine line between what would be tolerated and what would be punished." (Webber)

Meanwhile, Southern whites during slavery times were busily persuading themselves that the people they held in bondage were both stupid and innately loyal. Even a century later, Richard Weaver, a pro-slave-owner white conservative, wrote "...the Negroes went through the war and well into Reconstruction in a dense ignorance of what beyond the scope of their actual observation was going on." This tells us more about his own ignorance than about that of African-Americans. (Weaver)

African-Americans had an enormous advantage in understanding the political and social situation they shared with whites. From necessity, African-Americans knew almost everything important about Southern whites. By choice, Southern whites knew almost nothing about African-Americans.

A practically unanimous nation of four million people within a nation of less than 32 million, with centuries of experience and knowledge behind it, and with a crucial role in the economy, had substantially more power than a few thousand whites working on one of several issues close to their hearts. (U.S. Census Bureau, Population) This is true even though the enslaved were mostly illiterate and had no legal rights, while some white abolitionists were highly literate intellectuals with significant personal influence.

Why the Compromises Failed

During the United States' first 76 years, our white male élites spent much of their energy coming up with compromises, with ways to evade the crisis that all of them could see coming. Looking back, this may seem hard to believe. But after all, the white male élites of the early 21st century are treating the crisis of global climate change exactly the same way today.

So how did the process of evading the issues finally come to an end? And, more importantly, how did the war that did come become an anti-slavery war on the Union side?

There were differences of interests between North and South from the founding of the United States, as reflected in the shaping of the Constitution.

Slave-owners, though, in defending themselves against the intensifying liberation efforts of the people they claimed to own, made these differences more painful and more serious. They essentially went on the offensive against the rights and sensibilities of Northerners.

Slave-owners pushed a Gag Rule through Congress that blocked receipt of any antislavery petitions by Congress for more than a decade. Southern elected officials assaulted a Nothern Senator at his desk, burned mail deliveries of abolitionist materials, imprisoned white preachers opposing slavery, and insisted on their right to invade Northern cities seeking escaped captives and take them without due process. They talked about their own "state's rights," while ignoring the rights of those states that had chosen not to have slavery within their borders, and that wanted to protect their citizens from being stolen South.

While historians make a reasonable case that there was no "Great Slavepower Conspiracy," no coherent widely-agreed on plan for secession before Lincoln's election. But in the North, it looked to many people like there was "a South, united in abnormal conspiratorial control of democracy...." (Freehling, 1990).

The intellectual life of the white South was totally focused on "what would be the most effective propaganda to counter the stream flowing down from the North [so that] .. in the four decades preceding the war dispassionate opinion practically vanished." (Weaver) After noting this, Southern apologist Richard Weaver uses the "the Yankees started it" argument to justify this focus, but that's not too convincing.

During the same period, after all, there was also a Southern white critique of the North as money-grubbing, materialistic, and cruel to white labor. Yet somehow Northern intellectuals felt no need to spend every waking hour defensively rebutting the South. Instead, they found time to write novels, poetry and essays that are still read.

So, here's what I'm thinking. I'm thinking the Southern slave-owners were nervous about something other than expressions of opinion by a small minority of white Northerners, expressions that very few enslaved people would ever see or in most cases could not read if they did.

Why did the slavocracy to overreach so far? Why did people with powerful positions in the United States government, including Cabinet members and high-ranking generals, after decades of blundering from compromise to provocation back to compromise, eventually join a conspiracy to set up a pretend country, the Confederacy?

I believe they were driven by fear and by self-doubt, and fooled by their own ignorance.

Slave-owners, like the Norfolk judge quoted previously, constantly repeated fantasies that the Yankees, armed with magic abolitionist pamphlets, were going to take their slaves away, or somehow compel the slaves to murder their masters in their beds.

Behind the fantasies was the reality of the threat from enslaved people – a threat that needed no magic pamphlets to become real.

Fear probably loomed largest, but Southern slave-owners also showed signs of shame and guilt. John C. Calhoun, perhaps the best known pre-war defender of the South, admitted as much while arguing for a Gag Rule, a rule under which Congress would not accept antislavery petitions. He worried that if the Southern Congresscritters received such petitions "year after year, session after session, hearing ourselves and our constituents vilified ... we must ultimately be ... degraded in our own estimation and that of the world." (Freehling, 1990) In other words, eventually they might feel shame.

Or they might admit they already felt it.

There was only one consistent and unrelenting force that kept fear and shame alive, that actually increased the everyday costs of slavery and that genuinely threatened the lives of slave-holders. And it wasn't a few white abolitionists. It was four million people of African descent.

The masters knew, and yet would not allow themselves to know, that enslaved people themselves were **already** taking their slaves away. Probably far more often than we can guess, they were **already** murdering Ol' Massa in his bed. Nor did white Southerners have to read Yankee petitions to experience profound moral self-doubt. They only had to look into the eyes of those they ruled to be reminded, even if only for an instant, that in the words of a North Carolina slaveholder, "Slavery and

Tyranny must go together – and .. there is no such thing as having an obedient and useful slave, without the painful exercise of undue and tyrannical authority." (Oakes) And no Christian, they knew, had any business engaging in tyranny. Nor did any heir of the Declaration of Independence.

This is the force that was hounding the slave-owners from the 1600s on. This was the **real** abolitionism, the force of people of African descent unceasingly working for their own liberation. These endeavors included:

- Tens of thousand of resignations without notice that fed the Underground Railroad;

> **[The writer's mother] worked so long and so often that once she went to sleep at the loom. Her master's boy saw her and told his mother. His mother told him to take a whip and wear her out. He took a stick and went to beat her awake. When she woke up, she took a pole out of her loom and beat him nearly to death with it. She said, "I'm going to kill you. These black titties sucked you, and then you come out here to beat me." And when she left him he wasn't able to walk.**

And that was the last I seen of her until after freedom. She went out and got on an old cow that she used to milk...[and] she rode away from the plantation. (Sterling)

- Abolitionist organizing across the North and in Britain and elsewhere, at the center of which were the testimony and the strategies of ex-slaves, based on their unanswerable moral authority, influencing every sector of the white population, but especially the progressive and powerful Northern middle class;

She commenced a narrative of her early slave life, part of which was very affecting, calling forth many tears, especially from the female portion of the audience. She afterwards spoke at length on our condition in this country ... we should think it had a wholesome effect on the audience, many of whom were white. Description of a speech by a Miss Paulyon in the Weekly Anglo-African (Sterling)

- The never-ending possibility of rebellion, exemplified by the large well-organized attempt in

> Richmond in 1800 and the insurrection in Southampton County in 1831, but including at least ten other occasions in Virginia alone that led to the state executing 23 men for slave rebellion; (Death Penalty Information Center)

In January 1811, the people enslaved on Manual Andry's plantation, about thirty miles from New Orleans rose up in rebellion. After wounding and killing Andry family members, one hundred and fifty or more Africans marched towards New Orleans in military style. As panicked whites fled, federal troops and militia were mobilized. The rebel army avoided one ambush, but then were trapped in another and defeated. Almost one hundred rebels were killed in combat or were executed, making this one of the largest slave rebellions in the U.S. Perhaps because Louisiana had only recently become part of the U.S., or because some thought the rebellion was a Spanish plot, the rebellion was little known at the time or in subsequent years. (Paquette)

- Finding or creating places of refuge for self-aware and politically active communities of free African-Americans, at first with the Seminole refugee nation in Florida and in places like the Dismal Swamp, and then in Canada and the North, places where they could organize for their own needs, welcome others leaving slavery, and also fight for those they had left behind still in captivity.

"Florida proved unique in history – a place where a large community of ex-slaves could live hidden from enemy eyes ... Generations before Thomas Jefferson sat down to write the Declaration of Independence, Florida's dark runaways wrote their own...refuges from the Creek nation also settled there. This group called themselves "Seminoles" or runaways... Seminoles began to learn how to survive in Florida from these ex-slaves ... Georgia slaveholders were soon invading Florida, seeking runaways, and were soon meeting a united resistance by

red and black armed forces." (Katz, 1986)

- Enslaved people, despite their legal status as chattel, formed strong family bonds, and then defended those family bonds in every way they knew how.

"John C. Stanly, a successful free Negro barber, purchased and emancipated his wife and children in 1805, and two years later freed his brother-in-law. During the next eleven years Stanly ransomed another eighteen slaves...Other free Negroes .... lacked the patience, money or inclination to buy liberty ... So often did newly freed blacks rescue their families from servitude that masters looked to them first when slaves ran away."(Norton)

- And last but not least, the everyday resistance within slavery – sabotage, slowdowns, eavesdropping, pilferage, emotional manipulation, intimidation, and from time to time violence, even carefully disguised murder, by poison or as a result of an apparent accident.

> **"...Dr. Keitt [a white man] .. was chronically ill. Dr. Keitt's friend suggested to him that his slaves were perhaps trying to kill him...As soon as his friend left, a Negro woman brought him a cup of tea. In stirring it, a white powder became evident.... He dashed the tea in her face. 'You ungrateful beast, I believe you are trying to poison me.' Next morning, he was found with his throat cut from ear to ear...the woman, in league with two male slaves, was putting a poison in Dr. Keitt's coffee every morning and when discovered they murdered him outright.... the men successfully escaped but the woman was caught and hanged."** (White, Deborah Gray)

This is awkward for us who learned conventional history. It's hard to see the heirs of Jefferson and Madison and Washington essentially driven into a trap by the people they believed they controlled. But when it came to genuinely understanding the system they had created, the slave-owners were out of their league. And, in the words of that Yankee thinker Yogi Berra, a man never out of his league, "If you don't know where you are going, you will wind up somewhere else."

Of course, a few Virginia Gentlemen were smart enough to see what could happen, including the grandson of Thomas Jefferson, arguing for gradual emancipation in the Virginia General Assembly in the early 1830s:

> **"There is one circumstance to which we are to look as inevitable in the fullness of time; a dissolution of this Union.. and when it does come, border war follows it... Suppose an invasion by your enemy, in part with black troops, speaking the same language, of the same nation, burning with enthusiasm for the liberation of their race...."**
> (Randolph, Thomas Jefferson)

But, hey, nobody wants to listen to a party-pooper. This other guy was much more popular, especially once the war got going:

> **"Judging from what we know of the character of the African in America ... the idea that our slaves would embarrass and weaken us in time of war – even in a contest conducted for the express purpose of**

giving them liberty, appears to us to be totally groundless." This is Edmund Ruffin, writing in 1848. (Ruffin) Eddie was the secessionist freak who fired the first gun at Fort Sumter. He shot himself dead when he got the news of Appomattox. He did have some interesting ideas about agriculture, though.

EDMUND RUFFIN

In 1797, Prince Hall, founder of the African-American Freemasonry movement, gave a speech on the situation of African-American people. In it, he noted the Biblical account that "Jethro, an Ethiopian, gave instructions to his son-in-law, Moses, in establishing government... Thus, Moses was not ashamed to be instructed by a black man." (Foner, 1972) But none of the politicians of the early nineteenth century would have accepted instruction from anyone of African descent. Many of us still have a problem accepting it today.

Moral instruction is one thing. We 21st century U.S. whites can easily say that the whites of the 1840s or 1850s should have listened with mercy to African-American voices – as some did, by proxy, when Uncle Tom's Cabin was published. We can easily say that whites of that time should have had sympathy for the slave. But what about "being instructed in government," as Moses was? Did African-Americans have something to teach white Americans?

Yes, they did. The people with the best strategic grasp of the most crucial issue for the United States in those years were not white. That's not standard Virginia history, not even standard U.S. history, but it's true.

Excellent evidence to this effect is a speech, available online, that the Virginia-born writer, soldier and leader Martin Delany gave in October, 1855. In the speech, he summarizes the political situation for African-Americans in every state in the union, and also goes into detail about foreign policy issues related to Haïti, Canada, Cuba and other nations. Speaking as someone who has heard plenty of them, and given a few, the speech could stand without apology beside modern policy briefings in Washington DC. (Of course it was done without benefit of Powerpoint, email, or even the telephone.) (Delany) No white politician of the era, not even Lincoln, had this depth of knowledge about the issues that were moving the nation to war.

Nor was Delany unique. Frederick Douglass, Henry Highland Garnett, Harriet Tubman, Sojourner Truth and others all had a deep understanding of the nation on the brink of war – and all played some significant role in the war. Douglass, in particular, became the closest thing to a Black adviser that any U.S. president had ever had up till then.

SOJOURNER TRUTH AND LINCOLN

But these talented and brave people were much more than the Colin Powells and Vernon Jordans of their day. They were deeply rooted in a struggling and conscious population. Each of them had close relationships with the African-American masses, including many people who had lived most of their lives in slavery (or at least in Tubman's case, were still in slavery).

And what was going on with that population? I return to Vincent Harding for his picture of Black people as early as the 1830s, after Nat Turner's rebellion:

> **"Even where there were no actual uprisings, no battles in the road, no burning of barns and houses, it was yet possible to sense the profound disequilibrium building in the society, to feel the underlying restless eruptive movement of the river, gaining ground. Those who had the proper ears could hear and feel, in spite of laws and patrols and lashes.... Martin Delany said he had heard about Nat Turner in Pittsburgh, and it helped to shape the direction of his future. Harriet Tubman said she heard in Maryland, and pondered his meaning deep within her. Frederick Douglass said that he heard too.....**" (Harding, There is a River)

And this was thirty-four years before the war came. Twenty-two year old

Abraham Lincoln was splitting rails for a living, and Robert E. Lee, an untried lieutenant, was courting his wife to be.

When the war did come, at first it was not the war that African-Americans needed and had worked to bring about – the war against slavery. At first, it was a war that arrogant and fearful Southern slave-owners, never satisfied, had forced on the North – white against white.

The war became the war against slavery step by step. First, massive numbers of African-Americans showing up at Union lines made it impossible for the Union army to ignore them, and effectively freed themselves, not just as individuals, but as communities. Next, they made themselves indispensable to the Union army as laborers, guides and spies. Finally, they were accepted as soldiers, and provided crucial reinforcement of the Union Army. At that point, though neither Lincoln nor most white Union soldiers had ever intended it, "in the last two years of the war, Union soldiers acted as an army of liberation." (Foner, 1988)

No, Virginia, "your" African servants were not the bystanders you imagined they were. When the conflict came, and you were giddy with surprise and anticipation of victory, those "bystanders" were well prepared to carry out actions that were far more effective than the foolish war of the slave-holders. It's kind of like the Br'er Rabbit and other trickster stories, with the "weaker" creature controlling what the stronger creature does, by using its habits and prejudicies against it.

For slave-owners, the war they had felt they had to fight ended in disaster. For many Northern and Southern white families, it was an occasion for mourning or for coping with life-long disability. But for those who had been enslaved, though they certainly shared in the bitterness of war, it was above all a vital step on their way to full freedom -- another step in a long struggle they had already been waging for centuries.

Fraud and Fable Number Ten: White Virginia Rightfully Cherished A Noble Lost Cause

Purpose: Even though the Virginia Gentleman, if pressed, will admit the Union victory was a good thing, it is vital to him not to admit that the Confederacy was a terrible moral and political mistake, as well as a fiasco. So he makes it a kind of noble adventure story.

"[The Civil War] destroyed a social fabric of exquisite poise and picturesqueness which had endured from the beginning of the American colonization." (Eggleston)

Comments on Confederate History Month: "*Forget, Hell!*"

We critics of Confederate History/Hooray for the Losers Month are accused of erasing history. We are accused of trying to obliterate the memory of a crusade fought for "states rights." They say we want to burn books and smash monuments.

Well, there are some monuments I'd like to move to inconspicuous locations. But I definitely don't want to burn any books, because books are the best source of evidence for the truth.

No, let's never erase the history of the Confederacy. Let's remember that a Union is a compromise, never completely satisfactory to anyone. Let's remember that when an arrogant clique of elitists took up arms to preserve privileges they called "states' rights," the people fighting for real human rights soundly defeated them. Forget, Hell!

You Lost on the Battlefield? Well, Fight Back By Rewriting History!

> **"The glorification of the Confederacy and the deification of Robert E. Lee allowed the mythology of the "Moonlight and Magnolias" genre of writing to sweep the field, so infecting historical writing that much that issued from the book publishers in the guise of history was really fiction in disguise."** (Tarter 2007)

Jubal Early was one of Lee's generals in the Confederate Army of Northern Virginia. Along with Lee and the rest, he was defeated in war. Unlike some of his comrades in arms – the majority of those who survived – he never accepted this fact.

According to Charles Osborne's biography, Jubal, Early was not among those who surrendered at Appomattox. He considered himself still at war after Lee's surrender, and rode southwest to find rumored continued Confederate resistance. When he could not find it, he exiled himself, first in Mexico and then in Canada, where he indulged in various delusionary ideas about a revived Civil War that he could play a part in, while writing his memoirs. (Osborne)

JUBAL EARLY

He did not return to his native Virginia until 1869, settling in Lynchburg. Back in Virginia, Osborne writes, “He joined with a band or supporters, mostly Virginians and old soldiers, who fought a campaign to rationalize and vindicate the fate of the Confederacy.” This campaign was founded on their control of the Southern Historical Society, which published 52 volumes of papers mostly making their “Lost Cause” case.

The Glory That Was Lee

Key to that case was the glorification of Robert E. Lee, commander of the Confederate Army of Northern Virginia. Lee died in 1870, and Early and his collaborators then became leaders in gaining him "an image of moral purity and martial perfection that raised him – and by association, all male white Southerners – above the level of ordinary men." (Osborne)

The Southern writer Fanny Downing, for example, described Lee as all but godlike, shamelessly writing of him as "bathed in the white light that falls directly upon him from the smile of an approving and sustaining God." (Gallagher)

The cult of the Confederacy and of Lee continues to this day. In his book <u>Decline of the West</u>, Patrick Buchanan, the racist politician and commentator, refers to the controversy over a huge portrait of Lee planned as part of a Richmond mural. Many contemporary residents of Richmond, not only in the city's African American majority, thought honoring Lee was a mistake. Buchanan begins his description of the event by referring to "Richmond, which was defended for four years by [Lee's] Army of Northern Virginia...." (Buchanan) When Lee's army finally got out of the way, a lot of native Richmonders wildly celebrated the entry of the Union Army into Richmond. It wasn't Richmond that Lee was defending; it was slavery in Richmond.

There was one little problem with making Lee a Confederate saint. Lee was the leading general of an army that decisively lost its one and only war. So some other Confederate leader had to take any blame for defeat that might otherwise fall on Lee.

Longstreet Becomes The Loser

Jeffry Wert writes, in an essay "James Longstreet and the Lost Cause" in the collection The Myth of the Lost Cause and Civil War History, about the process by which Early's group victimized a fellow Confederate general, James Longstreet, to advance their myth-making. Wert notes that Longstreet had a good reputation as the Civil War ended, and that the first published histories of the war spoke well of him. (Gallagher)

However, Longstreet was among the first and most eager of the Confederate generals to adapt to post-war reality. In 1867, he published a letter urging cooperation with the Republican Party, and in 1869 he accepted a federal appointment from President Grant. These political choices made him a target for others less eager to accept their defeat.

JAMES LONGSTREET

The battle of Gettysburg, a turning point of the Civil War, now became a battleground of historical interpretation. In Wert's words, "to demonstrate that Lee was blameless at Gettysburg ... they needed a scapegoat, a subordinate officer whose conduct had been so egregious as to bring defeat...." In an 1872 speech, Early claimed that on the second day of the Gettysburg battle, Longstreet had been ordered by Lee to make a dawn attack, but had delayed until the afternoon, causing the loss of the battle. Wert describes the charge as "historically false," (Gallagher) and Osborne, though he is Early's biographer, agrees that "Lee gave no such order." (Osborne)

But Early and his co-conspirators overrode the truth. Longstreet was helpless in the face of a Robert E. Lee frenzy that at one point led to a proposal to "canvass every house in every town in the Southern States" to raise money for a Lee monument in Richmond. Even in the 1940s, the massive work Lee's Lieutenants by Douglass Southall Freeman, though it states that at Gettysburg Longstreet was not "the villain of the piece," nevertheless, according to Wert, "relegated ... Longstreet .. to a diminished stature." (Gallagher)

Wert, who has written a biography of Longstreet that casts him in a much more positive light as a soldier, may or may not be right about Longstreet's relative military qualities. But there seems to be little doubt that, in building up the Lost Cause myth and their hero Robert E. Lee, Early and his ilk libeled Longstreet.

In 1912, with Early dead for almost two

decades, we see in a children's history book about Lee this account of Gettysburg: "General Lee ordered an attack to be made on the Federals in the early morning of the second of July. But for some reason it was not made until four o'clock in the afternoon ..." (Whitehead)

Throwing Longstreet under the wheels of History's chariot was just one step towards totally reimagining the Civil War. Alan Nolan, also writing in <u>The Myth of the Lost Cause and Civil War History</u>, described their myth of the war as evoking a "heroic and romantic melodrama, an honorable sectional duel..." The real purpose of the Lost Cause myth, Nolan writes, "was to hide the Southerners' tragic and self-destructive mistake." (Gallagher)

Perfuming the Lost Cause

In his article, "The Anatomy of the Myth," Nolan describes as the first claim of the Lost Cause boosters, "Slavery was not the critical issue" between the North and the South. Nolan describes this claim as "decontaminating" the Confederate cause. (Gallagher)

Jubal Early was not the only Lost Cause celebrity. Sallie Ann Corbell Pickett was a Confederate war widow who worked for the federal pension department. But she had another identity under the more romantic name of LaSalle Corbell Pickett. She was a speaker and author on the Lost Cause and the preserver of the reputation of her late husband, General George Pickett. For half a century, she wrote and gave speeches about her husband, whom she called "the noble leader of that band of heroes whose deeds are sparkling jewels set in the history of the Army of Northern Virginia," and about the idyllic life of the Old South, complete with contented slaves. (Gallagher)

General Pickett is known mainly for the charge named after him, an assault on Union lines at Gettysburg that devastated the division he led. He graduated at the bottom of his West Point class, and after the war was said by other Confederate leaders to be on bad terms with General Lee. In fact, he was selected as one of the subjects of a paper, "Remembered Not for Their Greatness But Their Flaws," presented to the American Civil War Roundtable of Australia in 2005. (Kensey)

LaSalle Corbell Pickett had her flaws too. One writer has described her storytelling as fiction that "publicly reconstructed her past, not only to venerate the slaveholding South and the Confederacy, but like other scarred and discontented white Southerners, to find meaning, comfort and hope in her own troubled life." (Gordon)

Such claims as Pickett's, or the virtual sainthood of Lee and of General Thomas Jackson (often known by his thug name, "Stonewall"), helped to ease the tormented hearts of some former Confederates by rewriting their failed history. Much like today's gangsta rap, these legends found a twisted nobility in men fighting a useless losing battle against the law of the land.

And as on today's urban streets, "woofin'" – making threats your behind can't back up – was also part of the picture. As Confederate apologist Richard Weaver pointed out, Southern white males genuinely believed in their prowess on the battlefield. "Washington, Jackson and Taylor had led the South to believe that it possessed the fighting talent of the nation…In a sense the South was in the position of a professional expecting easy defeat of an amateur, and one should not wonder at the shock and humiliation expressed when the amateur won." (Weaver) Of course, the ex-Confederates never consciously faced the fact that the "amateurs" that had really defeated them – the driving force that led to the war and ultimately won it– were the population of African descent living among them. Still, even being defeated by white Yankees was traumatic.

THUG LIFE

Organizing Jim Crow

But the Lost Cause Myth was not just a kind of psychological mechanism to ease ex-Confederate minds. The Lost Cause Myth was also the organizing myth for a new nation within a nation – the Jim Crow South.

To understand how such a myth works, we can look to South Africa, whose history as a race-based settler state parallels that of the southern U.S.

The Afrikaans minority in South Africa, like the so-called Confederacy, suffered a total military defeat (by the British in 1902). Like the white South, this white settler group came back from defeat to be the dominant force in a society based on racial segregation – and on a powerful myth-- the Voortrekker myth.

The "most dramatic event" that embodied that mythology was "the symbolic ox-wagon trek of 1938, which celebrated the centenary of the Great Trek." (The Great Trek was a temporarily successful effort by some Afrikaners to migrate away from British control.) This propaganda event brought together "more than 100,000 Afrikaners" for "the ceremonial laying of the foundation stone of the Voortrekker Monument." Within ten years, the political goals of this event had been achieved. The apartheid system advocated by Afrikaner

Nationalist leaders was the law of the land in South Africa, and continued to be for some 40 years. (Thompson)

Both the Afrikaner/Boer cause and the U.S. white Southern Lost Cause were largely based on resentment of a government that had defeated them.

To Disgrace the White People of the South

In his 1879 autobiographical novel, A Fool's Errand, Albion Tourgée described how Southern whites saw what Yankees had "done to them:"

> **"The negro is made a voter simply to degrade and disgrace the white people of the South. The North cares nothing about the negro as a man, but only enfranchises him in order to humiliate and enfeeble us." (Tourgée)**

Tourgée, who came to North Carolina as a Union officer, and then tried to help establish a biracial and democratic society, knew better, but this is the rationale he heard all around him from the former slaveholders – the people who finally drove him out of the South with death threats.

Pat Buchanan, in yet another comment

on public art in Richmond, perpetuates this paranoia more than a century after Appomattox. Buchanan refers to Richmond's Monument Avenue, where, he writes, "statues of the four great sons of the Confederacy stand – Lee, Jackson, Stuart and Davis..." He then states that a statue of Arthur Ashe, added to the far end of the Avenue in 1996, was "put there to disrupt and contradict the symbolism." (Buchanan) Ashe was a very highly respected son of the Richmond African American community, and clearly someone worth memorializing. But those still suffering from CSA (Confederate Supporter Anxiety syndrome) believe that everyone else's only motivation is to hurt them.

The erection of the Monument Avenue array of Confederates began, of course, with General Lee. The unveiling of the Robert E. Lee Memorial in Richmond in 1890 paralleled the Voortrekker Monument event. The largest pro-Confederate event ever held, its four mile long parade also drew 100,000 or more spectators. It was, like the Voortrekker event, an occasion to remember the

inspirational, though ineffective, acts of those gone before. Like the Voortrekker event, it was above all an act of political mobilization.

A keen observer of and participant in Virginia politics, John Mitchell, editor of the Richmond Planet, wrote "What does this display of Confederate emblems mean? What does it serve to teach the rising generations of the South?" (Alexander, Ann)

Mitchell, a leading figure in the Richmond African-American community, knew quite well what the display meant. A few months later, he was chief marshal of an Emancipation Day celebration in which African-American militia units and fraternal groups had their own two mile long parade in Richmond, an event that "many black Richmonders saw ... as their answer" to the Robert E. Lee event.

Just over a decade later, Virginia created its new Constitution, which would effectively end African-American voting, and would establish the rule of the Virginia Gentleman's Jim Crow system for more than half a century.

By the way, Robert E. Lee generally manages to escape all responsibility for what was done in his name. He did die in 1870, and most of the lies of the Lost Cause were propagated after that by Early and his cronies. It is clear, as I note below, that Lee did have some sense of shame, which singled him out from his collaborators.

But we should not meekly accept the picture of Lee as a conciliator who sought to bring everyone together after the war. He did urge former Confederates to see themselves again as Americans. But this hardly means he genuinely accepted the lessons of the war, or that he ever transcended his white Virginian identity. In 1867, he wrote this in a letter to one of his former generals (which one is coyly disguised by his biographer):

> **"I think it is the duty of all citizens not disfranchised to**

qualify themselves to vote, attend the polls, and elect the best men in their power. Judge Underwood, Messrs. Botts, Hunnicut, etc., would be well pleased, I presume, if the business were left to them and the negroes. But I do not think this course would either for the interest of the State or country.... I look upon the Southern people as acting under compulsion, not of their free choice..." (Jones, John William)

Establishing The Ideology

Like other totalitarian élites, Jim Crow Virginia's rulers understood that constantly reinforcing their ideology was crucial to maintaining their system. Thus in 1912, the Winchester Star reported that "each county and city" in Virginia was authorized to spend taxpayer funds to send "Confederates from the state of Virginia" to the semi-centennial of the Battle of Gettysburg. (Winchester Star)

As Jim Crow became a full-blown system in Virginia, Mitchell wrote in an editorial, "The position of Southern Negroes is that while they submit to these persistent and continuing exhibitions of race prejudice ... they do so under protest. Like a rubber ball, they yield to continuing pressure but whenever that pressure is removed, whether it be this year or next year or the year after or a hundred years, they will return to their normal state." (Alexander, Ann)

Speaking to the Virginia State Bar Association in 1955, then-Senator Strom Thurmond of South Carolina gave an inadvertent shout out to this stance of Mitchell's:

> **"Those persons who sought to destroy the Constitution and the rights of the states did not meekly bow down to the doctrine of 'separate but equal' established under the Constitution by the *Plessy v. Ferguson* decision. Instead, for half a century they have conducted a propaganda campaign against the Constitution and against the decision of a respected court."** (Muse)

In a later section, rebutting the Fable and Fraud that **Virginia's African-Americans Have Been Kinda Quiet Since the War**, I describe the fight of African-Americans in Warren County, including my friend James Kilby, to end school segregation there. In September of 2006, the Historical Educational Movement, a Warren County group that I belong to, organized an event to commemorate the 50th anniversary of legal action by local African-Americans.

To our genuine "shock and awe," one of the great figures of the Virginia civil rights history, attorney Oliver Hill, showed up.

We had invited Hill, but really didn't expect him to show up. Hill was 99 years old, and in fact had less than a year to live. Nevertheless, he felt it was important to return to one of the scenes of the legal struggle he waged against segregation – and to speak to us. Assisted by his son, Hill spoke us to us briefly and with difficulty. He told about his own mentor, Professor Charles Hamilton Houston. Along with Supreme Court Justice Thurgood Marshall and other noted lawyers, Hill had studied under Houston at Howard University Law School. Hill told us how Houston had conceived of, and trained his students to carry out, the legal strategy that led to *Brown vs. Board of Education* and other key civil rights decisions. (Howard University School of Law)

It was thrilling to hear a revered elder tell us about the man that had in turn shaped his life. Though Houston died in

1950, and never saw the successes of his theory, Hill brought him to life for us in that room, and vividly showed us that we were part of a long and conscious struggle.

So while I hardly agree with Strom Thurmond that John Mitchell, Oliver Hill, and other Virginia freedom fighters sought to "destroy the Constitution and the rights of the states," he is certainly right that they "did not meekly bow down," and that they conducted a campaign of propaganda, legal action and mass mobilization, one that in fact lasted much longer than fifty years, to finally bring down Jim Crow.

The Lost Cause myth and the Jim Crow system, like the apartheid system, could distort normal human kindness and respect, but it could not extinguish them.

Jubal Early did not live to see the early twentieth century triumphs of his longest and most successful campaign, let alone its ultimate defeat. He died in 1894.

After Early's death, his niece published a tract he had written entitled The Heritage of the South: A History Of The Introduction Of Slavery, Its Establishment From Colonial Times, And Final Effect Upon The Politics Of The United States. (Early

Early had, for the reasons mentioned above, been silent on slavery in his later years. The Editor's note to The Heritage of the South, by Early's niece, stated that "the manuscript had lain unpublished for half a century, til passion having cooled...." His closing chapter, "Injurious Effect of Misinformation," included an attack on Harriet Beecher Stowe and her novel "Uncle Tom's Cabin." He wrote that it contained "misrepresentations of slavery and slanders upon Southern society." He insisted that "In his native land, [the negro] has never reached the status of a civilized being, and he has never been civilized until transplanted into slavery."

He also answered those who said the Confederacy could have survived had it emancipated its slaves with "What could the people of the South have done if 3,000,000 slaves had been turned loose among them and the whole labor system of the country deranged?" I kind of think that we found out the answer to that question by the end of the Civil War. But in any case, the tract reveals that Early was not the proponent of an ennobled Lost Cause that was all about the Constitution and heroic warriors. He was, to the end, a defender of slavery. (Early)

At his funeral, his former chaplain described a moment when he had seen the general "bowed almost to the saddle .... Bent under the storm, but unconquered and unconquerable." The moment the Chaplain referred to was after the Battle of Cedar Creek, Jubal Early's most serious defeat. (Osborne) He had in fact just been well and truly "conquered," and in less than a year the Confederacy would be demolished. But that minister's rhetorical trope was a good fit with most of this hateful man's life. Once again the brutal fact of defeat was somehow redefined as glorious success, thanks to the Virginia Gentleman's capacity for utterly shameless self-delusion.

Certificate of Cause of Death of Robert Edward Lee
Date of death: September 28, 1870
Place of death: Lexington, Virginia
Cause of death: Shame and guilt over the so-called Confederacy

Robert E. Lee knew he was not the heroic, almost saintly, figure later represented by the huge statue on Richmond's Monument Avenue. He knew his flawed actions and his shortcomings had contributed to a profound tragedy, and the burden of that knowledge killed him.

What others saw as his modesty was in fact shame. As the most beloved ex-Confederate leader, and one of the few who took responsibility for the results of his actions, he received desperate entreaties for help every single day after the end of the Civil War. Finally, his shame and guilt over the terrible problems that the War had created killed him. While he continued to subscribe to the racist ideas of his slave-owner caste, he understood at some level that he had been party to a terrible wrong, certainly to the white working people that given their sons to his command. Unlike others, he could not justify his actions with a phony pride in a gallant cause. Unlike others, he knew he had fallen far short of the Revolutionary generation he emulated. What was most remarkable about Lee was not his wartime record, but the fact that, unlike his comrades, he did not evade what he had done. And facing what he had done killed him.

"The great-hearted Lee must receive praise for setting before his countrymen a personal demeanour that remains unsurpassed in quiet dignity and forbearance. He suffered with his people and taught them how to suffer and be strong. Not a murmur escaped his lips." White, Henry Alexander, Robert E. Lee And The Southern Confederacy 1807- 1870, G.P. Putnam's Sons, 1897.

"Lee's physicians attributed his death in great measure to moral causes. The strain of his campaigns, the bitterness of defeat aggravated by the bad faith and insolence of the victor, sympathy with the subsequent sufferings of the Southern people, and the effort at calmness under these accumulated sorrows, seemed the sufficient and real causes that slowly but steadily undermined his health and led to his death." Lee,

Robert Edward, (son) author, Recollections and Letters of General Robert E. Lee

"I frequently think of shame as a Silent Killer ...Shame is a powerful and terribly painful emotiōn. It generates punishment for some quality of the Self that often leaves one feeling inherently and irreparably worthless, unlovable, not good enough, defective and so on. As such, shame, or even the threat of shame, initiates the construction of impenetrable defenses against closeness and contact with others thus giving rise to feelings of isolation, separation, and abandonment. " Blume, Michele, Psy. D., Understanding and Working Through Shame in Therapy, December 30, 2011, http://drmicheleblume.com/blog/understanding-and-working-through-shame-in-therapy/#more-29

"....simplistic, one-dimensional portraits offered of Lee are largely a product of the carefully crafted and manufactured campaign orchestrated following the war by Jubal Early and the other leaders of the Lost Cause movement.....Lee's father ... would die when Robert was only eleven, leaving nothing behind but heartbreak and shame, which stained the Lee reputation as one of the first families of Virginia..... we can see Lee as a man who grew up in an atmosphere marked by insecurity and shame, and who, under his mother's influence, became excessively self-controlled and prone to accept discomfort to a point where any sense of joy or pleasure was perceived as improper." Thompson, Robert, "Robert E. Lee, The Human Being," May 2, 2009, http://bobcivilwarhistory.blogspot.com/2009/05/robert-e-lee-human-being.html

Fraud and Fable Number Eleven: Virginia's Women Were Quiet Handmaidens To Men, Not a Countervailing Force

Purpose: The Virginia Gentleman, like most men, wants to see "his" female partner or relative as being on his side, and certainly not as challenging his major values and choices.

"..by the middle of the eighteenth century, Virginia's famous plantation aristocracy was in its heyday. Or, more accurately, it was the heyday of the male half of the plantation aristocracy." (Virginia Women's Cultural History Project)

In the 1700s, Virginia came into its own as a different kind of society than the ones its immigrant populations had come from.

In the early years of Virginia, many people of African descent who came to Virginia were those historian Ira Berlin calls "Atlantic creoles," people who had been exposed to a kind of multicultural world that included Atlantic seaports and islands, as well as parts of Africa that had been Christianized for some time, like parts of Angola and the Congo. They had at least some ability to adapt to the English Christian colony. (Berlin)

The Englishwomen who had come to Virginia early on had also had some advantages over those of later years. A more turbulent society, and one with relatively few

women, created opportunities for some women to "marry up," sometimes more than once, and even to exercise independence as land-owning widows. (Virginia Women's Cultural History Project)

There were, of course, limits to how far white women could go.

> **Whereas it doth appear to this court ... that Anne Fowler the wife of William Fowler of Linhaven, planter, did in a shameful uncomely and irreverent manner, bid Capt. Adam Thorougood Kiss her arse... [Thorougood was a local justice of the peace.] It is therefore ordered that the said Anne Fowler shall, for hir offense, receive twenty Stripes up on the bare shoulders and ask forgiveness**

> **of the said Cap. Thorougood here now in Court and also the ensuing Sunday at Linhaven.** (Lower Norfolk County Order Book, 1637)

The Virginia Gentleman was always in charge. But as time went on, that became even more firmly established.

By the early 1700s, people of African descent were unquestionably enslaved for life. Africans began to be imported in much larger numbers, and increasingly from the interior of Africa. Instead of coming to Virginia with some ability to assimilate and a possibility of freedom, they were immediately stripped of all identity and put into a labor barracks.

Enslaved women were not spared from this process, but their experience was different from that of enslaved men, as shown in Deborah Gray White's Ar'n't I a Woman?:

> **"Female slave bondage was not better or worse, or more or less severe, than male bondage, but it was different. From the very beginning of a woman's enslavement she had to cope with sexual abuse, abuse made legitimate by the conventional wisdom that**

black women were promiscuous Jezebels. Work assignments also structured female slave life so that women were more confined to the boundaries of the plantation than were men. The most important reason for the difference between male and female bondage, however, was the slave woman's childbearing and child care responsibilities." (White, Deborah Gray)

As children, White contends, enslaved girls "probably grew up minimizing the difference between the sexes while learning far more about the difference between the races." The latter, of course, was more critical to their survival.

"...adult female cooperation and interdependence was a fact of female slave life," according to White, who notes that while enslaved women did hard labor that white women did not do, they most typically did it with other women. They also cooperated to deal with pregnancy and with health issues. Finally, "the female network and its emotional sustenance was always there – there between an 'abroad' husband's visits, there when a husband or son was sent or sold off or ran away."

Enslaved women of African descent clearly created, or sustained, many practices that kept them and succeeding generations alive and strong. Nevertheless, "only enslaved women were so totally unprotected by men or by the law." (White) Ultimately, white male power determined their lives.

White women's lives were limited in a different way. Increasingly, they were now only to be modest and humble and to reflect well on their husbands.

Survival tasks – cooking, sewing and taking care of children – started to become elaborate and culturally complicated rituals, especially for the wives of wealthier men -- rituals that they were under increasing pressure to perform correctly. In particular, this was the first wave of popularity for cookbooks in North America.

The eighteenth century, of course, was a revolutionary century in Virginia and the other states-to-be. But the Revolution was pretty much for white men only. The few rights womenhad had in colonial society were taken away by post-Revolutionary legislation, while the pressures for more rigid domestic roles grew stronger.

> **"… the American Revolution retarded those social conditions that had given colonial women their unique function and status in society, while it promoted those that were leading toward the gradual 'embourgeoisement' of late eighteenth century women. By 1800 their legal and economic privileges were curtailed; their recent revolutionary activity minimized or simply ignored; their future interest in politics ignored; and their domestic roles extolled, but increasingly limited."** (Wilson, Joan Hoff)

While slaves were controlled and worked collectively, for the most part, as part of an agricultural labor force or a team of household servants, white women were controlled individually, as wives and daughters. Living in the household of their controlling patriarch, giving birth to and raising large numbers of children, and managing household functions, were all conditions that made being involved in social change incredibly difficult.

Nevertheless, as the nineteenth century began, A Share of Honour records an emerging collective social role for white women. In 1803, a group of women in Fredericksburg organized themselves to provide a boarding school for girls from low-income families. Across Virginia in the next decade, similar "female education" projects were started in at least five cities. (Virginia Women's Cultural History Project)

One of the earliest and longest-lived of these voluntary associations [in Richmond] was the Female Humane Association. Founded in 1805 as a nonsectarian charity of leading Protestant women, the association operated an asylum for white girls. At any given time, the asylum housed fifteen to twenty orphans and half orphans, who received basic education and training in 'domestic business'... part of a larger network of such benevolences founded in this era: the growing towns of Fredericksburg, Petersburg and Norfolk also established female-run charities in this decade. (Green)

We 21st century folks have lived with nonprofit charitable organizations like this all of our lives. These small efforts don't seem like remarkable achievements to us. But these women were, if only indirectly, challenging the central assumptions of the society they lived in.

Virginia Gentlemen had established a selfish society. What else could a slave society be? And what else could a society be when all of its decisions were made not for the common good, but to increase the wealth drawn from a single cash crop?

On a national and even transatlantic, scale, the Gents were reinforced in their selfishness by radical new ideas that treated making money as positive, and that encouraged contempt for the poor – an evangelical Protestantism that was closely tied to the emergence of laissez-faire capitalism.

> **"... evangelicalism's emphasis on personal moral responsibility led to a further demonizing of the 'unworthy' poor. Evangelicals saw poverty as the product of a moral defect in the individual and stressed individual**

morality as the key to overcoming poverty…. rather than relief, the poor needed habits of temperance, thrift and self-denial. … a southern evangelical editorialist wrote that poverty was the result of 'dissolute habits, intemperate living, idleness and vice.'" (Green)

Just as with Virginia's slavery system, we make a mistake if we see this as the old bad way things had always been done. In fact, English people had come to Virginia with a very different approach to charity.

"The English poor-relief system viewed relief as both a civic and a religious duty, an obligation that members of the community owed one

> **another. As such, the poor received assistance as a right, an entitlement…. applicants were neither stigmatized nor ostracized for receiving public charity.”** (Green)

This Biblically based way to respond to the needs of the poor had been in place for centuries, but now it was radically changing.

> **"As market relations supplanted traditional economic relations in the commercial centers of Northern Europe, preoccupation with the control of vagrancy and beggary grew. What had been a right in the traditional community -- the right to seek alms -- now became a crime...Something important was at stake, and the propertied classes said clearly enough what it was. If the poor were allowed their traditional right to charity, they might evade wage labor."**(Piven)

But as this increasingly cruel system was imposed, some Virginia women had a different vision – at least for poor whites. As their husbands and fathers established a society which included “the freedom to starve,” women were establishing orphanages and “benevolent societies” of various kinds. They also organized and carried out the events that raised money for these activities, raising “countless thousands of dollars.” (Virginia Women’s Cultural History Project)

For the next century and more, this was the main social and political work of women. Women were blocked from voting, passing legislation, or even proposing policy in a narrow sense. But they were creating and directing change in their own communities and even beyond.

What would Virginia history have been without these efforts? We don’t have any statistical way to measure their results. But these women were responding to real problems right in front of them, so they were surely having some impact.

Something similar happened in the 1980s, as homelessness suddenly and rapidly increased. There were government responses, but as someone working in nonprofit housing from 1981 to 1995, I can tell you those responses were pathetically inadequate. But alongside the government response was a massive volunteer response, from concerned individuals, congregations, and nonprofits. Such a volunteer response, of course, always includes not only the organized meals, but the immeasurable moments of human contact and the small favors and gifts that can make a difference in the lives of desperate people. (I am not one of those that believes a smile can substitute for a meal or a warm dry bed, but the combination of the three is a good thing.)

We can safely assume that Virginia women in the nineteenth and early twentieth centuries “fixed” at least some of the results of the Virginia Gentlemen’s social program of selfishness, and that they made Virginia a safer and more humane place than it would have been if they had not acted. We can also assume that they created connections and provided human affirmation in some of the areas of life where the Virginia Gentleman offered only punishment and humiliation.

Ladies Undermining Slavery

Generally, Virginian white women’s organized benevolence did not extend to slaves. Standing on the side of slaves was dangerous business.

Earlier in this book, I mentioned Margaret Douglass, who went to jail for teaching free African-American children to read the Bible.

Mary Berkeley Minor Blackford of Fredericksburg was another of these rare Virginia ladies.

Mary "descended from prominent Virginia landed families." Her husband edited a Whig newspaper, and briefly served as a diplomatic representative in Bogotá, so he was well-connected, though not wealthy.

Both Blackfords were strong supporters of the American Colonization Society, which worked to send free African-Americans to Liberia. However, Mr. Blackford saw colonization "as a means to rid the state of its free black population," a common reason for white support of colonization. (Tarter, "Mary Berkeley Minor Blackford")

Mary Blackford, on the other hand, opposed slavery itself. As early as

1827, at the age of 25, she freed her own two "house servants," and then, when they refused to go to Liberia, hired them as paid servants. (Degler)

In 1832, not long after the Nat Turner rebellion, Mary Blackford intervened to have a slave mother be allowed to say goodbye to her son, who had been sold South. When the white guard who had refused the mother also turned Blackford down, she wrote in her diary "I warned him that such cruelty could not long go unpunished and reminded him of the affair at Southampton which had just occurred." Few members of the Virginia's gentry would have said out loud in 1832 that Turner's rebellion was "punishment" for "cruelty." (Degler)

Liberian Stamp

Mary Blackford raised funds for and donated to the American Colonization Society, and also worked with freed African-Americans to prepare them to go to Liberia. She also ran a Sunday school for slave children, which was an illegal activity in Virginia, writing "I have myself been twice threatened by the Grand Jury for teaching on Sunday a few colored children to read their Bibles." Unlike Margaret Douglass, though, she never served any time for this crime.

Another of Virginia's wealthy white women took her opposition to slavery far beyond teaching free African-American children to read the Bible. Elizabeth Van Lew grew up in a slaveholding family with a mansion in Richmond's Church Hill, but became an abolitionist. When the Civil War came, she was part of a Union spy ring that was active in Richmond throughout the war, with a focus on communicating with Union prisoners held in the city.

The Encyclopedia Virginia suggests that many of the details of that spy ring's work are still unclear, including the identity of an African-American woman that worked in Jefferson Davis' "White House." Whatever the precise facts, the fables and self-delusion of the Virginia gentry certainly protected the spy ring. The Virginia Gentlemen and their Confederate colleagues apparently could not fathom that they could be betrayed by "one of their own," and also could not imagine an African-

American woman being infiltrated into the center of their power and being able to comprehend and report back on their plans.

After the war (as some still say in Richmond), Van Lew was ostracized by Richmond's gentry. She was the city's postmaster and helped to establish a library, in both cases to the benefit of Richmond's African-American population. However, in 1877, with the Tilden-Hayes Compromise and the subsequent retreat of the national Republican Party from the South, she lost her position, and she was a poor woman when she died in 1900.

Van Lew and Blackford went far beyond charity, risking their identity as Southern ladies and even their lives on behalf of the people who, they had been taught, were hardly people at all.

Hundreds of Virginian men went to war proclaiming that they were defending their "colored servants" from the devastating impacts of freedom. Van Lew and Blackford showed what it really meant to defend – and respect – African-Americans.

Continuing the Tradition of Mutual Aid and Service

After the war, with the end of slavery, African-American women were able to join in the public tradition of collective charity, and did so with vigor. Our Share of Honour records the contributions of African-American women teachers – women who were creating from almost nothing a tradition of service that still continues today, in hundreds of Virginia schools as well as in places that bear their names, like Lucy Sims School in Harrisonburg, now a community center, or Rosa Bowser School in Richmond, now a Black History museum. These women and their male professional counterparts were not only teachers. They were career counselors, social workers, and above all role models, projecting ideas of African-American identity and destiny to a people that had just gone through an almost incredible change. African-American women, of course, were also very much part of the network of community organizations that took on Jim Crow.

One of the first African-American women's clubs in Virginia, the Richmond Mothers' Club, as its first project raised funds for the defense of two African-American women charged with murder of a white woman in rural Virginia. (Lebsock) That Club was in turn a founding member of the Virginia State Federation of Colored Women's Clubs.

The Federation's president, Janie Porter Barrett, had already

established the Locust Street Social Settlement in Hampton, which was on the model of Hull House in Chicago, and for which Barrett got national recognition from Jane Addams and others. For the Federation's main project, she suggested what became, in 1915, the Industrial Home School for Colored Girls – an alternative to prison for African-American girls.

A Share of Honour, notes "coincidentally, the other major figure in rebuilding the lives of girls in trouble was also a Barrett."

Kate Waller Barrett, white and married to a minister, was originally from Stafford County. Her husband was serving the Richmond neighborhood of Butchertown. A young woman came to their home seeking shelter for herself and her baby. Barrett found herself wondering "Where was the terrible degradation, the hopeless depravity ... which I had always been taught to associate with the fallen woman?"

Kate Barrett obviously came from a very different environment than Janie Porter Barrett. The latter merely opened her door to her neighbors and her work began. For the sheltered white woman, the reality of suffering young women had to be thrust upon her.

Kate Barrett never stopped being a member of her class, a helpmeet to the Virginia Gentleman. When she died in 1925, she was the State Regent of the Virginia Daughters of the American Revolution, as reported on the website of the DAR Chapter which she helped start in Arlington,

Virginia, and which bears her name. (Kate Waller Barrett Chapter) She also was a delegate to the 1924 Democratic Convention, and gave one of the speeches nominating Virginia's Carter Glass. In her speech, according to a biographical essay by another member of the gentry, Pocahontas Wight Edmunds, she spoke against "the disparagement of Wall Street" by another speaker. (Edmunds)

Despite her being completely at home with the conservatism of Virginia Gentlemen, Barrett's life's work can only be described, in the context of her time, as genuinely feminist. Her work with "fallen women," for which she was best known, led her to found "rescue homes" for them, usually against strong neighborhood opposition. In 1909, she became the President of the National Florence Crittenton Mission, which eventually had more than 50 homes around the country. While their mission of "saving and rescuing the fallen and degraded" seems ugly to us today, it was far preferable to the traditional choices of prostitution or starvation. (Edmunds)

Kate Barrett also joined the struggle for the vote for women. The DAR website notes that she was "Vice President of the Virginia Equal Suffrage (1909-1920), and was a charter member of the League of Women Voters." (Kate Waller Barrett Chapter)

Few women succeeded as Kate Barrett did, in achieving both high respect from Virginia Gentlemen and genuine changes in women's lives. But every Virginia woman seeking to make change faced the same dilemma – managing both to survive in the Virginia Gentlemen's world and to act on behalf of those the Virginia Gentleman had no respect for.

As the twentieth century opened, white women and, in a very different way, African-American women had been actively reshaping Virginia for at least a century, and actively undermining the dog-eat-dog model that Virginia Gentlemen sought to enforce. Increased public visibility, and then ultimately the vote, would merely add new techniques and methods to the work they had been doing. Though the comment was made just about the Progressive Era, it has always been true that the "social justice movement within progressivism was largely a women's movement." (Virginia Women's Cultural History Project)

Women involved in the early twentieth century reform efforts are also among the first to appear by name in the pages of the historical work Lesbian and Gay Richmond. Of course, none of them were "out" in public in those days; even the most well-connected openly lesbian or gay Virginians might have gone to prison in those days – and still could. (Marschak)

(One of Virginia's first executions, in 1624, was for the crime of sodomy. Jefferson, in an unsuccessful attempt at reform, urged that the punishment for that crime be reduced to castration. In 1800, the penalty for free people committing sodomy was reduced to one to ten years in prison. Slaves still faced the death penalty for the crime until 1860. From 1800 until today, the punishment for sodomy has remained a prison term of between one and ten years.) (Painter)

Lesbian and Gay Richmond identifies several of the era's reformers who "lived as companions" with a person of the same gender for many years and never married. These included Equal Suffrage League members Adele Clark and Willoughby Ions and Lucy Randolph Mason and Katherine Gerwick. Mason was also the General Secretary of the Richmond YWCA and president of the League of Women Voters. In addition, Grace Arents, who inherited a tobacco fortune and gave much of it away, especially in the working-class white Oregon Hill neighborhood, lived with and left much of her wealth to "her close companion."

As Lesbian and Gay Richmond notes about Mason, "Like many socially progressive women of her time, Mason had her closest relationships with women." (Marschak) We can't know whether this might have been less visibly the case for decades before, and not only for women of privilege, but for many others.

Among women's social justice accomplishments of those days that Our Share of Honour cites are the YWCA branches (white and "colored") in Richmond, the Instructive Visiting Nurses' Association, NAACP branches, and support for college opportunities for women.

There is no question that obtaining the right to vote, to serve on juries, run for office, and generally to be citizens were vital steps for women in Virginia, and that that struggle for full democratic participation is far from over.

But when a group of women gathered in Fredericksburg and began serious conversation about establishing a school for working-class girls, they were taking a major political step. To the Virginia Gentleman, those girls were meant to be maids or prostitutes or serving wenches; they didn't need reading or even moral teaching. But to the organizers of the school, the girls were human beings like themselves, who deserved some small measure of self-respect and self-determination.

Two conceptions of humanity – the hierarchical and the humanitarian – were contending for ascendancy, even if few of those involved fully recognized it.

As Anne Firor Scott wrote in the Introduction to <u>A Share of Honour</u>, "the creation of state responsibility for public welfare was largely the work of women who used their own voluntary associations to create a political voice." I would only add that they used “their own voluntary associations” to take responsibility themselves for public welfare when the state was backing away from its responsibilities in the nineteenth century – as it is again today.

The Virginia Gentleman, while deluding himself that he was a kind patriarch, was quite willing to create a Hell on Earth for his inferiors. To the extent life in Virginia has been something else than that Hell on Earth, it has been the women of Virginia who have been largely responsible.

Alternative Lifestyles of the Richmond Famous

In December of 1870, Susan B. Anthony spoke at the federal courthouse in Richmond. I have yet to find an account of the meeting with much detail, but these are some basic facts.

The meeting was organized by Anna Whitehead Bodeker, President of the Virginia Woman Suffrage Association. She had gathered together enough folks to create that organization earlier that year, and only a few months later, had brought one of the great names of that day's (and any day's) women's movement to Richmond.

Two of the most prominent targets for white contempt in Richmond were probably in the room. Both are known to have supported Bodeker and women's suffrage, and probably would not have missed the event.

John C. Underwood was a federal judge, as a result of having been part of the Union effort in Virginia. But, more notoriously, he had headed up the Constitutional Convention that had brought Virginia back into the Union – at the price of agreeing to "universal manhood suffrage." As historian Jeremy Boggs wrote, "The passage and implementation of the Underwood Constitution brought abundant protest from native white Virginians, who despised the imposition of the constitution by Northerners and black Virginians." (Boggs)

Underwood had also proposed suffrage for women at the convention, but that idea had little support from the guys there.

Elizabeth Van Lew's career has already been described. She was also probably present, given her support for feminism and a general activist approach.

From a Confederate point of view, that little meeting was like a nest of serpents.In other words, it may have been a connection point for some of the most intriguing and important Virginians of the era.

Richmond has rarely been a center of mass activism. But that evening is similar to many others – some public meetings, some more private gatherings -- where potent and radical ideas were transmitted, and the transgenerational process of movement building took place.

The Virginia Woman Suffrage Association did not last long. Not only did it face the usual male resistance, but many white leaders "associated the issue of a potential federal or state voting amendment with the hated politics of Reconstruction." (Virginia Department of Historic Resources)

But in 1907, a similar small meeting founded a successor organization, the Equal Suffrage League of Virginia, an organization that was active until women in the U.S. finally gained the vote. Again, a remarkable group of people were involved, though all were wealthy white Richmond woman. (Virginia Department of Historic Resources)

They included:

- Lila Meade Valentine, who continued the tradition of Virginia women engaged in independent social service. In 1900, she founded and became President of the Richmond Education Association, which in its first four years "raised funds for a new high school, founded programs designed to help train kindergarten teachers, called for better training and higher wages for all teachers, and created initiatives designed to help poor white and African American students receive excellent educations." Valentine also "helped found the Instructive Visiting Nurse Association of Richmond, ... [which] became a model for health-care reformers throughout Virginia." All this was before her involvement in the Equal Suffrage League. Like many other women of the time, she saw woman suffrage as key to making the social reforms she supported. (Encyclopedia Virginia) Many people are skeptical that this came about. But would we have Social Security, Medicare, and civil rights legislation if women had never had the vote? No one can prove the point either way, but I think it's worth a thought.

- Ellen Glasgow, perhaps the best novelist who wrote mostly about Virginia, was also at the meeting. Glasgow was a key figure in Richmond's arts and feminist communities for many years. But her real strength was in her writing. Her novels give us a wide range of characters living through the 19th and early 20th century changes in Virginia. Her characters are always closely accompanied by the sights and smells and structures around Virginia. The natural and the human-built world of Virginia of that day live on in her work.

- Adele Clark, whose mention in Lesbian and Gay Richmond has already been referred to, was a graphic artist committed to "making the art of painting and its kindred crafts a more functional thing in the life of the community." As such, she helped to found the Virginia League of Fine Arts and Handicraft in 1920. During the New Deal, she served as Director of the Arts program for the Works Progress Administration in Virginia. (Irwin)

- Anne Clay Crenshaw, the host of the meeting, was the daughter of Cassius Marcellus Clay of Kentucky. You may recognize that name. Cassius Clay was also the name that the great boxer Muhammad Ali was born with. This is no coincidence; the first Cassius Clay was one of the few publicly active white Southern abolitionists and an adviser to Lincoln. But he was not a good husband, and his wife divorced him – a radical step in 1878. Mrs. Clay and her four daughters were left in poverty, and the daughters committed themselves to justice for women and were active in the suffrage movement in Kentucky. Anne married an upper class Richmonder in 1886; while she put a lot of energy into her family, she played a key role in getting the Equal Suffrage League going, serving on the first Board of Directors and helping to get its first national speaker. (Bonis)

These four women, despite their common class and racial background, brought very different qualities to the political opening they were part of. They also connected it to past and future efforts, from the abolition of slavery to the New Deal.

I spent fifteen mostly good years in Richmond. I was at a lot of parties, dinners, meetings, and in a lot of random conversations that in their small way moved history forward. Just a few memories of women at work in Richmond come to mind:

- At a Democratic precinct meeting, I helped Beth Marschak, who has had a finger in most feminist activity in Richmond since the 70s, to take the first step towards becoming a Jesse Jackson delegate at the national Democratic Party convention.
- I went to the wake of Estelle Smith, who I knew mainly as the President of Richmond United Neighborhoods, and learned how many lives she had touched, especially those of so many foster children. And I saw her granddaughter Regina Chaney with frankness and kindness take on and handle the task of helping folks deal with homeownership realistically.

- I strategized with Sara Motley from Pittsylvania County about stopping uranium mining (the first time it was talked about, in the 1980s) and heard from her about how the issue there crossed race lines.
- I saw the great power and dignity of Sandra Parker, a Black woman principal, descend on a white banker and change his life, despite all his resistance.
- I watched Janine Bell work with others in the community to forge the Elegba Folklore Society, an exciting force for positive African culture in a community that has attacked everything African for centuries.

There have been, are, and will be, hundreds of women like these in Richmond. In fact, I have come to know more remarkable women just in Richmond even since I left there in 1988-- women who hold and pass on embers of the social justice fire. I am so grateful for what I have gained from them, including pretty much my career.

One of my many nights at the old Main Street Grill, one of the places in Richmond where social barriers came down most often, I was invited over to a table by a woman friend. Most of the women at the table were Lesbians, and one in particular was a very butch truck driver. A beer or three later, I had been declared "an honorary Lesbian truck driver." A year or so later, one of the women who met me at that table that night turned me on to a job – my first serious job, running the small library at the City Jail. (I went from one random blue collar job to the next until I was 30.) So I sort of owe the start of my sort of professional career to one of those encounters.

But we all owe more than we can calculate to these encounters and interactions.

I don't know the details, but I know that this year – 2012 – once again, encounters and connections like this changed Virginia history. I am thinking specifically of the protests at the State Capitol on February 20 and March 3, 2012. These actions were organized quickly and efficiently, and were extremely powerful, both as spectacle and in their state and even national political impact.

The legislation that inspired them – a requirement that women intending to have an abortion first undergo an intrusive and unnecessary procedure, a transvaginal ultrasound– was stalled, amended, and nationally ridiculed as a result of the actions. Most of the participants were women.

In fact, as I was going to press with this book, Congresscritter Akin of Missouri made his disgusting comment about "legitimate rape." An Associated Press analysis article mentioned the Capitol demonstrations. The article went on, "Perhaps because of that...." and then described the "swift and thundering" efforts by Virginia Republican candidates to distance themselves from Akin's comments. (Lewis, Bob) Perhaps.... Yeah, like "perhaps" there is a relationship between burning your hand on a hot stove and being careful next time.

Actions like this can only come from a group of people who have grown, over years of encounters, to trust each other and to know how to work together. In a real sense, those actions were rooted in the steps that a few women took in Richmond to establish the Female Humane Association, or during the first days in slavery, getting to know each other and learning how to take action together in a hostile world. From then to today, the torch has passed without a lapse.

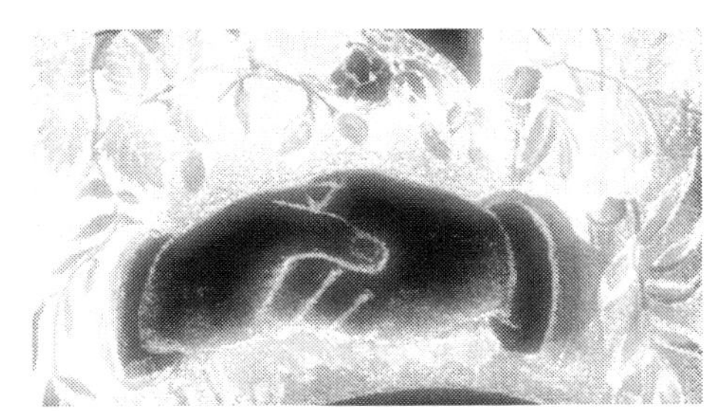

Fraud and Fable Number Twelve: Virginia's African-Americans Have Been Kinda Quiet Since the War

Purpose: It is the Virginia Gentleman and his media and schools that have been quiet on this subject, because information about effective and aroused African-Americans in Virginia contradicts their picture of calm and unchallenged white dominance.

One way white supremacy was established and maintained was by erasing the memory of a powerful and responsible black citizenry, by excising the history of whites and blacks working together on more or less equal terms. These erasures, conscious or not, had the effect of making white supremacy seem natural, inevitable, rock solid by virtue of having been in place forever.” (Lebsock)

This is an interesting myth, because it contradicts the myth the Virginia Gentlemen told in earlier days. Up until the 1890s, the Virginia Gentlemen perceived a terrible situation in Virginia --“an actual and very lawless government by the worst elements of society, exalting ignorance above culture, vice over virtue, and setting a horde of half-savage and suddenly emancipated slaves to direct the destinies” of the beloved Commonwealth. (Eggleston)

But once the crisis was over (for the white élite) with passage of the Jim Crow 1902 Constitution, the Gentlemen did not want to actually examine or understand what had happened. There had just been "chaos." Now it was all over, and the new line was that African-Americans had done nothing significant. White rule was always inevitable. Reconstruction had not been an attempted African-American revolution, just a mistake by over-zealous Yankees that the Virginia Gentleman had had to fix.

Organized Black Power Fights The Slaveholders' Comeback

Over the years, I have collected several books of jokes from back in the day, and in a couple of cases they have had specific sections of jokes about African-Americans. (Though African-American is not, of course, the word such books use.) The major themes of these ugly jokes are laziness, stealing, and lack of education. Or as I would like to put it, avoiding exploitation, expropriation, and sounding dumb to fool white folks.

But I recently found a couple of jokes that speak to a very different issue – organized Black Power.

One of the jokes runs like this:

An NAACP official calls the Library of Congress and tells them they have a week to remove all 18,000 books that contain the "n word." The librarian protests that this would be a terrible precedent, and says "We have 55,000 books with the word 'bastard ' in them."

The punch line? The NAACP leader says "I know. But you bastards aren't organized."

The other joke is more insulting to African-Americans, with a punch line about the "Grand All-Powerful Invincible Most Supreme Unconquerable Potentate" of a fraternal organization. (Actually, it sounds to me like a title the Lost Cause might have used for Robert E. Lee.)

Even the second joke, though, speaks to the existence of organization in the African-American community. Elaborately named lodges and fraternal organizations are a staple of white-written comedy about African-Americans, showing up for example in the lives of characters like Amos and Andy and Jack Benny's servant Rochester. But the comedy was a white distortion of real and vital organizations in the Black community.

Of course, white working people have also belonged to such organizations. But in the years from the end of slavery to the early 20th century, fraternal and civic organizations were especially important to African-Americans. Those were terrible years, and years in which "the bastards" **were** organized. But the organizing that African-Americans did for self-defense and for survival made a huge difference, though it was unable to prevent decades of apartheid and quasi-fascism in Virginia and throughout the South.

Peter Rachleff in his Black Labor in Richmond, 1865-1890 tells the story of some of this organizing. His detailed research of social patterns in political clubs and fraternal organizations in Richmond at the time brings the struggle to life. As he describes,

> **"Richmond Afro-Americans built an impressive community ... the initial building block was the church...Built on this foundation, a broad network of social organizations called 'secret societies' fulfilled a multiplicity of purposes; funerals and death benefits, trade organization, collective self-education and self-improvement, religious advancement, political expression, socializing, and the like..."**

FREED PEOPLE IN RICHMOND, 1865

When the war ended, many of Richmond's African Americans already belonged to such organizations, which were necessarily secret under slavery.

Church membership, experience working together in factories, and the connections made within these organizations combined to make Richmond's African-Americans a more cohesive force than most whites could imagine.

The former masters saw only a seething and dangerous black mass, as did the 1910 conservative chronicler of the period, Professor Preston McConnell, who approvingly quoted this June 12, 1865 Lynchburg Virginian editorial:

> **"Large numbers have deserted the plantations and seek to congregate in the cities, so that the most stringent police regulations may be necessary to keep them from overburdening the towns and depleting the agricultural regions of labor. The military authorities seem to be alive to this fact and are taking measures to correct the evil. But the civil authorities also should be fully empowered to protect the community from this new imposition."** (McConnell)

Rachleff reports that in that same month, 800 African-Americans, some former slaves and others born free, and "including children," were arrested in Richmond for not having "passes" and being considered vagrant, that is, for not having a signed statement from their white boss approving their whereabouts. (The South African apartheid government and Nazi Germany later adopted similar policies.)

African-Americans quickly began to organize against this oppressive practice. A June 10 meeting at the historic First African Baptist Church sent a delegation to President Johnson to protest the pass system. Their actions were successful; the Confederate Mayor of Richmond, who had been reinstated, was removed, as were several Union officers administering Richmond, who were replaced by General Alfred Terry. Rachleff writes "These events ... taught [Richmond African-Americans] that they did have the power to address their problems, that they could organize and struggle for what they wanted."

FIRST AFRICAN BAPTIST CHURCH

In January 1866, the Virginia legislature passed a law based on their understanding that:

> **"there hath lately been a great increase of idle and disorderly persons in some parts of this Commonwealth, and, unless some stringent laws are passed to restrain**

and prevent such vagrancy and idleness, the State will be over run with dissolute and abandoned characters to the great detriment of the public weal.." (McConnell)

This law would have required anyone (in practice, any one dark-skinned) who was unemployed to be required to work, burdened with a ball and chain if the judge so ordered, or to serve three months in jail on bread and water. Even McConnell noted that "The language of this act applies alike to all persons, both white and black, but it was enacted primarily to suppress vagrancy among the negroes."

General Alfred Terry, who had been appointed after African-American protests, annulled this act immediately, stating that "The ultimate effect of the statute will be to reduce the freed men to a condition of servitude worse than that from which they have been emancipated, a condition which will be slavery in all but its name."

So at this stage, Union forces still controlled the state, and organized African-Americans in Richmond had the ear of Union officials. (Rachleff)

Rural Virginia, however, was a different story. At the same time that many whites were complaining about the influx of African-Americans to the cities, county-wide groups of white farmers were meeting and instituting restrictions on ex-slaves. In different counties white farmers set a maximum wage, agreed not to rent to any African-Americans, and, as a condition for being hired, required African-Americans to provide "testimonials or recommendations from their last employer, which practically meant that a negro could not find employment unless he had the endorsement of his former owner." (McConnell)

Some rural African-Americans did fight back, and "sometimes adopted bolder tactics, gathered into crowds in remote parts of the counties, killed the hogs, sheep and cattle of the white farmers and plundered their orchards and fields." (McConnell) Given that these people were responding not only to hunger and desperate poverty, but to the theft of their labor for centuries, I am not sure I would categorize this as "idleness and vagrancy" as McConnell did.

But the power imbalance in the rural areas was too great. Urban Virginia, and especially Richmond, was the front line of the struggle. There the organized African-American held parades and events. There unions, like the Stevedore Society, went on strike. There, African-Americans played a central role in the Republican Party.

While the Republican Party is often seen as the main organization for the advancement of African-Americans in those days, African-Americans understood they had to use their independent base within that party. The Party was largely controlled by "white political bosses," people "powerfully connected to the Republican party machine in Washington and to the Federal military director of Virginia." So African-Americans acted independently on issues that concerned them. (Rachleff)

One example was the action of 200 participants in the 1868 Emancipation parade who, to protest an oppressive toll on a footbridge across the James, left the parade and crossed the bridge without paying the toll. Another sign of independence and progressive thought, in Nansemond County, now the City of Virginia Beach, was "a negro meeting [that] advocated negro equality in every respect and female suffrage." (McConnell)

In 1870, the genteel politics of Richmond Gentlemen showed their collective rear end.

George Chahoon was the young white liberal Republican mayor of Richmond, born in the North but having lived most of his life in Richmond. He had been appointed by the Federal military government.

In January, Virginia was readmitted to the Union. The more conservative Republican Governor Walker appointed his own Richmond City Council, and they chose Henry Ellyson as Mayor. Ellyson, a prominent Baptist layman for most of his life, had held elective office before the war and was Sheriff of Richmond under the Confederacy. He had also begun his long service on the Board of what is now the University of

Richmond. Despite not being an Episcopalian, he was a pretty sound Virginia Gentleman.

Chahoon refused to recognize Ellyson's appointment as Mayor, and he and his police force barricaded themselves in the municipal building located in the Old City Market area. Ellyson deputized 200 white men in his support; Chahoon then turned to the African-American community and appointed his own deputies. What some called the Municipal War began.

Ellyson's forces surrounded and besieged Chahoon and his forces; an African-American crowd in turn surrounded Ellyson's "troops." Police fired into the crowd, and one African-American was killed and others wounded. Finally, a Federal general intervened and enforced a truce until the issue could go to court – and eventually neither Chahoon nor Ellyson took the Mayor's seat. (While I have followed Rachleff's account fairly closely here, I first heard this story from Jeff Ruggles, who ran the Main Street Grill in the Old City Market area in the 1980s, and who is a remarkable self-taught historian of Richmond.)

Rachleff's book, and his knowledge of the era, go deeper than I can here. There were ups and downs – and unfortunately more of the latter – for

Richmond's African-American community. But his book clearly shows that the community was neither chaotic nor cowed; that it was a community that made a serious effort to determine its own destiny, against overwhelming odds.

Rachleff notes early on that "the leadership of the black community," and of the organizations he describes, "emerged from families that had deep roots in Richmond." One such person was John Mitchell, who has been mentioned previously. In 1863, Mitchell was born on the estate

of Virginia Gentleman James Lyons, at the time a member of the Confederate Congress, to two house servants, Lyons' coachman and a seamstress.

Born just days after the Battle of Gettysburg, Mitchell represented a younger generation than most of those that Rachleff wrote about. At eighteen, he became a public school teacher. Soon he began to write for African-American newspapers, and in 1884 became editor of a “start-up” newspaper, the Richmond Planet. Soon, he was its publisher, and continued to be until his death in 1929.

RICHMOND PLANET OFFICE

No African-American "fighting editor" could be just a journalist in the era of slowly encroaching Jim Crow in Virginia. Mitchell served on City Council until the election of a Black man was no longer possible. He led protests against lynching and streetcar segregation. He founded other businesses, though with less success than other African-American Richmonders, especially Maggie Walker. (Alexander, Ann)

But above all, as his biographer Ann Field Alexander wrote, "he and other black journalists kept alive the dream of full citizenship" for African-Americans.

When I moved to Richmond in 1973, the successor to Mitchell's paper, the Richmond Afro-American and Planet, was still publishing. One of the most important decisions I made in Richmond was to subscribe to and read that paper.

In many respects, it was a small town paper – serving the small community of Richmond's African-Americans, especially the "social set." The layout was not great, and typos were not rare. But at the same time, it published voices like that of Manning Marable, the socialist writer and activist and Rev. L. Francis Griffin, a civil rights leader from Prince Edward County -- because they were clearly part of the African-

American oppositional tradition. Most importantly, the newspaper gave me another perspective on Richmond. Once African-Americans gained a majority on City Council, the daily papers in Richmond (there were two then, but both came from the same publisher) hammered away on any theme that might bring down Black politicians. (No, it didn't start with President Obama.) The Afro gave me an alternative viewpoint.

In 1996, after I left Richmond, the Afro-American newspapers, based in Baltimore, stopped publishing in Richmond. Technically, that was the end of the Planet. But today the Richmond Free Press carries on the tradition, published and written by several former staffers from the Richmond Afro.

Community-based business was another tool of African-American survival. In Martinsville, Virginia, a key figure in the African-American community, Dr. Dana O. Baldwin, owned or participated in the Baldwin Pharmacy, the Baldwin Hospital, the Douglas Café, and Booker T. Washington Park, an amusement park that included a baseball field. Baldwin also helped start Martinsville Brick Manufacturing, Inc. This latter business created more than 25 jobs and had 40 local stockholders. According to Fayette Street, A Hundred-Year History of African-American Life in Martinsville, Virginia, "buildings using Baldwin's brick still standing today include the Gordon Building ... and Pilgrim Missionary Baptist Church.." (Fayette Area Historical Initiative)

While not every Virginia African-American community had a business leader as ubiquitous as Dr. Baldwin, similar activities occurred on Henry Street in Roanoke, in Jackson Ward in Richmond, and in other cities around the state.

Another critical element of African-American self determination has been the HBCUs -- Historically Black Colleges and Universities.

On September 17, 1861, a Virginia woman of African descent, Mary Peake, held a class, which consisted of about twenty students, under an oak tree. Mary Peake was a free woman; her students were "contrabands," people escaped from slavery who had gathered under the protection of Union General Benjamin Butler near Fort Monroe, Virginia. That oak tree is now a feature of the campus of Hampton University, among the earliest of the Historically Black Colleges and Universities to founded in the South. (Hampton)

As with most HBCUs at that date, Hampton's first president was a white man, Brigadier General Samuel Armstrong, who was also in charge of the Freedmen's Bureau in the area. Booker T. Washington, who went on to found Tuskegee University, another renowned HBCU, wrote of Armstrong in 1900, after Washington was himself a famous man, "I do not hesitate to say that I never met any man who, in my estimation, was the equal of General Armstrong." (Washington, Booker T.)

For Washington and many others who began their lives as slave children, Hampton created opportunities they did not even know existed.

> **"One of the rooms in the Old Folks Home for Colored in Portsmouth, Virginia, is occupied by an ex-slave – one of the first Negro teachers of Portsmouth .... Miss Mary Jane Wilson...**
> **'When I was free, I went to school.... they builded a school building that was called Chestnut Street Academy, and I went there. After finishing Chestnut Street Academy, I went to Hampton. In 1874 .... I graduated.'**
> **'After two years my class grew so fast and so large that my father built a school for me in our back yard. I had as many as seventy-five pupils.'"**
> (Library of Congress)

Of those who served Virginia's African-American community during the bitter years of Jim Crow, probably no single person is more revered than Ms. Maggie Lena Mitchell Walker.

MRS. MAGGIE WALKER

She is most commonly remembered as U.S. Congressperson Bobby Scott referred to her in a speech of praise he gave in 2001 – " the first African American female bank president." (Scott, Representative Robert) The title is accurate – in fact she was the " first female bank president" in the United States. And the bank she established survived as an African-American owned bank for over a century, and still is in business today, though as part of a larger white-owned bank.

To call Maggie Walker a bank president, though, is like calling Ida Wells-Barnett a reporter, or Harriet Tubman a wilderness guide. Her mission was far greater than that of the typical banker.

When I lived in Richmond, I knew a few older women who quite likely knew Maggie Walker, and who certainly knew people who knew her. These women were retired teachers, with the diction and phrasing of people who preserved the oratorical strength of Victorian English. They had spent their lives in the service of "uplifting the race" – and so did Maggie Walker.

The book sitting by my computer that tells Maggie Walker's story was originally published in 1931 by Associated Publishers, the publishing arm of what is now the Association for the Study of African-American Life and History. So the book, Women Builders, comes right from the fount of Black History, from Carter Woodson's organization. When it was published, Carter Woodson was still alive, and so was Maggie Walker.

Its author, Sadie Iola Daniel, stated in her foreword that "books depicting the achievement of the race in various lines of endeavor are necessary." So in 1931, she and Dr. Woodson and Ms. Walker were all engaged in the tough work of bringing facts and hope to an oppressed people. (Daniel)

At that time, Herbert Hoover was President and leader of a Republican Party that had long since lost any commitment to racial justice. The Great

Depression was underway. Jim Crow was a half century old, and no one saw it collapsing any time soon.

These African-American leaders had seen the 1920s, the highpoint of the revived Klan, and the bitter race riot year 1919. But they never stopped their work of those "uplifting the race."

Maggie Walker was born in 1867. Her mother and stepfather worked for Elizabeth Van Lew, the abolitionist, Union spy, and feminist described earlier in this book.

When she was a girl, her widowed mother took in washing and ironing. Maggie, the older daughter, helped while she kept up her schoolwork. In high school, she was part of a student strike against "separate and unequal" graduation exercises; this 1883 protest "stands recorded as the first school strike of Negroes in America." (Daniel)

She resigned from teaching after marrying, and became deeply involved in the Independent Order of St. Luke, one of the many community organizations that Rachleff wrote about.

Maggie Walker moved up in the Order's structure, being seen as pious, alert and energetic. She started taking on staff roles – as Executive Secretary, and then as secretary-treasurer of the new endowment department. Daniel

describes one of Maggie Walker's tasks as being "to win those who had to be taught loyalty to a cause and enabled to see the folly of selfish motives." In other words, the work of the Order was never just financial in the narrow sense. (Daniel)

Maggie Walker went on to establish a magazine, The Saint Luke Herald, the Saint Luke Penny Bank, and the Saint Luke Emporium, a department store. The Order also had an Emergency Fund of over $150,000 by 1931.

Along with these business activities, the Order had a program for 15,000 juvenile members, who met in small groups weekly with a program including

"Bible instruction and lessons in thrift and hygiene."

At an event honoring Ms. Walker in 1924, one speaker noted that during her time with the Order:

> **"...in twenty-five years, a small spiritless company of men and women is converted in a compact army; a dilapidated dwelling house is replaced by a magnificent office building... The pencil has yielded to the typewriter, and the pen to the press.. the once empty treasury, like the widow's oil, is being constantly increased. The once unknown school teacher becomes a national figure..."**
> (Daniel)

In 1926, as she proposed an Educational Loan Fund, she stated "Any organization desiring to secure and hold its place as a permanent factor in modern progress must justify itself in continuous service to humanity."

Maggie Walker was also the longtime President of the Richmond Council of Colored Women, which funded an African-American visiting nurse and a settlement house.

Rep. Scott, in his speech about Maggie Walker, also noted that she “set the groundwork for the local women's suffrage movement and ... boldly challenged the political establishment in 1921 when she ran for State Superintendent of Public Instruction on the ‘Lily Black’ Republican ticket.” (Scott, Representative Robert)

John Mitchell and Maggie Lena Walker were heroic figures of Richmond’s African-American history, and of the golden age of the Jackson Ward neighborhood. During their lifetimes, a less celebrated but still prominent citizen, James Edward Jackson, Sr., ran a pharmacy in Jackson Ward. I couldn’t find out much about him, but he and his wife, Clara Louise Kersey Jackson, had two quite remarkable children.

Their son, James E. Jackson Jr., was memorialized with a New York Times obituary. Initially, he followed in his father’s professional footsteps and became a pharmacist. However, in his last year of pharmacy college at Howard University, he helped to organize the first meeting of the Southern Negro Youth Congress, held at Fifth Baptist Church in Richmond in February of 1937.

The Congress brought over 500 delegates to Richmond, “who had come in response to an appeal to cast off their chains and continue the tradition of struggle against second-class citizenship..." The delegates went out and organized hundreds of tobacco workers into union membership while they were in Richmond. (Strong)

Jackson went on to hold important positions in the Communist Party USA, including serving as the editor of its national newspaper. In 1953, he was the main author of "The Southern People's Common Program for Democracy, Prosperity and Peace."

This program for organizing had as its central goal "to eliminate anti-democratic, feudal and autocratic political and economic relations, laws, institutions and practices from the South." (Southern Regional Committee) Jackson was also one of the defendants in the federal case against the Party under the Smith Act (authored by Harry Byrd associate Howard "Judge" Smith, discussed in ***Fraud and Fable Number Sixteen: Modern Virginia Conservatism Has Broken with***

the Jim Crow Past.) Jackson went underground for five years to avoid arrest. He died in Brooklyn, New York, in 2007.

Jackson's younger sister, Alice, was also a remarkable character.

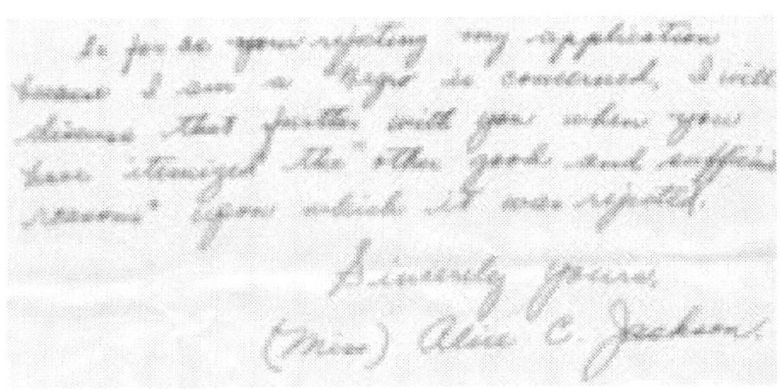

In so far as your rejecting my application because I am a "Negro" is concerned, I will discuss that further with you when you have itemized the "other good and sufficient reasons" upon which it was rejected.

Sincerely yours,

(Miss) Alice C. Jackson

After graduating from Virginia Union University, she applied to the University of Virginia's graduate school. Since she was very well qualified, her application precipitated a crisis. The General Assembly created a fund to pay for her to go to graduate school at Columbia University, the first time for such a step, and she went on to have a long teaching career. (University of Virginia Library)

The world that created James and Alice Jackson, and that was created by ex-slaves, was invisible to most whites. Even to the whites who knew that world existed, the idea that it could matter in any significant way to them would have seemed absurd.

But soon the Freedom Movement, one of the most powerful political forces in US history, emerged from this world.

A Speech I Delivered in Capitol Square, Richmond, Virginia at a Move-On Rally in Solidarity with Wisconsin Workers, February 26, 2011

(*Capitol Square landmarks referred to in my speech include a more than life-size statue of Harry Byrd Sr. and an office building named after civil rights attorney Oliver Hill. At the time of this speech, Wisconsin unions and their supporters were fighting anti-labor legislation proposed by a right-wing governor.*)

A lot of Virginians think that what's happening in Madison has nothing to do with us – that Madison, Wisconsin is as different from us as the moon.

They want to ignore our Virginia history of solidarity -- our history of fighting for public institutions that serve all the people. But that history is reflected right here around us – as well as in the Northern Shenandoah Valley where I live.

Virginia Teachers Association's Struggle

75 years ago, there was a meeting of the Virginia Teachers Association (the association of African-American teachers) in Hampton. They made a decision – that Virginia deserved good schools for every child – and that a key step was getting equal pay for all Virginia teachers. They set up a fund and an alliance with the NAACP, and, according to the official history of the VTA, the approximately 1000 delegates left knowing that they had put their hand on the plow and there was no turning back.

Now the guy who ran Virginia in those days – Harry Byrd – whose statue is right up there – probably was not too impressed by that meeting. Even less impressed than Gov. McDonnell is by our little group. Black Virginians mostly couldn't vote, and our nation was in the depths of the Great Depression. But they didn't give up.

By the 1950s, Harry Byrd, who lived about nine miles down Route 7 from where I live, took them more seriously.

Thanks to both brilliant lawyers and determined movement solidarity, Virginia's schools were going to be one system, open to all. That's when Harry Byrd showed that, like Scott Walker, and like Bob McDonnell, he really didn't give a damn about schoolchildren or teachers of any color. If he couldn't have schools the way he wanted them – segregated and underfunded – he would shut them down.

> **"One of the leading Southern segregationists, Editor James Kilpatrick, of the Richmond News-Leader, was reduced to Latin by his dismay at the contrast between the quiet manners of Negro sit-inners and the crudities of white bystanders. "Eheu," he said, "that the South should witness Negroes teaching whites manners." But the South has always witnessed this without trying to understand it. Who taught whom the manners of the South? I can still hear the voice of my Negro nurse, 'Child, ain't you shamed?'"**
> Who Speaks for the South?, by James McBride Dabbs, 1964

Warren County & Massive Resistance

One of the schools Byrd shut down was Warren County High School, about 20 miles from his own home in Berryville.

A few years ago, I had the privilege of helping to organize an event at the Warren County Courthouse commemorating the response NAACP members and the Front Royal area African-American community made to Byrd's action.

One speaker was a 99 year old man, who as it happened was in the last year of his life. He used a wheelchair, and spoke with difficulty. But what had happened in Warren County mattered to him, and he wanted to be part of that commemoration. Since that day, that man has passed on, but he is not forgotten. Yes, Harry Byrd has a little statue up the hill. But that man, Attorney Oliver Hill Sr., a civil rights titan, has that entire state government building on Capitol Square named after him.

Rev. James Kilby also spoke at that event. James was one of the students that Oliver Hill argued for in court, and James' father was the local NAACP leader. The Kilby family was threatened, and their property and livestock were harmed, but they persevered. James was one of the first Black graduates of Warren County High School.

This week, James sent me an e-mail. Warren County Schools fourth and fifth graders are studying the history of 50 years ago – the civil rights movement. And they have a wonderful resource. Rev. James Kilby, who at 14 walked past a nasty yelling mob with 22 other students to integrate Warren County High School, is speaking in their classrooms, telling them what actually happened – how his father, and Oliver Hill, and a movement of parents and teachers and attorneys – rocked Virginia.

Virginia and Wisconsin

What is happening in Madison, the occupation of the State Capital and the massive marches by labor, is wonderful, but it is not new. And it certainly is not alien to us in Virginia. The teachers who have been standing up under the Wisconsin Capitol dome have a real kinship with the Virginia Teachers Association as it stood up in 1937.

Harry Byrd is just a memory or a name in the history books for most of us. Before too long, Scott Walker and Bob McDonnell will also be forgotten. But – if we do our jobs, standing up for Wisconsin teachers, standing proudly in the tradition of the Virginia Teachers Association 75 years ago – the peoples' movement that Wisconsin has sparked will live on. It will be remembered in good schools, good public services, and in proud unions and grassroots organizations. We stand on mighty shoulders, and, like Wisconsin, we too have a strong history of solidarity here in Virginia. We have put our shoulder to the wheel, and we can't turn back now.

Two Relevant Books :
History of the Virginia Teachers Association by J. Rupert Picott, 1975.
The Forever Fight by James Kilby, 1998.

Danville and Petersburg: Struggles All But Forgotten

> **"My mother was a slave and she belonged to Dick Belcher in Chesterfield County... You know there was an overseer who use to tie mother up in the barn with a rope round her arms up over her head, while she stood on a block... This ol' man, now, would start beating her naked 'til the blood run down back to her heels.... Lord, Lord, I hate white people and the flood waters going to drown some more..."** Interview with Mrs. Minnie Fulkes, Petersburg, Virginia, 1937 (Library of Congress)

The Freedom Movement is best known for its work in Alabama and Mississippi, and no one can take away the enduring glory that surrounds the great work done there.

But the Freedom Movement was at work in every state in the old Confederacy – and in the north, where it especially was critical in energizing campuses and the networks of liberals and radicals that had withered under

McCarthyism. It was certainly at work in Virginia.

The struggles led by the Danville Movement and the Petersburg Improvement Association were among the two largest Freedom Movement struggles in Virginia. They are rarely mentioned today.

The Virginia Historical Society describes events in Danville in 1963 as "the most violent episode of the civil rights movement in Virginia." The violence, of course, was white violence, and mainly police violence.

The most brutal episode was Bloody Monday, on June 10, 1963. African-Americans in Danville had been marching frequently since May 31. Danville authorities had made no attempt to have a conversation about the issues, responding only with police force and harsh arrests. On June 10, two demonstrations, one in the morning and one at night, were attacked with fire hoses and nightsticks. According to the Virginia historical marker commemorating Bloody Monday, at least 47 were injured and 60 were arrested. The marker says that the "events swelled sentiment in favor of civil rights legislation" in the period leading up to the March on Washington in August. (Virginia Historical Society, Danville)

A pamphlet published at the time of the March by the Student Nonviolent Coordinating Committee (SNCC) described the event like this:

> **"Chief McCain bellowed, "Let 'em have it" and the firemen turned hoses on the people, many of them women and teenagers. Nightstick-wielding police and deputized garbage collectors smashed into the group, clubbing Negroes who were bunched for safety against parked cars. Some were washed under cars; others were clubbed after water had knocked them down. Bodies lay on the street, drenched and bloody. Police and garbage collectors**

chased those demonstrators who were able to walk for two blocks."

While this was the most violent day of the struggle, it was typical of the City of Danville's reaction. A few days before, leaders had asked to meet with the city's mayor. They were told he was unavailable. Then the police attacked them, knocking one minister down a flight of stairs, and arresting two ministers for "inciting to riot."

Mary King was a staffer for SNCC who came to Danville a few weeks after these events. She wrote in her memoir of the movement, Freedom Song, about "being surrounded by police, state troopers, and deputized militia" with "choppers in the distance." There was one unpaved dark road in Danville's African-American community, King said, where the police never followed the SNCC workers. When she asked why, other SNCC staff told her "the police knew they might be picked off by sniper shots" there. (King)

The Roanoke Times, then as now one of the less conservative mainstream Virginia newspapers, still described these events as an "ordeal of racial tension brought on by those not content to rely on the procedures of law to gain what they assert to be Negro rights." "Not content to rely on the procedures of law" is actually an excellent description not of the Freedom Movement, but of Virginia's political leaders, when they instituted Massive Resistance a few years before.

Mary King felt a special call to Danville, since her family dated "back to the seventeenth century in the five-county area around Danville on either side of the state line." Her father, one of six ministers in five generations of this family, wrote to the governor of Virginia about the violent treatment of nonviolent African-American protestors. The governor's staff forwarded his letter to Danville's mayor, who assured him that "in the last few weeks, lawless mobs have undertaken to break up and destroy the orderly pattern of life in existence here between the colored and white population since reconstruction days..." (King)

The Virginia Historical Society states that "The Danville protesters' demands were never met by local authorities, and they had to wait for action to be taken at the national level, namely the Civil Rights Act of 1964 and the Voting

Rights Act of 1965, to see their complaints answered." (Virginia Historical Society, Danville) However, Avon Rollins, a SNCC staffer assigned to Danville, prepared a memo that listed a number of small victories, including the hiring of African-American sales people in local stores and the elimination of "all physical signs of segregation" at Dan River Mills, the dominant employer in Danville at the time. Also, the City of Danville hired two African-American social workers and "One Negro policeman," as well as replacing the chairs in the library. The chairs "had been taken out previously in an attempt to keep the races separated.." (Rollins)

The history of the Petersburg Improvement Association (PIA) is not marked by one vivid event like Bloody Monday. It is best known for its leader, Rev. Wyatt Tee Walker, who went on from Petersburg to become the Executive Director of the Southern Christian Leadership Conference in 1960.

In Aldon Morris's crucial analytical work, The Origins of the Civil Rights

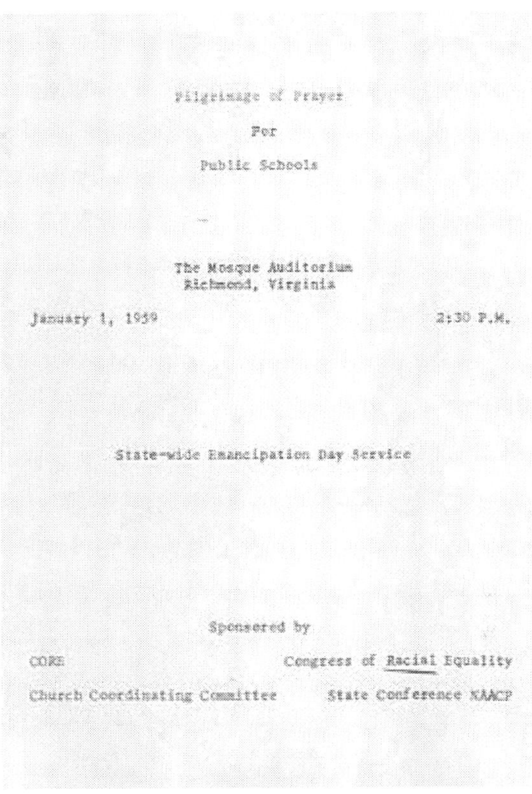

Pilgrimage of Prayer

For

Public Schools

The Mosque Auditorium
Richmond, Virginia

January 1, 1959 2:30 P.M.

State-wide Emancipation Day Service

Sponsored by

CORE Congress of Racial Equality

Church Coordinating Committee State Conference NAACP

Movement, the PIA is identified as a model of the "movement center," which Morris saw as the basic building block of the Freedom Movement. Rev. Walker's church, Gillfield Baptist in Petersburg, 'became the headquarters and the focal point for organizing demonstrations' across Virginia, according to his SCLC colleague Dorothy Cotton. This network organized a march on Richmond on January 1, 1959 to oppose the state policy of closing schools to avoid desegregation.

Walker drafted a letter for Dr. Martin Luther King to send to African-American ministers across Virginia, in which he asked each to one to "let it be your personal responsibility to send at least 50 persons to Richmond from your church community" on January 1.

Despite heavy snow on Richmond that day, the march, as Rev. Walker described it in a letter to Rev. King, went "for twelve or thirteen blocks, men, women and children; the halt and the lame; the young and the aged; orderly and with dignity..."

Years later, in a 1978 interview, Rev. Walker described what gave Dr. King "his tremendous influence and power" -- "he was able to get more warm bodies in the street at one time than anybody else we've seen in American history." (Morris)

Despite the growth of social media and other electronic tools. Rev. Walker's description of where power comes from– which also speaks to the courageous Danville demonstrators – still stands.

In addition to Rev. Walker, another key leader of the Freedom Movement was born in Virginia. Ella Baker left Norfolk as a child to move back to her mother's native North Carolina, so Virginia doesn't have much of a claim on her. But even a small claim on this remarkable social justice figure is worth having.

Ella Baker was one of the great organizers – on any issue – of the twentieth century. She played a significant role in building first the NAACP, then the Southern Christian Leadership Conference, and then, as its "elder" mentor, the Student Nonviolent Coordinating Committee – SNCC. She was a radical democrat, who always sought to involve the young, the poor and the forgotten in their own liberation. (Ransby)

While she did not spend much of her life in Virginia, she did connect to the Movement here in many ways. The author of a biography about her has posted online several weeks of her schedule during her work for the NAACP in the 1940s. The schedule not only shows us Ms. Baker's dedication, but also gives us an outline of some of the key institutions and locations for African-American justice work, before and since, some of them mentioned in these Notes:

April 11: Richmond, Va., meeting with staff of Richmond Beneficial Insurance Company

April 12 : Baptist Minister's conference
April 15 : 9 a.m., Southern Aid Society staff meeting; 9:30 a.m., staff meeting of N.C. Mutual Life Insurance; 7 p.m., campaign report meeting
April 16 : Independent Order of St. Luke meeting
April 17 : 10 a.m., Apex School of Beauty; 11 a.m., School of Modern Beauty Culture
April 17 : Peaks, Va., 8:30 p.m., staff meeting, Peaks Industrial School
April 18 : Peaks Industrial School student assembly
April 18 : Richmond, Va., meeting with staff of Mutual Insurance Company
April 21 : Meeting of Interdenominational Ministerial Alliance; 2 p.m., luncheon meeting of branch
April 21 : Victoria, Va., 8 p.m., meeting at Lunenburg County Training School re organizing branch
April 22 : Richmond, Va., closing meeting of branch campaign
April 24 : Mass meeting of student chapter, Virginia Union University
April 24 : Danville, Va., 7:30 p.m. conference with branch officers to plan campaign
April 27 : Opening mass meeting of Danville branch campaign
April 28 : Meeting held in county
April 28 : Martinsville, Va., meeting with group interested in organizing branch

April 29 : Youth council meeting at high school
April 29 : Farmville, Va., meeting with branch officers, mass meeting of branch, Moton High School meeting
April 30 : Nottoway County, Va., branch meeting held at Blackstone, Va (Grant, 1998)

Each of Ella Baker's stops in April, 1941, represents a site of African-American influence and struggle. There are many more such sites. Every Virginian lives in the midst of an invisible web of African-American history – history we should all be proud to be associated with, and that we should take to our hearts as the best of what Virginia has been and can be. And that history is far from over.

Fraud and Fable Number Thirteen: Virginia's native people vanished long ago, replaced by whites and Blacks

Purpose: To put indigenous Virginians safely in the past, rather than see them as independent peoples in a complicated world with claims on all of us.

The Monacan Nation: Surviving Virginia's Race Fantasies

In 1984, the Virginia Women's Cultural History Project published "A Share of Honour":Virginia Women 1600-1945. This 167 page large format book, with a diversity of glossy illustrations, proclaimed its origins in "resurgent feminism," which had caused "many women to wonder about the lives and experiences .. of all the other women who had lived and died" in Virginia, with "some even" wondering about "the women who were here when the Europeans arrived and about the African women brought here against their will." But the book only had two sentences about one group "who were here when the Europeans arrived":

> "In the Piedmont lived a number of Siouan speakers. About these groups we unfortunately know little."

Yet only five years later, in 1989, one of "these groups," the Monacan Nation, was recognized by the Commonwealth of Virginia, not only as an existing tribe, but as one that had had a continuous presence in Virginia since before English settlement.

What explains this invisibility of a

people who have always been in Virginia, especially to as culturally sensitive a group as the Virginia Women's Cultural History Project?

The Monacan Indians: Our Story, by Karenne Wood and Diane Shields, is available from http://www.monacannation.com/. (Wood) It's brief and powerful, and no Virginia library is complete without a copy. (A good companion to it is Markings on Earth, a book of poems by Karenne Wood, an active Monacan Nation member and a remarkable poet.)

From the beginning of Virginia (after a millennium or ten of pre-Virginia residence in their present territory), the Monacan

Nation was a small group caught up in the power politics of Virginians, Pennsylvanians, Iroquois, and others. Finding a more or less invisible refuge was the survival mode of choice for the Monacans, as well as for other small Virginia communities. Fortunately, the Monacan people did not, like some other native peoples, such as their Siouan kinfolk the Tuscarora, have to relocate hundreds or even thousands of miles away from their home ground.

One of the legends collected by the Virginia Writers' Project, recorded in Spotsylvania County, about 100 miles northeast of the Monacan territory, was called "The Indian Who Lived in a Cave." In the story, a young chief was captured and then released by the whites. All alone, and later with an "Indian Princess" bride, he carved "a square room" out of rock, and lived there by permission of the landowner, whom he occasionally provided with wild game. (Barden) This legend reflects the reality that faced many of Virginia's native people – the need to find an inconspicuous and safe place and means of survival.

No one knows how many such sanctuaries there were, off the main roads and away from the cities and best farmland, up and down the east coast of the U.S. I remember as an environmental organizer talking to a man from a group that had completely lost its traditions, but still hung together over the years, not knowing who they were, but knowing they shared a common identity. Only in this century did they learn that they were a lost remnant of the Leni Lenape, or Delaware, people.

The Monacan nation reached the

twentieth century without losing their identity, and kept a geographical center for their people on Bear Mountain, not far from Lynchburg.

Then, in the twentieth century, they faced their most serious threat – from a man who considered Nazi eugenicists his colleagues, and who used the power of the Commonwealth in an aggressive attempt to erase the Monacan nation – and all native nations – from Virginia.

In 2004, the Norfolk Virginian-Pilot published a detailed story on this man, Walter Ashby Plecker. The story, "The Black-and-White World of Walter Ashby Plecker" reported that Plecker, as Virginia's registrar of Virginia's Bureau of Vital Statistics from 1912 to 1946, "led the effort to purify the white race in Virginia by forcing Indians and other nonwhites to classify themselves as blacks." (Fiske, Walter)

No one, of course, has an "objective" racial identity or heritage. Racial categories are political, not biological. So they are subject to change along with political and cultural changes; and in any family, there are wide variations of appearance, reflecting the complexity of ancestors we all have had since our earliest days as humans in Africa.

Plecker, however, believed that every individual Virginian could be racially defined, and that they were all either "white" or "colored." And he believed he personally could, and indeed had a duty to, carry out this task.

The Monacan people, who knew they were in neither group, were a special target of Plecker's. They began the twentieth century in a weak position, as mostly landless agricultural laborers. But then Plecker's work took away their identity, made their access to schools more complicated, and even made existing marriages illegal, since some Monacan were deemed "white" and others "colored." At this point, many Monacan left Virginia, to form exile communities in Baltimore and elsewhere, beyond Plecker's reach. (Wood)

Rosemary Clark Whitlock, a South Carolinian of Monacan descent, also wrote a book on the Monacan, based on a number of interviews. One of Whitlock's interviews was with a non-Monacan, William Sandidge, who was Clerk of the Court in Amherst County and dealt directly with Plecker. On official trips to Sandidge's office, Plecker threatened Sandidge with imprisonment if he did not follow Virginia's Racial Integrity Act of 1924 as Plecker interpreted it.

Sandidge described Plecker standing in the Amherst courthouse square, and pointing to different Monacans and ruling on their racial identities, as in "This one to our left is a mixed breed." Sandidge told his interviewer "Plecker didn't realize ... that he had pointed .. in some instances to brothers, fathers and sons" as being of different racial backgrounds.

Sandidge said in his 1997 interview, long after his retirement, "I realize most of the Monacan Indians in this area must hate me... [but] I didn't want to be imprisoned as [Plecker] kept reminding me I would be if I did not do exactly as instructed." (Whitlock)

Sandidge's fear was not irrational. The Racial Integrity Act did prescribe a year in prison for violators. According to the Virginian-Pilot, the law was also the basis for 8,300 mandatory sterilizations.

But brutal enforcement of the Act did not satisfy Plecker. The article also details a 1935 letter Plecker wrote to the director of Nazi Germany's Bureau of Human Betterment and Eugenics. In the letter, "Plecker complimented the

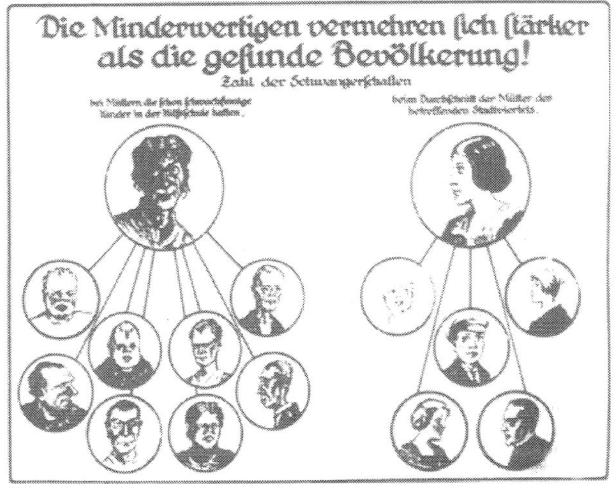

Third Reich for sterilizing 600 children in Algeria who were born to German women and black men." He wrote in the letter "'I hope this work is complete and not one has been missed.. I sometimes regret that we have not the authority to put some measures in practice in Virginia.'" (Fiske, Walter)

Plecker was the final authority not just on the racial identity of groups like the Monacan Nation, but on individual cases across Virginia. He wrote in an official letter to a mother, who had recently given birth to a child she considered white, "This is to inform you that this is a mulatto child and you cannot pass it off as white...You will have to do something about this matter and see that this child is not allowed to mix with white children. It cannot go to white schools and can never marry a white person in Virginia. It is a horrible thing." (Fiske, Walter)

And here we come to the center of this despicable man's impact. He created enormous tragedies for the Monacan Nation and for individuals whose identities were irrevocably severed from others in their families and communities. But at the heart of his activity was white Virginia's profound and fearful rejection of African-Americans – a people that white Virginians had grown up alongside, not just individually, but as a society. His life's work was the maintenance of a completely imaginary barrier between white and black, to the terrible disadvantage of African-Americans.

> **.. the negro arrived in Virginia, not only a wretched slave, torn from his country, but also an indescribably raw and bestial savage, as hideous in aspect as he was brutish in instinct and mean in intelligence.** (Bruce, 1907)

Walter Ashby Plecker was a powerful and respected Virginian in the second quarter of the twentieth century. He was also, by any reasonable standard, completely insane.

Phyllis Branham Hicks, a Monacan woman who is now an Episcopal priest, was correct in her interview in Whitlock's book, when she said "This pitiful lichen of a man had to have been backed by Virginia's Legislature and by the acquiescence of Virginia's governors" during his time in power. (Whitlock)

In the 1950s and 1960s, the Freedom Movement successfully challenged the whole Jim Crow system. One of the results was the Supreme Court decision Loving v. Virginia. This criminal case began with the arrest, in 1958, of Mildred Jeter Loving and Richard Perry Loving for violating the Racial Integrity law. Their crime was getting married, though they knew she was defined as "colored," and he as "white." A judge waived their prison terms if they left the Commonwealth for 25 years.

The Encyclopedia Virginia records that, when they appealed, their judge denied the appeal with these words:

"Almighty God created the races white, black, yellow, malay and red, and he placed them on separate continents. And but for the interference with his arrangement there would be no cause for such marriages. The fact that he separated the races shows that he did not intend for the races to mix." (Encyclopedia Virginia)

TYPES OF THE HUMAN RACE.

Of course, the supposed "interference" was done mostly by white people transporting people across the Atlantic. It's not clear to me why the judge's "Almighty God" didn't just zap slave traders to stop "race-mixing."

Speaking of abusing the Bible, when I was a child, one of my uncles, who I think of as the "white sheet" of the family, told me that "colored people" were inferior because of the curse on Ham in the Bible. Not only is this "curse of Ham" racist interpretation ugly theology, it doesn't even make sense. It supposedly describes the origin of the Semites, from Noah's son Shem, of the Europeans, from his brother Japeth, and of the black Africans, from their brother Ham. It kinda leaves out the "yellow, malay and red."

The Bible was written long before modern races were invented. It has no more to say about the imaginary world of racial identity than it does about the rules of backgammon.

Eventually, the judge who interpreted the will of Almighty God for the Lovings was overruled by the United States Supreme Court.

With this decision, ending enforcement of Virginia's Racial Integrity Act, the Monacan people were free to reclaim their identity in Virginia. Monacan people began to return to Bear Mountain, to conduct events there, and talk to other people about who they were.

MONACAN MUSEUM AND CULTURAL CENTER

In April of 2010, I had an opportunity to learn firsthand about the Monacan people from George Branham Whitewolf, then the assistant chief and spiritual adviser to the Monacan Nation. (I had already attended the annual Monacan Powwow in 2008.) I met Whitewolf at the Monacan Museum, formerly the schoolhouse operated for Monacan children by the Episcopal Church. He showed me the Museum's exhibits, and generously gave of his time to an enquiring stranger.

As it happened, I was very fortunate. Whitewolf died less than two months later, at the age of 67.

I did not take notes on our conversation, but I do remember him talking about his childhood in the Baltimore area, and his travels as a youth. I especially remember him talking about his time with the Lakota. The Lakota belong to the same language group as the Monacan, and probably have other links with them over the long history of pre-1492 North America.

Like many native nations in the Plains and Northwest, the Lakota have a much more recent connection to their pre-conquest history than the Monacan do. After all, the first impact of white people – disease -- devastated the Monacans before Jamestown was even settled, and by 1661 they were paying tribute to Virginia. The Lakota certainly saw major changes due to whites even at this point, but about 150 years went by before they found it necessary to interact officially with the white government. So Whitewolf seemed to feel that he gained some important wisdom from spending time with the Lakota, before finally moving to traditional Monacan territory in 1991, in a sense coming home for the first time at the age of 48.

Whitewolf told me that he worshiped according to what he understood of Monacan tradition, up on Bear Mountain. He also told me he really especially enjoyed talking to Monacan youth and passing on what he could about the millennia that the Monacan have been in the Bear Mountain area.

If the Virginia Gentlemen had had their way, if they had not experienced their Second Appomattox in the 1960s, I could never have had that conversation with Whitewolf.

While the Commonwealth of Virginia has had a continuous relationship with several tribes going back to colonial times, that relationship began to be formalized in the 1980s. The Chickahominy; the Chickahominy, Eastern Division; the Mattaponi; the Upper Mattaponi; the Pamunkey; and the Rappahannock tribes were recognized by the General Assembly in 1983; the Nansemond tribe in 1985; and the Monacan tribe in 1989.

The Monacan Indians: Our Story closes by reporting the Monacan Nation's activities since 1989, including elections of leaders, opening of the museum, contact with other Siouan Indian groups in North Carolina and Canada, and a wide variety of cultural and educational outreach, including the annual Powwow. (Wood)

The Powwow I attended in 2008 was a wonderful event, but hardly a life-changing one for me. It reminded me of other events I have been involved in – community carnivals and celebrations, even church suppers and game nights. But that is as it should be.

The Monacan do not exist to provide me or other Virginians with an exotic connection to "Native American secrets." (Try searching the Internet for that phrase; you will find Native

American healing secrets, secret herbal remedies, and all kinds of "cool" items for sale. I wonder how many are being sold by Native people.)

Like any community, and especially one with a long history tied to a homeland, the Monacan continue for many reasons. Those reasons are their own, just as they were in 1492, before white impact. If the Virginia Gentlemen had been a less greedy tribe than they were, the Monacan – and many others in Virginia – might have had an uninterrupted history of ordinary daily life in all its sacredness.

The Reverend Phyllis Branham Hicks closed her interview in Whitlock's book by saying "It is with thanksgiving to God I can now stand at my grandfather's grave and say, 'Chief, your dream has come to pass for us, and we can now lift our heads and proudly say, 'We are Monacan Indians.'" (Whitlock)

To say "I am a Virginia Gentleman" proudly is easy. No one is persecuted for doing so, even if the claim is absurd. (Though, hey, maybe that will change after this book gets real popular.) But the Virginia Gentleman has made it painfully difficult for those he fears and despises to stand up and say "I am..."

A Personal Remembrance of Ms. Bessie Pryor

tie firmly knotted,
and on time,
i turned the corner
onto Decatur
and saw the
cemetery

i'm here, i thought,
this is the time i'll
say goodbye to
you

at the gate, a
young woman in
dark clothes
casually told me
the funeral had
been held
four hours before -
-
"it was too late to
get it in the
paper".

Ms. Pryor, you've
eluded me again.

two months ago, I
talked you into
letting me take
your picture;
it was the last time
i saw you, and
you were feeling
old,
not worth taking a
picture of.
when i got the
film back from the
drugstore,
there was no
picture of you in
the envelope.

i used to argue
with you,
telling you how
smart you were
and how much
you'd done,
and you would
contradict me,
and laugh about it,
call yourself worn
out and useless

and all the time
those shrewd eyes
watched.

you did what was
right, Bessie,
and not -- you'll
understand this --
because you were
nice and sweet.
you said what you
saw,
about neighbors or
big shots,

and laughed when
you said it
sometimes.
you never took
any credit,
even when i got
you to tell how
you
started the first
Black Girl Scout
troop
in Richmond,
or about tough
times living in the
country,
raising kids,
even when you
had to stand up
to a pompous city
official
because those that
should have
wouldn't.

doing right isn't
fun,
and life has no
guarantee of
reward
included in the
box it comes in;
tired, in pain, and
still being leaned
on
even in old age,
you knew better.

right is just right.
right is what was
given us to do
as God's creatures,
so we can walk
with dignity
on the face on the
earth.
and that you
always did.

one evening this
year,
i went over to
your house after a
meeting.
the night was
warm,
and the wind was
soft.
you told me about
the big trees in the
yards
of your childhood
and how all the
women would
gather there
and talk about
what mattered to
them
while the children
played.
you talked about

the good in those
days,
and i could hear
the warmth in you
for neighborliness
and family,
for support long
since lost.

but your clear
mind remembered
it all,
not just the
pleasant parts.
people worked so
hard in those days,
you remembered,
and segregation
held them down.
we couldn't go
back, you said.

even in the solace
of memory,
in your last
months,
you found no easy
answers.

we are who we
are,
you taught me,
and we know what
we must do
to do right.

no point in making
a big deal about it,
so you didn't.

i sometimes
thought i would
see that you
got something for
doing right,
i wanted to see
you recognized
and praised;
you've slipped by
that plan too.

you gave so much
to us, Bessie,
and never even
allowed us to talk
about it.

you can't escape
this time.
wherever you are,
this goes to you
directly.
you gave us so
much,
and i say it.
you got so little
for it here,
and i say that.

you can't escape

this,
wherever you are.
Bessie Pryor,
i've never known a
clearer mind
or a life
that was such a
gift.

November 20,
1987

Fraud and Fable Number Fourteen: Modern Virginia Conservatism Expresses Traditional Christian Values

Purpose: Most people in Virginia are or used to be Christians. So the Virginia Gentleman tries to look Christian too.

Was Slave-Owning Virginia a Christian Society?

Whereas some doubts have risen whether children that are slaves by birth, and by the charity and piety of their owners made partakers of the blessed sacrament of baptisme, should by virtue of their baptisme be made ffree; It is enacted and declared ... that the conferring of baptisme doth not alter the condition of the person as to his bondage or ffreedom..."
Virginia Statute, 1667

"On the Sabbath after church, I was going, according to the general custom, to dine out; but the spirit of God spoke better counsel ... I shut myself up in my room, where my soul was engaged with the thoughts of judgment and eternity. While thus engaged in my chamber, an old blind negro woman was led in, who was a dear child of God. We began a conversation in which she used expressions respecting entire confidence in Christ... I think I owe her,

under God, much of my religious joy in after years. Dear old creature, I often visited her in her cottage, and witnessed the evidences of her triumphant faith. She was a living example of Christ formed in the soul, the hope of glory." Anne Randolph Page (1781-1838), wife of the "owner" of 200 human beings in Clarke County, Virginia, about 10 miles from where I live.

"I see a book kissed here which I suppose to be the Bible, or at least the New Testament. That teaches me that all things whatsoever I would that men should do to me, I should do even so to them. It teaches me, further, to "remember them that are in bonds, as bound with them." I endeavored to act up to that instruction. I say, I am yet too young to understand that God is any respecter of persons."
John Brown speaking at his trial, 1859

HANGING OF TWO OF JOHN BROWN'S PARTY, COOK AND COPPOCK

When John Brown was hanged, among those present as part of the military force were Robert E. Lee, J.E.B. Stuart and Thomas Jackson, later to be known by his thug name, Stonewall.

While all three were there as part of their military duties, they all certainly approved of the execution. Each of the three, of course, considered himself a Christian, and Jackson was especially pious. After the event, Jackson wrote this in a letter to his wife:

> "I **was much impressed with the thought that before me stood a man, in the full vigor of health, who must in a few moments enter eternity. I sent up the petition that he might**

be saved. Awful was the thought that he might in a few minutes receive the sentence, 'Depart, ye wicked, into everlasting fire!' I hope that he was prepared to die, but I am doubtful."

By "prepared to die," Jackson did not mean, as we might today, mentally or emotionally ready. John Brown's emotional and mental readiness to die for his beliefs had been obvious long before Harpers Ferry. Jackson's question was whether Brown's soul was prepared.

Even that question, though, seems strange. Clearly, if anyone ever lived and died for Biblical principles, it was John Brown.

One could see Jackson and Lee as just

having a different interpretation of Christianity than Brown. But that was not how John Brown saw it.

Brown wrote to an abolitionist minister who contacted him as he awaited execution:

> "There are no ministers of Christ here. These ministers who profess to be Christian, and hold slaves or advocate slavery, I cannot abide them. My knees will not bend in prayer with them, while their hands are stained with the blood of souls."

To a Southern minister who defended slavery as a "Christian institution," Brown responded "I respect you as a gentleman, of course; but it is as a heathen gentleman."

While there are still plenty of Virginians who would defend Jackson and Lee's Christian characters, certainly many Virginians would be willing to admit that support of slavery is not compatible with Christianity.

I am not a Christian. But I am very committed to the specific set of moral ideas that Jesus taught. I think they represent our best hope in Virginia to find some common moral ground. And I believe we can trace the degree to which those ideas have been followed by the masters of Virginia over the years.

If John Brown was right, and Virginia was not a Christian society in 1859, when, if ever, did the society of his "heathen gentlemen" become a Christian one, as so many claim it is today?

The Civil War and Christianity

The common view today is that the Civil War was an ugly business, with both sides praying to the same God as, in the cliché, "brother fought brother."

But, with God perhaps taken a bit more seriously in those days, that was not an acceptable view to either side. Neither the Union nor the Confederacy was willing to see God as neutral in their conflict.

Historian Drew Gilpin Faust, in The Creation of Confederate Nationalism, elaborates on the Christian claims of Confederate leaders. Key to the rhetoric of Confederate leaders as well as Confederate ministers was a literal belief that the Confederate nation was a chosen people, doing the work of God. This was reinforced by the Southern habit of finding appropriate Biblical verses. These two from the first book of the Book of Jeremiah were popular (Faust):

> **Verse 14: Then the LORD said unto me, Out of the north an evil shall break forth upon all the inhabitants of the land.** 
>
> **Verse 19:**
> **And they shall fight against thee; but they shall not prevail against thee; for I am with thee, saith the LORD, to deliver thee.**

It seems to us today like quite a stretch to see the Confederacy as "the new Israel." And Confederates did have to

make a somewhat convoluted case. We can see an example in the sermon that Methodist minister Robert Newton Sledd preached in Petersburg in September of 1861 to cadets heading off the to the war. (Sledd)

After making the customary exhortations to the cadets to be courageous and valiant, Sledd closed his sermon with his view of the two key war aims of the Confederacy. The first was the fight for liberty -- *"to shield our gray-haired sires and honored mothers, our noble wives and lovely daughters, our tender children and faithful servants, from the wanton violence of a despotism whose deeds would disgrace the annals of the Middle Ages..." and to protect "the liberty to think, and speak, and act for ourselves."* This is rhetoric that most of us have heard, as much as it clashes with our values and our understanding of history.

But the second aim that Sledd described would generally seem less likely to us – and yet in a different way, very contemporary. Sledd stated that *"The cause of Christ, the interests of religion are involved in this direful conflict."* This was, he argued, because the "fanaticism" of abolition had resulted in "an open rejection of the Word of God." Sledd's argument was that, since the Bible sanctioned slavery, opponents of slavery were challenging God's law.

We hear a similar argument in today's Virginia. Those who tolerate abortion and homosexuality are characterized as rejecting the Bible. Of course, then and now, such claims won't stand up. The Bible is a complex text with subtle and many-layered messages that one can study for a lifetime, not a 3 page illustrated booklet with a quiz at the end. Those who trivialize Scripture in this way are surely the ones who, in Sledd's words, *"infuse into a pure christianity (sic) the poison of their own infidelity."*

Christianity and the Union

For most of us, the moral arc of the Union cause is a lot clearer than that of the Confederacy. We have grown up with Lincoln as an icon, not Jeff Davis, and we know the Battle Hymn of the Republic, not "God Save the South." We may think of John Brown or Frederick

Douglass or Thaddeus Stevens as extremists, but we do not think of them as atheists – and they certainly did not see themselves that way.

Charles Sumner was so demonized by the Confederates-to-be that he was brutally attacked on the Senate floor by a South Carolina Congressman. But when he first stood against the Fugitive Slave Act, he justified his actions by “the Supreme Law, which commands me to do no injustice, by the comprehensive Christian Law of Brotherhood,” and only then by the Constitution. (This was cited in the eulogy of Sumner by Carl Schurz.)

Of course, Confederates had faith, attended church, sang hymns, and so on. But it is a universal tenet of Christianity that not everyone who claims to be a Christian really is one. Thus the great division of the faith into Catholic and Protestant, but also into Orthodox, Anabaptist, and many other sectarian divisions, each of which generally considers the others not really 100% Christian.

Where did real Christianity find a home during the Civil War?

I found my answer to that question on September 11, 2002.

I was living in Arlington, Virginia, on "the" September 11th, a year before. I felt the agony of Greater New York with the rest of the nation; but the attack on the Pentagon was in my neighborhood. So when the anniversary came around, I looked for someplace local to commemorate it.

I found that place at Mount Zion Baptist Church, a few blocks from my home. I haven't worshipped there before or since. But on that day, it was where I needed to be.

Mount Zion begins its record of its history on its website with these words:

> **After the close of the Civil War, a number of Christians banded together to establish a Baptist church in Freedman's Village. This site is now the National Arlington Cemetery. They called this church "The Old Bell Church". Members worshipped under the leadership of the first pastor, Reverend Robert S. Laws. When the federal government moved the congregation from**

this location, they settled in nearby Alexandria County, which is now Arlington County, Virginia.
(Mount Zion)

Freedman's Village, as its name suggests, was a settlement for people coming out of slavery. Mount Zion Baptist, in other words, is a church founded by people whose lives were personally changed by the Civil War – who came out of slavery. Over the decades, its members have seen their chances in life grow, especially with the expansion of government job opportunities, and today it is a prosperous church beginning to expand its ministry to the outer suburbs.

When I stood with that congregation and sang "As He died to make men holy, let us live to make men free," it was clear to me that I was deeply privileged to be right in the center of the best common ground of Christianity and U.S. patriotism.

I have been to a service at Saint Paul's Episcopal in Richmond, where Lee and Davis worshipped (today a liberal urban church.) I am very familiar with the monuments of Confederate Richmond, including the pyramid that honors anonymous Confederate dead in

Hollywood Cemetery, in the neighborhood I lived in for nine years.

I will say unequivocally that I experienced more of the Christian meaning of the Civil War in that one service at Mount Zion than all the Sledds that lived then and since could

have summoned up in all their services, with all their fine rhetoric and scholarship.

No one who seriously thinks about Jesus, the man who challenged the privileged and explicitly identified himself with the prisoner and the hungry and the poor, can put Jesus on the pulpit next to Rev. Sledd. And no one can imagine him not choosing to be present at Mount Zion on that day of grief and of celebration of justice and heritage.

Christianity: Ninety Years of Patient Effort 1866-1956

"...amicable relations between the white and Negro races ... have been created through 90 years of patient effort by the good people of both races."
from the Southern Manifesto, 1956

"'You used to could tell a n*** something and they'd listen to you, but that time's gone by,' a white Virginian exclaimed in exasperation, directing his anger at a young black woman who had ignored his instructions. 'She as much as said she knew more than I did, and I'd rather be called the meanest name there is than have a n***** tell me that.'"**
Highways and Byways of the South, 1904, quoted in (Litwack)

"..the well-born Virginian of our era was tutored to revere himself as being the dispossessed heir to an all-perfect and all-admirable state in the Old South. We were taught that we had been robbed; that our rights had been taken away from us at Appomattox..." (Cabell)

"A [slaveholding Georgia] Methodist Bishop had been ordered to desist from performing his episcopal duties until his status as a slaveholder had been cleared.... Separation was the only alternative... [In} May 1846, the Methodist Episcopal Church, South, met in Petersburg, Virginia, in its first official General Conference."
from The Negro in the Methodist Church by Mason Crum, 1951.

The Commonwealth of Virginia, from the destruction of the Confederacy to the beginning of the end of Jim Crow, was engaged, as the Southern Manifesto said, in "90 years of patient effort" around the issue of race. But the goal of that effort was to find a way to ensure white supremacy and African-American subordination, not to establish "amicable relations." Whatever was "amicable" about interracial relations was in spite of, not because of, Jim Crow.

How did this "effort" fit in with the white South's claims to be a Christian society? Well, there have been plenty of voices that answer, quite simply, it didn't. The white South's commitment to maintaining an unjust system was sinful and hypocritical, say these voices, mostly from outside the white South.

Hey, I'm OK with that.

But in 1995, a voice from the heart of white Southern history, and of Virginia history, joined the discussion. I think it makes sense to include the document in its entirety:

> **Resolution On Racial Reconciliation On The 150th Anniversary Of The Southern Baptist Convention**
> **June 1995**
>
> **WHEREAS, Since its founding in 1845, the Southern Baptist Convention has been an effective instrument of God in missions, evangelism, and social ministry; and**
>
> **WHEREAS, The Scriptures**

teach that Eve is the mother of all living (Genesis 3:20), and that God shows no partiality, but in every nation whoever fears him and works righteousness is accepted by him (Acts 10:34-35), and that God has made from one blood every nation of men to dwell on the face of the earth (Acts 17:26); and

WHEREAS, Our relationship to African-Americans has been hindered from the beginning by the role that slavery played in the formation of the Southern Baptist Convention; and

WHEREAS, Many of our Southern Baptist forbears defended the right to own slaves, and either participated in, supported, or acquiesced in the particularly inhumane nature of American slavery; and

WHEREAS, In later years Southern Baptists failed, in many cases, to support, and in some cases opposed, legitimate initiatives to secure the civil rights of African-Americans; and

WHEREAS, Racism has led to discrimination, oppression, injustice, and violence, both in the Civil War and throughout the history of our nation; and

WHEREAS, Racism has divided the body of Christ and Southern Baptists in particular, and separated us from our African-American brothers and sisters; and

WHEREAS, Many of our congregations have intentionally and/or unintentionally excluded African-Americans from worship, membership, and leadership; and

WHEREAS, Racism profoundly distorts our understanding of Christian morality, leading some Southern Baptists to believe that racial prejudice and discrimination are compatible with the Gospel; and

WHEREAS, Jesus performed the ministry of reconciliation to restore sinners to a right relationship with the

Heavenly Father, and to establish right relations among all human beings, especially within the family of faith.

Therefore, be it RESOLVED, That we, the messengers to the Sesquicentennial meeting of the Southern Baptist Convention, assembled in Atlanta, Georgia, June 20-22, 1995, unwaveringly denounce racism, in all its forms, as deplorable sin; and

Be it further RESOLVED, That we affirm the Bible's teaching that every human life is sacred, and is of equal and immeasurable worth, made in Gods image, regardless of race or ethnicity (Genesis 1:27), and that, with respect to salvation through Christ, there is neither Jew nor Greek, there is neither slave nor free, there is neither male nor female, for (we) are all one in Christ Jesus (Galatians 3:28); and

Be it further RESOLVED, That we lament and repudiate historic acts of evil such as

slavery from which we continue to reap a bitter harvest, and we recognize that the racism which yet plagues our culture today is inextricably tied to the past; and

Be it further RESOLVED, That we apologize to all African-Americans for condoning and/or perpetuating individual and systemic racism in our lifetime; and we genuinely repent of racism of which we have been guilty, whether consciously (Psalm 19:13) or unconsciously (Leviticus 4:27); and

Be it further RESOLVED, That we ask forgiveness from our African-American brothers and sisters, acknowledging that our own healing is at stake; and

Be it further RESOLVED, That we hereby commit ourselves to eradicate racism in all its forms from Southern Baptist life and ministry; and

Be it further RESOLVED, That we commit ourselves to be doers of the Word (James

1:22) by pursuing racial reconciliation in all our relationships, especially with our brothers and sisters in Christ (1 John 2:6), to the end that our light would so shine before others, that they may see (our) good works and glorify (our) Father in heaven (Matthew 5:16); and

Be it finally RESOLVED, That we pledge our commitment to the Great Commission task of making disciples of all people (Matthew 28:19), confessing that in the church God is calling together one people from every tribe and nation (Revelation 5:9), and proclaiming that the Gospel of our Lord Jesus Christ is the only certain and sufficient ground upon which redeemed persons will stand together in restored family union as joint-heirs with Christ (Romans 8:17).

While there are serious questions, a decade and a half down the road, about how well the Southern Baptists have lived up to this commitment, the document sums up the history well from a Christian point of view. In a sense, it brings the Baptist movement back to where it began in the South, as a grassroots faith that united rather than separated slave-owner and slave. John Poindexter, a white man converted to the Baptist faith in 1791, spoke in the spirit of this faith in 1797.

> **"I have been an advocate for Slavery, but thanks be to God, My Eyes have been Opened to see the impropriety of it, and I long for the Happy times to Come, when the Church of Christ shall loose the Bands of Wickedness, undo the Heavy burdens, and let the oppressed go free."** (Sobel)

But since Poindexter's time, "Wickedness" has continued, even taken over, Christian denominations.

When the conservatives of the 1870s put repayment of the state debt (largely owed to them and their friends) above public education and other critical state services, ignoring the desperate needs of recently freed African-Americans and of whites also devastated by war, they were sinning.

When the Democrats of the 1890s began to segregate streetcars and trains, and to make Black voting all but impossible, they were sinning.

When the Byrd Machine maintained its white power, and supported cruel eugenics laws and Jim Crow schools and facilities, they were sinning.

Virginia history, let's face it, makes Sodom and Gomorrah look like Disneyland – once we understand what its central sin was – and is.

MICKEY GOMORRAH AND DONALD SODOM

The Virginia Gentlemen who have piloted white Virginia have quite a record of losing, though they have managed to resurrect their machinery of power over and over. It never seems to have occurred to them is that maybe they lose so often because God is punishing them.

Reverend Charles Minnigerode, the rector of St. Paul's Episcopal Church in Richmond during the Civil Warwas pastor to the man himself, Bobby Lee. On New Year's Day, 1865, only a few months before his famous parishioner's surrender at Appomattox, he gave a sermon entitled "He That Believeth Shall Not Make Haste." In it, he recognized the serious trouble the Confederacy was in – it was hard not to – but expressed certainty that all would be well if the pretend Confederate "nation" turned to God, recognizing its troubles as "a fatherly chastisement for our sins, to make us more humble before him and dependent on his alone saving grace." But did Rev. Minnigerode suggest a humility before the African-Americans that Virginia had repressed for centuries? Not a chance.

Until the Virginia Gentleman engages in an effort to make amends, he can hardly be said to be a Christian. Such an effort would be easy to recognize, because it would take as much energy and time and commitment as it has to invent and maintain racism.

In Matthew 25, Jesus spoke of several types of people that Christians must help in order to see eternal life. If the Virginia Gentleman is judged only on the basis of how he treats the prisoner, that will be enough right there to condemn him. (For more details, see the section **Virginia Is and Always Has Been Fair and Moderate in Punishing Crime**.)

Can any of us humans actually meet the standards that Jesus set? I don't know. But those standards are laid out so clearly in the Gospels that it is pretty easy to recognize someone who falsely claims to do so. I don't need to tell anyone how loudly the conservative élite that governs Virginia proclaims their dedication to faith. By their fruit you shall know them.

> **".. a Friend in company began to talk in support of the slave-trade, and said the negroes were understood to be the offspring of Cain, their blackness being the mark which God set upon him after he murdered Abel his brother; that it was the design of Providence they should be slaves, as a condition proper to the race of so wicked a man as Cain was. Then another spake in support of what had been said.**
> **.. I was troubled to perceive the darkness of their imaginations, and in some pressure of spirit said, "The love of ease and gain are the motives in general of keeping slaves, and men are wont to take hold of weak arguments to support a cause which is unreasonable. .. I believe liberty is their right, and as I see they are not only deprived of it, but treated in other**

respects with inhumanity in many places, I believe He who is a refuge for the oppressed will, in his own time, plead their cause, and happy will it be for such as walk in uprightness before him." And thus our conversation ended."

John Woolman reporting on a conversation with fellow Quakers in northern Virginia in 1772 (Woolman)

Fraud and Fable Number Fifteen: Modern Virginia Conservatism Has No Links to Slave-Holders

Purpose: Though the Virginia Gentlemen softens the facts of slavery, he still wants to give the impression that he has somehow not inherited one trace of that evil.

> **" ..something happened a long time ago in Haiti, and people might not want to talk about it. They were under the heel of the French... they ... swore a pact to the devil. They said, 'We will serve you if you will get us free from the French.' True story. And so, the devil said, 'OK, it's a deal.'**
> "Televangelist Pat Robertson, on his show The 700 Club on January 13, 2010

Reverend Marion "Pat" Robertson has been a controversial figure for a long time, and has made outrageous statements before. So his callous comment about Haïti at a time of terrible suffering got a lot of attention, but was generally just seen as one more 'gaffe' – an inadvertent and random foolish statement.

Robertson, of course, is no mere television preacher. A recent article notes “Robertson was once a highly influential figure. He is founder of American Center for Law and Justice, Operation Blessing International Relief, Development Corporation, Regent University, and a few other organizations. In the 1988 presidential election, he was a candidate for the Republican presidential nomination.” He was also the founder of the Christian Coalition, at one time a powerful national organization. (Kumar)

And while Robertson’s national influence has waned, he is still a player in Virginia. Virginia’s current Governor, Bob McDonnell, received at least $59,000 in donations from Robertson and his son, (Virginia Public Access Project) and got his law degree from Robertson’s Regent University, which he chose because of its “faith-based mission that really tried to integrate faith and learning." (700 Club)

Haïti Comments Decoded

Public discussion of Robertson's "gaffe" revealed that Robertson was apparently talking about Boukman's Oath, a defining event of the Haïtian revolution.

This was a religious ceremony conducted by Dutty Boukman and other Haïtian leaders in 1791, and centered on a revolutionary anti-slavery oath. Boukman is believed to have closed his oath or prayer with these words: **"We all should throw away the image of the white men's god who is so pitiless. Listen to the voice for liberty that sings in all our hearts."**

Robertson's comment on TV may have been off the cuff. But it grew out of a heritage that few of us know about, though Robertson is proud of it – descent from Virginians who owned large numbers of slaves.

Robertson's Personal Connection to Slavery

In his 1997 book, The Christian Coalition, Justin Watson describes Robertson as perceiving "a solid phalanx of enemies manipulating the machinery of history for evil purposes ... [an] analysis embedded in a total worldview...." That view of history and the world can be traced back to, as we say in the South, "his people" – his family history.

Though most of us are unaware of it, Robertson's father was a U.S. Senator from Virginia, a key member of the Byrd Machine, and deeply complicit in the Massive Resistance effort to maintain segregation. But, as Robertson's own website highlights, his family connections to Virginia's racial evils go back much farther, to slavery days.

On a page of the website pretentiously titled "Pat Robertson's Bloodline: Living Descendants of Blood Royal (in America)," we learn that Robertson's ancestors included numerous powerful and wealthy men of colonial and early independent Virginia, living in the Tidewater region where slavery originated.

> **"Well she got her rawhide down from de nail by de fire place, an' she grabbed me by de arm an' she try to turn me 'cross her knees whilst she set in de rocker so's she could hol' me. I twisted 'way so dere warn't no chance o' her**

> **getting in no solid lick. Den old Missus lif' me up by de legs, an' she stuck my haid under de bottom of her rocker, an' she rock forward so's to hol' my haid an' whup me some mo'. I guess dey must of whupped me near an hour wid dat rocker leg a-pressin' down on my haid... dat rocker pressin' on my young bones have crushed 'em all into soft pulp...** Henrietta King, formerly enslaved Virginian, West Point, born 1843, interviewed in the 1930s. (Neely)

One of Robertson's proudly claimed ancestors, Nathaniel Harrison (1677-1727), willed each of his two sons a plantation, including "all slaves, stock, etc.", and "To each daughter now not married one Negro ten years old." (Harrison) Another ancestor, Robert "King" Carter, was described by the editor of his papers as "the richest and most important man of his day in Virginia, who owned at his death at least 300,000 acres containing many farms and plantations that produced tobacco and other crops for sale, some 750 slaves to work those plantations, and large sums of money invested in Virginia and in England." (Berkeley)

The descendants of these men were

profoundly threatened when the slaves of Haïti liberated themselves. As Virginia Gentleman John Randolph said in Congress in 1811, “God forbid that the Southern states should ever see an enemy on their shores, with these infernal principles of French fraternity in the van...” (Randolph, John)

The God Randolph appealed to, and that Robertson still worships today, is a God of authority, who supports slavery as a divinely ordained and Biblical institution -- the deity that Boukman referred to as “the white men's god who is so pitiless.”

Boukman’s anti-slavery God, then, was the antagonist of the slave-owners’ God – which meant, to them, Boukman worshipped and dealt with the Devil. (Many people might think the slave-owners got that one backward.)

Robertson’s Revisionist U.S. History

In his book The New Millennium, Robertson wrote that “In God’s eyes, the United States of America did not begin on July 4, 1776, but on April 29, 1607.” On that date, he claims, the English invaders of Powhatan territory conducted the first Christian service in what became the United States.

(Robertson, 1991)

Presumably to Protestant Robertson, the first mass held by Spanish Catholics in Florida in 1565 doesn't count as Christian, and means as little as 1776 does to him. (Cathedral Basilica) For Robertson, his Virginia Gentleman heritage of English Christian conquest in 1607 is what counts. As a "Living Descendant of the Blood Royal," he apparently feels quite the kinship with Englishmen engaged in the King's business, and even more when they get into the slavery business.

Haïti and the United States: Battling Revolutionary Republics

Ten years after Boukman's Oath, the Haïtian revolution under Toussaint L'Ouverture had liberated all of Haïti, ending slavery on their island. Napoleon asked the new President of the United States for help against the new African-American republic. Thomas Jefferson, the great voice for liberty, but also a Virginia slave-owner, told Napoleon "nothing will be easier than to furnish your army and fleet with everything and reduce Toussaint to starvation."

Well, Toussaint's revolution was not reduced to starvation, and Haïti became the first republic founded by rebels against slavery to survive into the modern era.

The United States did not give up its feud against Haïti. It did not recognize Haïti's nationhood until 1862, at which time there were few Southern members in Congress to oppose it.

Then, in 1915, the first Virginian in the Presidency in almost a century, Woodrow Wilson, ordered an invasion of Haïti. Marine Colonel Littleton Waller, from York County, Virginia, commanded the expeditionary forces. (Waller had previously led troops against the Boxer Rebellion in China and against nationalist rebels in the Philippine Islands.)

In 1920, journalist Herbert Seligmann wrote "The Conquest of Haïti" for the magazine The Nation, and described "black men and women ... put to torture.. theft, arson, and murder .... [and] actual slavery.." Seligmann also reported he heard "officers wearing the United States uniform ... talk of 'bumping off' (i.e. killing) 'Gooks' as if it were a variety of sport..." Seligmann also reported on Haïti as "a new field for American investors," with U.S. investors taking ownership of Haïti's national bank and railroads and other major industries.

This occupation lasted until 1934. Then, beginning in the 1990s, U.S intervention began again, mainly directed at undermining the pro-poor Lavalas movement and its leader, Jean Bertrand Aristide. Aristide himself has said of this situation, “Racism should not maintain a black holocaust in Haïti, where African descendants proclaimed their independence 200 years ago.” (Aristide.org)

Even today, the hostility by United States leaders towards Haïti continues. And at least in Robertson’s Virginia Beach studio, the cries of enslaved people to God for freedom are still being heard as a pact with the Devil. Robertson, true to his heritage, is still following the slave-owners’ religion.

When I get dar, Cappen Satan was dar..
Says, young man, young man, dere 's no use for pray..
For Jesus is dead, and God gone away,..
And I made him out a liar and I went my way... (Higginson)

Fraud and Fable Number Sixteen: Modern Virginia Conservatism Has Broken with the Jim Crow Past

Purpose: This is today's "decontamination" plan. Like the Lost Cause denials of being pro-slavery, constant repetition of "we're Republicans now" is supposed to create a barrier disguising the many links with Jim Crow politicians of past generations.

Obsession Confession: My Harry Flood Byrd Sr. Story

> **"Mixed schools prohibited. – White and colored children shall not be taught in the same school."**
> **"Every person having one-sixteenth or more of negro blood shall be deemed a colored person, and every person not a colored person having one-fourth or more of Indian blood shall be deemed an Indian." (**Virginia State Board of Education)

> **"May 17, 1954: [date of the Brown v. Board of Education decision] Senator Harry Flood Byrd, leader of the Party, said that the decision 'will bring implications and dangers of the greatest consequence.'"** (Smith, Bob)

In August of 2011, I was accused of being obsessed with Harry Flood Byrd Sr. My accuser was a man who works for a newspaper that Byrd Sr. formerly edited, and which the Byrd family still owns. He and that newspaper (and others in its little chain of papers) still carry on the political pathology that the Byrd Machine stood for in this state – an especially elitist and conformist politics of reaction. My accuser writes laudatory columns about the fine gentlemen of the Byrd days on a regular basis.

Yeah, it's pretty funny. Clearly my accuser is more than obsessed with Byrd. He's pretty much an appendage of the old guy – sort of a mini-clone.

But what about me? Am I obsessed with Byrd?

Well, I certainly think and write about Byrd Sr. more than most people do 45 years after his death. While I hardly think I am obsessed with the man, I do find him important to think and write about. Here's why.

Byrd and Virginia

First, I live in Virginia. Byrd Sr. personally controlled Virginia's politics for 40 of the last 90 years. And before him, the Martin organization was in power for a quarter century. Harry's uncle "Hal" Flood "was called the wheelhorse of .. Martin's machine." Harry Flood Byrd Sr. was named after him. (Edmunds) After him, many of the components of his machine stayed in place, including some of his main local leaders – and now their sons.

That earlier history takes us back to the years during which Virginians like Jubal Early spread the Lost Cause propaganda and Virginia adopted Jim Crow laws and a constitution that mostly eliminated the African-American vote.

This poem about the Valley, Byrd's home turf, and the "knights" that emerged to defend the slave system, is the kind of literary horror that was popular in Byrd's circles in his childhood. The textbooks he learned from were carefully vetted to fit the offical Lost Cause party line.

> **"We thought they slept! – the sons who kept**
> **The names of noble sires,**
> **And slumbered while the darkness crept**
> **Around their vigil fires;**
> **But aye the 'Golden Horseshoe' knights**
> **Their old Dominion keep,**
> **Whose foes have found enchanted ground,**
> **But not a knight asleep!"**
> From "Virginians of the Valley"

by Confederate poet Francis Orrery Ticknor

"'June 30, 1932.... Rebels United Confederate Veterans meeting in annual reunion in Richmond .. adopted a resolution calling for all veterans and affiliated organizations to protest against history books which fail to present the southern accomplishments, ideals and heroes in a fair light." (Raffle)

"The Virginia history which I used ... set forth in great detail what the southern generals did and how successful they were. To the student reader, it was obvious that the South won the war ... Imagine the letdown we felt about two days before the end of the school year when the history book ... declared on the final two pages that General Lee surrendered at Appomattox and the war was over." (Raflo)

It seems to me that to live in Virginia, and especially in the Shenandoah Valley, and not think about the Byrd Machine is like living in Russia and paying no attention to Stalin.

But a more appropriate analogy might be to living in Nicaragua and never thinking about the Somoza family that ruled that country for roughly the same period as Byrd rule in Virginia. Particularly since the two machines were, at least once symbolic ally, connecte d.

In 1973, the iconic position of Queen of the Winchester Apple Blossom Festival was given to Edda Maria Sevilla Somoza Sacasa. Yes, the granddaughter of the founder of the dictatorial Somoza dynasty got the highest symbolic honor in Byrd's Winchester. This occurred a year after the massive Managua earthquake and the subsequent humanitarian crisis. For most of the world, that crisis was the inescapable sign that the Somoza regime stank to high heaven. No problem, though, for the Byrd Organization.

Byrd and National Politics

I moved to Virginia with my parents in 1964, and almost immediately got involved in social justice activism. My first involvements were with fair housing and local Democratic Party work. I was a liberal in high school – though I have wandered somewhat left of there since. And liberal Democratic Party work in those days meant fighting the Byrd Machine. This was true not just locally and statewide, but even nationally.

Byrd and his Machine cronies had had few effective challengers for four decades. This political security had given them a base from which to build seniority in Congress and to organize nationally against social justice measures. In the 1930s, Byrd Sr. was one of the major opponents of the New Deal, and especially of labor and welfare rights. When he retired in 1965, he was fighting both the Freedom Movement and the Great Society, and one of his last battles was against the Voting Rights Act.

Of course, Byrd was not alone in his stand for injustice and the Confederate Way. Byrd crony Howard "Judge" Smith came to the U.S. House of Representatives in 1930. By the 1950s, he was Chair of the Rules Committee, and had the power to stop civil rights and other legislation from moving in the House. (This power was diminished somewhat in the 1960s.) He was also notable as author of the Smith Act, under which Marxists were imprisoned for organizing and speech that advocated overthrow of the US government.

In 1956, Smith read the Southern Manifesto to the House of Representatives. This document, written mainly by Senator Strom Thurmond of South Carolina, and signed on to by most Southern members of the House and Senate, said in part:

> **"This unwarranted exercise of power by the Court ... is destroying the amicable relations between the white and Negro races that have been created by 90 years of patient effort by the good people of both races... outside agitators are threatening immediate and revolutionary changes in our public-school system...We commend the motives of those states which have declared their intention to resist forced integration by any lawful means."**

Ten years later, Smith was defeated in a Democratic primary by George Rawlings, a liberal. This was a major turning point for the Byrd Machine and the Virginia Democratic Party, almost as serious a turning point as Byrd Sr.'s death a few months later. I did not live in Smith's district or work on Rawlings' campaign, but I understood how important it was and cheered him on.

Post-Byrd or Neo-Byrd?

In 1965, the year before, the last Byrd Machine Democratic governor, Mills Godwin, was elected. Godwin had been a solid supporter of the Byrd Machine's last big issue campaign – Massive Resistance. This was, of course, the fight against the Supreme Court's Brown vs. Board of Education decision, and the last serious attempt to preserve legal segregation of schools. By the time of Godwin's election as Governor, though, that fight was lost.

Like all Virginia governors, Godwin could not succeed himself, and his successor was Linwood Holton, the heir to the patrician moderation of the Republican Party of the Valley of Virginia. That Republicanism had been a tiny and mostly ineffectual opposition to the Byrd Machine. Holton's election was a vindication of years of struggle against the Byrd Machine and for honest government.

But Holton's successor in 1973 was none other than Godwin – this time elected as a Republican. Godwin's "conversion" and election signaled a new era --- not so much for Virginia, but for those that run Virginia. Just as Byrd Sr. had come into power with a new look, but with most of the same cronies that had run the Martin Organization, now the Byrd Machine began to move into and take over the Virginia Republican Party.

Me and Byrd

I lived through this process, albeit as a very young man who did a little Democratic campaign work every year. (Virginia, by electing its state officials in odd years, ensures that the political process never takes a break.) Party politics, though, did not impress me as much as serious efforts to make change in this nation, especially the Freedom Movement.

As part of my work against housing segregation, I marched several times with a group organized by Freedom Movement leaders with SNCC backgrounds, picketing a large segregated housing complex in Arlington. So I learned the songs, walked the picket line, and even participated in a bold action at JFK's grave, where we sang "America the Beautiful" until threatened with arrest.

My father, by the way, was the one who took me to my first fair housing meetings, and who also told me about growing up in the South (though not in Virginia) and how important the New Deal was for his community. He also talked about his service in World War II. When the hero of his generation and his community, FDR, died, he heard about it from the guards at the Luftstalag where he was a prisoner of war. So I knew, not just for myself, and not just for current issues, but for generations, what damage Byrd Sr. had done or tried to do to my country.

Traces of Byrd in Richmond

At the age of 23, I moved to Richmond, Virginia, to be part of the arts and music scene there. I had wearied of the D.C. suburbs, where organizing never seemed to find firm ground. I had also burned out along with the New Left, one more victim of impatience, inexperience, and Cointelpro.

Soon, I was living in Oregon Hill, a working-class white downtown neighborhood, next to Hollywood Cemetery, the burial place of Richmond's élite – and of Jefferson Davis and hundreds of anonymous Confederate soldiers. Though I only learned this after living there a while, Oregon Hill was also the former site of the mansion named Belvidere, built in 1758 by the man who then owned most of Richmond – William Byrd III. And yes, he was Harry Flood Byrd Sr.'s great-grandfather.

The home I owned there was built around the time that Belvidere fell into ruins, in the 1850s.

Oregon Hill was an interesting anomaly – a white low-income inner-city neighborhood. Just before I moved there, a highway went through, taking out several blocks, and soon after Virginia Commonwealth University began to act on plans to demolish the rest of the neighborhood.

In the process of working with my neighbors to fight this destruction, I got a lesson in Byrd Machine politics. First, I watched as the long-time residents of Oregon Hill persisted in the belief that if only they could reach some of the nice people on the University's Board of Visitors, people like the wife of a former Congressman, everything would be fine. This illusion ran deep, and I came to understand that it was based on the real experience of back in the day. Under the Byrd Machine's monopoly of power, Virginians abjectly depended on those in high places to take care of them. But sometimes at least those in high places came through.

In fact, one of the last vestiges of Byrd patriarchal benevolence did help Oregon Hill. My neighbors had no luck getting through to the University Board, but they did get through to Ed Willey, our state senator and the Chair of the Virginia Senate's Finance Committee. Senator Willey toured the neighborhood, harrumphed a bit about how run-down it was, and then told the University they could not use eminent domain to take the neighborhood, and would have to settle for buying homes one by one. And since he was a major "decider" of university budgets, his word was obeyed.

(The longterm result was that, unable to get the property it wanted cheaply, the University decided to target the African-American neighborhood to its north, Carver, for its expansion plans. Oregon Hill still stands much as it did when I moved there.)

Byrd's Shadow on the Democrats

The patriarchal and deferential habits of the Byrd era (and really of four centuries of Virginia politics) showed up somewhere else in the 1970s – in the supposedly renewed and liberal Democratic Party. With the statewide candidacy of Chuck Robb, Virginia Democrats set the pattern they have followed since – liberal on a few issues, conservative on most, and mainly different from the Republicans in the relative racial and gender diversity of those they bring to public office.

> **The Virginians as a body were as conservative at heart as the English themselves, and conformity to the Church of England was but one phase of loyalty to the established**

> **order in the State... the whole power of Virginian society even in the times when universal suffrage prevailed, was directed by the landowners.**
> (Bruce, 1907)

The fights that George Rawlings and populist gubernatorial candidate Henry Howell had waged for the party, as well as the energy of the Freedom Movement in places like Petersburg and Prince Edward County, seemed to leave little trace in Democratic Party circles, especially in the policies of the conservative (they would say "moderate") Virginia Democratic governors that have followed in Robb's footsteps.

Byrd's Blank Spot

While in Richmond, I became Executive Director of the Virginia Housing Coalition. I had some success in pulling together a coalition of very different housing groups in very different parts of the Commonwealth. I managed to get rural Appalachian housing groups to find common ground with groups in Arlington and other urban areas, and to get them to understand each other's issues. But there were a few "blank spots" on my map of the state – places where there were no housing nonprofits, no public housing authorities, apparently little or no activity at all to meet low-income housing needs. Surprisingly to me at first, supposedly backward Appalachian Virginia teemed with housing groups. Several were organized by the Catholic women religious that have made such a difference in U.S. grassroots organizing. Even the Eastern Shore, still pretty much run like a plantation economy with exploited migrant labor, had one or two groups at work.

But the Shenandoah Valley was a desert as far as such efforts were concerned. During the five years I worked on statewide housing issues, I continued to try to find some group in that area, and found only one or two, none of them strong and none willing to get involved at the state level.

The Socialist Republic

From 1988-2003, I worked for national organizations. I lived in Arlington, a locality that prides itself on not being like the rest of Virginia, and certainly does not have the monuments from the Byrd era that mar the rest of the Commonwealth. It elects a lot of women to office, and has elected Virginia's only Hispanic official and only openly gay official. In Richmond, it is mockingly referred to as the Socialist Republic of

Arlington. So I did not think about Byrd Sr. all that often for a while.

Maybe I should have. One of the dominant institutions in the area where I lived is the Shirley Highway, the massive corridor of Interstate 95  that feeds suburbanites from Virginia to the Pentagon and into D.C. It's named for Henry Shirley, the highway boss for the Byrd Machine – a key figure in Byrd Sr.'s vaunted highway system. The dominant employer in Arlington, the Pentagon, was built there by FDR's administration, but it couldn't have hurt to put it in the state of FDR's powerful frenemy, Harry Byrd Sr. Byrd's hand still rests, if only lightly, even on the Socialist Republic of Arlington.

To The Valley

In 2003, my wife and I moved to the Shenandoah Valley, and in 2010, to Winchester, and to Berryville Avenue, a road which runs east nine miles from my house to Rosemont Manor, where Byrd Sr. lived.

So I came to live in the "blank spot on the map." Working here as an organizer, and involved in grassroots activities, I found clear evidence that the Shenandoah Valley's blank spot on the map was not a chance phenomenon.

I tried to organize a demonstration in Berryville, a few miles from the Manor.

I found out the Town of Berryville had the most repressive restrictions on demonstrations I had ever seen. (The restrictions were so blatantly unconstitutional that a letter from the ACLU ensured they were voted off the books at the next town council meeting.)

I watched as the Northern Shenandoah Valley gained a community action agency, more than 40 years after most of the rest of Virginia got one of these Great Society anti-poverty nonprofit organizations.

I was told, though I have not been able to verify it, that the Shenandoah Valley is not part of the official defined Appalachian region because Senator Byrd decided it wouldn't be. (The map of Appalachia used by the federal Appalachian Regional Commission shows Appalachian counties bordering Frederick County, where Winchester is located, on three sides, and an indentation in the eastern boundary of Appalachia precisely corresponding to the counties of Virginia's Shenandoah Valley.)

Today in Byrdland

In Berryville, in Winchester and in nearby Warren County, I have seen racism still at work, from surrealistically long prison sentences to constant postponement of needed public works in African-American neighborhoods to the spreading of vicious rumors about Latino immigrants. I have come to know personally African-American leaders who were the first in their families to attend integrated schools, and to learn about the courage with which they and their parents faced white mobs. And I have seen all of these things treated as minor matters in comparison to the civic orgy that is the Apple Blossom Festival, a holiday comparable to Christmas in its impact on Winchester.

(Byrd and his fellow apple growers instituted the event to promote their product. Now, with apple growing a decreasingly small part of the local economy, it's just a bad habit.)

So here I am, living at the geographic center of Byrd Sr.'s nasty work. The paper that lands on my front porch in the morning is his newspaper. His son's name is emblazoned on the Shenandoah University Business Building, which stands at a key local intersection a few blocks from my house.

By all accounts, Byrd Jr. is a man who would have led a very undistinguished life, if his career had been based on his talents and not on his name. And in fact, his many years in the Virginia Senate and his term in the U.S. Senate seem to have left no significant traces behind.

The last chapter of Byrd Jr.'s life will be the glowing obituaries and fulsome elegies that mark his death, after which he will be decently forgotten. Then serious politicians and officials will go back to the work of Byrd Sr. – controlling the Commonwealth with patronage and deception. They will continue to rely on what I call deference and lack of self-respect on the part of many, if not most, Virginians – what they would call civility, or "the Virginia Way." It is, of course, precisely the opposite of the Virginia Way of my Virginia heroes like Gabriel Prosser and Elizabeth Van Lew.

Confessing My Obsession

I began this essay by noting that I was accused of being obsessed with Harry Flood Byrd Sr. The man who made that accusation in his editorials rarely or never mentions Byrd, the Byrd "Organization," or its continuing impact. Clearly, when he calls me obsessed, what he means that I am obsessed with **mentioning** Byrd.

I am violating a kind of taboo, in Winchester as a community and in Virginia politics in general. According to this pervasive but unspoken rule, we must never mention Harry Flood Byrd Sr., and especially never mention the characteristic which defined him – his enormous political power.

Unlike many political bosses, Harry Byrd preferred to present himself as a quiet and dignified country gentleman.

This, of course, was posturing. Byrd inherited relatively little wealth, and was first a hard-nosed businessman and then a self-serving politician. But the image was consistent with the centuries of posturing by Virginia Gentlemen and their phony claims to aristocracy. Everyone knew how hard Harry labored to get and keep control of Virginia. But even when he was alive, it was offensive to say these things out loud.

It is particularly offensive, of course, to mention the orgy of racism that marked the end of his regime – the Massive Resistance campaign. After all, unlike many politicians of the Deep South, Byrd "did not use disparaging, condescending or rabble-rousing racial language," as biographer Ronald Heinemann noted in Harry Byrd of Virginia. Virginia had a much smaller active Klan presence than most Southern states, and even lynchings were less common than in other parts of the region. (As noted elsewhere, this does not mean crimes, or what looked like crimes to Byrd's people, went unpunished. Virginia has an especially cruel prison system, and certainly did so under Byrd.)

The Byrd machine, like all smart

political machines, used the carrot as well as the stick, and many Virginians, not just white ones, got enough from the machine to make it worthwhile not to protest.

However, by the 1950s, as Virginia changed demographically and thus politically, Byrd's political machine depended more and more on the votes of Southside Virginia – tobacco country, Nat Turner's old stomping grounds – and the core of segregationist sentiment. Clearly, this influenced Byrd's actions of those years.

Perhaps understanding that he was losing control, in the face of school integration Byrd abandoned the calm demeanor that had marked his long career. Heinemann wrote of Byrd's thinking in 1957, "His hyperbolic statements about villainous federal judges, a ruthless president, and an apocalyptic vision of the end of segregation were the delusions of an embittered, frustrated man whose world was collapsing around him."

The supposedly charming, reasonable and dignified Harry F. Byrd showed himself as what he was – a man unwilling to give up his political power, and equally unwilling to give up the Jim Crow system he had grown up with. On his watch, Virginia closed schools, and

committed itself to rhetoric about state interposition that sounded great to him and to his followers, but ultimately meant nothing. Byrd did not wave any ax handles or use the "n word." But when my friend James Kilby and 22 other children walked up the hill to Warren County High School, Byrd might as well have recruited the screaming mob that was so frightening and ugly to fourteen year old James.

But we are not supposed to learn from Harry Byrd's moral weakness. We are supposed to pretend that his dignity was never ruffled. We are to keep Virginia on the course he set – to be a wealthy state, but spend like a poor one. We are supposed to continue to claim a Revolutionary legacy, while deferring to a quasi-aristocracy.

So, I suppose, I am obsessed. Unlike my accuser, I believe that that the habits the Byrd Machine taught us are still a major force holding us back. Unlike

Byrd, I believe that there is a potential in our Commonwealth for real democracy, real multiculturalism, and real justice. And I certainly am obsessed with those goals. Because I have not forgotten Byrd, but I have also not forgotten those who successfully stood up against him.

> **The kids were all there, and they had such high morale. We still intended to tell them go on back to school, but they were so, I don't know they. . . were just so persuasive that we told them if they could get their parents to agree, we would no longer file suits charging inequality, that we were going to challenge segregation per se from then on. And, if their parents would back them, we would file suit for them. .. we agreed to hold a county meeting on Friday a week after. And on that Friday, the church was standing room only. They discussed it going and coming, and the vote overwhelmingly was for supporting the children. So we accepted the case and proceeded to file the suit against Prince Edward County.**

Oliver Hill, interviewed by Julian Bond, on the grassroots origins of the Brown v. Board of Education decision. Two Virginia counties, Prince Edward and Warren, were parties to this case. (Bond)

SOME FURTHER READING (ONLINE)

Voices of Freedom: Oral histories of leaders of the Civil Rights movement in Virginia.
http://dig.library.vcu.edu/cdm4/index_voices.php?CISOROOT=/voices

We the "White" People: Race, Culture, and the Virginia Constitution of 1902
by Jeremy Boggs; Master's Thesis, Virginia Tech Department of History
http://scholar.lib.vt.edu/theses/available/etd-10302003-171358/unrestricted/jeboggs_thesis.pdf

Massive Resistance: Virginia's Great Leap Backward, by Ira Lechner, Virginia Quarterly Review, Autumn 1998
http://www.vqronline.org/articles/1998/autumn/lechner-massive-resistance-virginias/

Virginia Politics: Winds of Change

by Murat Williams, Virginia Quarterly Review, Spring 1966
http://www.vqronline.org/articles/1966/spring/williams-virginia-politics/

Crossing The Line: Racial Healing In A Family And Community

By ***Phoebe Kilby*** | *June 15th, 2011*
http://emu.edu/now/peacebuilder/2011/06/crossing-the-line-racial-healing-in-a-family-and-community/

Action Resources

And here are some multi-issue statewide organizations seeking to reverse the damage done by the Byrd Machine to Virginia:

Virginia State Conference NAACP
http://www.virginianaacp.org/
(Also check for local branches)

Virginia Organizing
http://virginiaorganizing.org

Virginia New Majority
http://www.virginianewmajority.org/

Virginia Interfaith Center for Public Policy
http://virginiainterfaithcenter.org/

New Market Battlefield: Spring Snow Flurries

it's April in
Virginia, and
Tuesday of Holy
Week,
and my birthday

and
snowflakes
stream in bright
sunlight
light but
disturbing riders
on an
unseasonable
and bitter wind

I am walking up
this sloping field
of dry
broomsedge and
wild carrot
and Indian
Hemp
here and there
overlooked
by dark cedars

the field
that was named
Bloody Cedars
after part of the
Battle of New
Market
was fought here
in another bitter
season

it could have
been fair and
temperate today
and I could be
watching
the Dutchman's
breeches dangle
on a calm and
pretty hillside
or the bluebells
glow
in the company
of a sparkling
river's
smoothness

I could be

instead I am
walking this high
field
and looking
across the tamed
valley
to the mutable
and complicated
sky
exhaling light

and inhaling
shadows
onto the ridges
of Massanutten
Mountain
across the way

I am this one
walking in this
high field
where
along the edge of
this path
the tiny flower
named Pearly
Everlasting
inconspicuously
grows
its paleness
almost invisible
in this day of
blue and gray
and rust
of fickle sunlight
and unreliable
shadow
this spring day

we have a long
history with
spring
we who live
towards the
north
so to distinguish
their worship
from that long
history
which they name
pagan
some have
renamed Easter
Resurrection
Sunday
perhaps a
distinction
without a
difference

I could have
been somewhere
else
but I am this one
that was born
almost sixty
springs ago

I am this one
and Jesus died
to make men
holy
and, bleeding on
cedars
whose seed still
flourishes here,
some men died
to make men
free,
and others died
otherwise,
but most

with hope of
resurrection

in the perhaps
pearly
everlasting

and I am this
one
so I am here
hooded against
the cold
on a path I never
knew about
until this day of
my birth and
Holy Week
and vacillating
spring

I am this one
passing last
summer's dead
flower heads
that are still
trembling
passing worn
and fissured
cedar fence posts
standing plain
alongside
the gloomy
intricacies of the
living cedars

I am this one
walking in the
footsteps of the
warring dead
and of the
peaceful ones
that came in
respect
some of whom
are also dead

and where they
passed,
amid the pale
broomsedge
on the hillside
this path climbs
there's one
great-growing
sycamore

the water-loving
tree is
a sign of a spring
deep in the
hillside

so I am
walking above a
spring I will
never see
and
feeling no spring
in the chill
around me
seeing none in
the broomsedge

alive only to the
wind

for each stalk of
the broomsedge
seen close
is dead
and almost as
pale as paper
yet a tint and
hint of red
haunts the full
field of the grass

haunts this field
that is now
reserved
from the smooth
green
of the farmed
valley below
for the honored
dead

and here I am
on this
particular path
as the sphere
unhesitatingly
turns
to take away
even this erratic
sunlight

as battles
continue

as every day
some die to
make persons
free
I am this one
in this moment
when the
calendar's
pledges
can't be trusted
and on this path
worn by those I
will never know
in this field
that was fertile a
season ago
that was fatal a
season ago

I am this one
with

every now and
then

a glimpse of the
Pearly
Everlasting

Fraud and Fable Number Seventeen: Today's Virginia Politics Is Colorblind

---

Purpose: This myth, common to most of the United States, insists that no one does, says or thinks anything racist any more, that racism is as obsolete as the problem of cleaning horse poop off our city streets. I wish.

"Despite the doubt and terror which gripped me, I finally made my way out of the white crowd and took my place with the Negro protesters... Among the white spectators, I saw here and there faces I remembered from my childhood... The rancor I felt by one elderly woman, whom I vaguely recalled..., was apparently too much for her to contain. With no warning, she marched up and spat in my face."
From "Richmond Journal, thirty years in black and white" by Edward H. Peeples, a white native of Richmond Virginia who has been an anti-racist activist since that day in 1960. Published in the collection Race Traitor, edited by Noel Ignatiev and John Garvey, Routledge 1996.

The Story of Tim and Chuck and Bo

Cast of Characters:
Tim Kaine, Richmond fair housing lawyer, City Councilman, Mayor, Governor and candidate for Senate.
Henry "Chuck" Richardson, former Richmond City Councilman
John "Bo" Flynn, activist, Front Royal, Virginia

When we were both younger, and he had no elected office at all, I broke bread at Tim's table. I remember a day when heavy snow democratically rendered us all equally unable to go to work, and free to wander Northside Richmond on slippery feet. I came by his home and hung out with his family. I remember another day, walking in a park with him, talking about remedies to housing segregation. I suppose I told him that, when he was 8, I was one of the teen followers of an organization marching against Jim Crow housing in our Commonwealth. He told me about his fair housing legal strategies, and I still remember details of them, part of the fabric of change and movement in that organizers like me see when we look at the world.

When I met Chuck, a few years earlier, he already had a title. He was a Richmond City Councilman. I never even saw his home or his family, and all I knew about was his public life, and gossip, and what was, more and more sadly, in the press. Nor did I ever tell him my stories.

I used to hang out with musicians, and once marched with a motley band in a city parade. We won a title like Most Likely to Disturb the Peace from a panel of judges that included Chuck. The next time Chuck saw me, he half apologized.

He didn't know me well enough to be sure I was proud of the title. Tim could have been in the band, had he been so inclined; he knew a few of us who marched, and he was only a little younger than most of us.

5th District
Richardson (B): 2,508
Craigie (W): 1,027
Johnson (B): 533
from the table "The 1978 Councilmanic Election, (W=white, B=Black)
(Moeser)

My neighborhood, Oregon Hill, was the white remnant in Richmond's inner city. Widows, disabled folk and those chronically in trouble were well-represented in the population. Many of the other white folks had fled to the suburbs, and now my kind were coming in, ex-students braving territory we'd been warned off of, making it ours here and there with a food co-op, a shared garden. The neighborhood was the political hole in Chuck's mostly African-American district; mine was one of the few votes there he could count on.

The comparisons to Marion Barry are obvious. But Chuck never risked his life with SNCC, and hadn't organized urban street life into grassroots power. He certainly hadn't said Hell No, I Won't Go, as I had been heard to do, and as Freedom Movement organizers like Barry did. In fact, Chuck did go to Vietnam, and in later years said war injuries and experiences led to his heroin habit. But he came back and went to college and took his handsome light-skinned self into politics.

Tim volunteered a year in Honduras as a teacher and missionary, giving his time in the framework of his Catholic faith. Anyway, there was no war to go to in 1977, when he turned 18. But there was college, and law school, and there was marriage to a governor's daughter. When I knew him, he never talked to me about the trajectory that was likely from there, but I saw what it could be, and was mildly pleased about it, and intrigued. Someone in my orbit, I thought, someone in my crowd, might be governor. And Tim was a good looking young man too.

Then, around the time Tim was in Honduras in 1980 and 1981, in Oregon Hill the discussions of the need for recreation solidified around the idea of a swimming pool. We deserved that from the city, went the word on the street. Cleanups of basketball courts and of a pocket park had whetted the appetite for city-provided recreation.

And I am all for poor folks asking for more from the cities that mostly feed the development machinery that chews up neighborhoods.

But there already was a pool.

There was a city pool that was easily close enough to walk to. And one day, Chuck organized a walk from our neighborhood to the pool, mostly of young kids in their bathing suits and T-shirts, and a few do-gooders like me that had no plans to go in the water but were ready to plunge into the micro-struggle. And we all walked the few blocks across the invisible race line. And Chuck did what he had to do, in his usual fine vested suit and sharp shoes – he let himself get thrown in the pool. And a fine time was had by all on a sunny Saturday. And then most of the kids from our white neighborhood never made that walk again.

> **"The Vietnam War created thousands of Black addicts... With roadside access to heroin, opium, and hashish in Vietnam, many Black soldiers became addicts... Although there was clear evidence that drug abuse among both combat and support soldiers was growing, the U.S. Armed Forces refused to implement**

any serious treatment program…" <u>Pipe Dream Blues: Racism and the War on Drugs</u>, by Clarence Lusane

Chuck blamed his Vietnam time for the heroin use, and I accept that it started there. But I wonder what other pain he felt.

Tim and Anne and the kids came to my wedding in 1993. He wasn't on City Council yet. We had a good time. I had been away from Richmond for five years by then, and I didn't see him for a while after that.

I never had a meal or even a cup of coffee with Chuck. The closest I got to Chuck was with a letter to the editor. I wrote it after he took a bigger chance than at the pool, and with even less results. He pushed the President of the university that was his district's biggest employer (as well as his own alma mater) to sit down with what the President clearly saw as the low income white trash of my neighborhood. Chuck gallantly tried to make peace between the two. It was a lost cause, but I admired him for his effort, one that neither side really welcomed.

The next day, one of the local white people daily papers (there were two then) published an article on the meeting. It didn't mention Chuck, who had organized, led, and sweated at the meeting. Yup, not a word. Apparently the reality of an African-American politician acting as mediator between two white groups was too much for the white media to handle.

> **"For the most part television and the movies depict a world where blacks and whites coexist in harmony although the subtext is clear; this harmony is maintained because no one really moves from the location white supremacy allocates to them...." Killing Rage: Ending Racism by bell hooks**

Well, I've been a fan of Orwell's 1984 for a lot of years, and when I saw the racial memory hole in action, I felt I had to respond. And for some reason they printed my letter castigating them.

A while later, I talked to Chuck at some event, and he thanked me. He pointed out that he could not have written the letter, and said this happens all the time.

This certainly didn't happen all the time to me. And it certainly didn't happen all the time to Tim.

I think the last connection I made with Chuck was when I contacted him about my idea for some kind of newspaper that would cross the race lines, and push a different vision for Richmond. It was a very vague idea, one that bobbed to the surface many times. It wasn't Chuck's style; he was working the inside game. But he was the only person that gave me anything concrete. He connected me to the woman who was just beginning to publish The Newspaper.

The Newspaper didn't last long. But it changed me. I got in print in my community with assigned articles, not just letters to the editor. And I worked for the first time with an organization where I was the only white person. I surprised folks, and to some extent myself, by continuing to show up, sometimes even on my bike in "their neighborhood" at night. That connection to The Newspaper was Chuck's gift to me, like the gifts he gave to Oregon Hill of letting himself be thrown in the pool, or getting a meeting with the arrogant university president.

I think I at least thanked him. Damn, I hope so.

I left Richmond in 1988. I'd run out of interesting jobs, and had a good offer in DC. And so I was out of touch, really, in

1994, when Tim got elected to his first office, to the Richmond City Council that Chuck also served on. It was that year, a year after my wedding, that I wrote the letter to Tim.

I can't find a copy of it now, but essentially I wrote to Tim and suggested that he build a relationship with Chuck, that Chuck was a decent guy and the two had more in common than Tim might realize. I don't believe I got any answer.

A year or so later, Chuck got arrested on another heroin charge, and it was the end of his political career. Three years later, Tim became mayor, and a lot more folks saw the trajectory of his career. Obviously, that career was not going to include Chuck, regardless of letters from well-meaning old friends.

The first time I saw Tim as Governor, I happened to be in a room of Virginia environmentalists. A good and ambitious friend had ushered my wife and me to the front row of the room. The room was packed with environmentalists hungry and hopeful to get something from Kaine. He walked in, saw me, and came over and gave me a hug. It was pretty exciting, especially thinking about all those enviros who were wondering who the hell I was and why Kaine singled me out.

I haven't worked much in recent statewide Virginia campaigns. Back in the 70s, after the Virginia Democratic Party snuffed out its working class populist element for a managerial approach, I stopped being very interested. There were plenty of other things to do that were more fun, more effective, and that seemed to put me in the room with a better class of people. (You know, the working class. At statewide Democratic celebrations in Richmond, I always seemed to end up talking to a stockbroker or a Main Street lawyer.)

So I didn't work in Tim's campaigns, for Lieutenant Governor or Governor. And so he didn't owe me anything, and by then he was surrounded by people who I am sure kept track of his obligations.

I contacted him a few times during his term, and despite the hug, I never really got through. I embarrassed myself by insisting that he would do something about racial profiling, even discussing it with him face to face a couple of times. That coin fell down my wishing well without even a splash.

Then, almost at the end of his term, I brought him face to face with Bo. Now Bo has served some time on a drug charge, and certainly knows the street life. But I am not saying Bo is some Chuck equivalent. Bo is way darker-skinned than Chuck, never had a college education, and has never run for, let alone been elected to, office. Instead, he has ground out grassroots victories since he was in the Freedom Movement, when Chuck was a child and Tim was in diapers. He was passing out flyers for candidates before Chuck ran for office the first time. And he kept doing it despite not having his voting rights after his drug charge. But he wanted those rights back. Face to face at a community event, he asked Tim to take care of it, and I backed him up. (It's the governor's prerogative in Virginia to restore the rights of ex-felons.) And Tim said he would deal with it, and passed it on to an aide, and Bo never heard anything else. That happened twice.

If I had a more politically moderate little brother, and he was Catholic, he could be Tim. Chuck emerged from and went back into African-American worlds I may never see.

I have no idea where Chuck is today; I don't even know who to ask. Tim is currently asking for my support – by email and postal mail – for a Senate campaign.

In 1994, I wrote a letter that fell into the abyss. Despite that charming hug, I don't think Tim and I have really connected since. No reason why we should. I know the rules of his game, and none of those rules require that he acknowledge my game, unless I make him do it. (As Frederick Douglass said, power concedes nothing without a demand.)

And those rules certainly don't require, or even allow, him to look back at a City Councilman who tried to serve the public, including his obstreperous white constituents who didn't particularly want to be served -- but who couldn't beat heroin.

Water under the bridge.

Since I left Richmond, they have knocked down the old Lee Bridge. They built a new bridge to carry Route 1 across the James River. It looks quite different, and I have some nice pictures of it. But it is also named after Robert E. Lee. The water under the bridge changes, even the bridge changes, but the names don't change.

They had another bridge in Richmond. As part of a downtown development boondoggle, before Tim was elected, there was a bridge built over Broad Street, symbolically uniting Black and White Richmond. That bridge was eventually torn down, and not replaced.

I am lucky to know Bo. For one thing, Bo is the acid test for the question, can the system be made to work? And Tim can't answer that question. Sure, he's worked hard, and done some good things that the other guys he ran against would never have done. But really, he just slid into place. Yes, he and many others worked their asses off; yes, hundreds of thousands of dollars were spent. But really, he just slid into place.

Nobody ever gave Bo anything for free. Just like nobody ever beat up and arrested Tim when he was on his way to the courthouse to see justice done. (Yes, that happened to Bo.) But from Bo's position, where he can see what Tim and I never will be able to see in the Black community, there have been real victories. And every victory had a cost.

One of the several phrases that Bo uses a lot is "It's not the person, it's the issue."

I hope Tim gets elected to the Senate this year. Like I hope it won't rain right when I am ready to go out and mow the lawn. It would be nice. But whoever gets elected, there is no turning back. Whoever gets elected, she or he is going to get pushed by Bo and by me.

The first time I ever saw Chuck's name was on the front page of the Richmond Afro-American, in its issue in 1977 celebrating the Black majority on City Council. The Virginia Gentlemen had held that win off for years with legal maneuvers, but finally Chuck and his colleagues broke through. I remember holding that paper in my hands. I remember thinking about all that it meant, all the struggle that had been waged to lead to this moment. I didn't know many details then; I know a few more now, some from reading, some from personal experience.

I didn't know that I would be Chuck's constituent, his supporter, and now in a way his mourner. I am angry, it's true, at how the white machinery ran over him, both when he was doing the right thing and when he lost all control. I kind of hope he will see this book and know he is remembered as something other than an addict.

But that's not so important. Because it isn't the person. it's the issue. The years move forward, and we do what we can, and all of our names will someday be forgotten. But what we attain, if we are good enough at what we do and also lucky, will remain.

Rights and powers and opportunities and even hopes, though they are mocked these days, are more lasting than any one person. It's not the election results, or the time served behind bars, it's the movement. It's not whether the handsome young man flowers or fades. It's the old man, my mentor and partner Bo, that matters. Because he has persisted on the issues, undeterred by failure or success. As I hope I have and hope I will.

Being raised up doesn't really matter, not even to the Presidency, not all that much. Nor does being cast down, as cruel as it is.

It's the persistence that matters. The invisible unstoppable persistence that is the human hunger for justice. It's not the person, it's the issue. Because the issue is all of us, Chuck and Tim, indistinguishable in our humanity, prodigal son and Samaritan, outcast and priest, pretty and ugly, dark and light.

Barbed Wire Poem

suppose you're
on your way
somewhere
in a hurry

and suppose,
taking a
shortcut,
you get caught
on barbed wire -
-

say, stepping
through it

and your leg's
hung up
behind you

and you're in a
hurry

you want to just
run on ahead

but you can't do
that

you want to rip
loose
and walk on
with your pants
still fresh and
untorn

but you can't

you want to
curse and yell
maybe you do

but when you're
through
you're still
hung up on
barbed wire

there's no better
choice

you've got to
turn around and
look at it
and work
yourself loose

that's where we
are
with racism
in this country

Don't Virginia White Working People Suffer Just as Much As People of Color? A Response to Senator Jim Webb's "Diversity and the Myth of White Privilege"
(Webb)

(The original version of this essay was sent to Senator Webb, and also published online in AltDaily, a Hampton Road online journal. I never had a response from the Senator.) (Yates)

In an age when so many politicians hardly dare think a thought that some fundraiser has not endorsed, the Junior Senator from my state of Virginia, Jim Webb, stands out as not afraid to say what he thinks.

He cares deeply about the frontline serviceman and servicewoman, and he certainly makes that known. Recently, he has spoken up on the catastrophe that is our "justice system," and I think he might actually spur some action with this bold initiative from an unexpected direction. [That was then; I'm more pessimistic now, especially since Webb chose not to run again. LLY 2012]

But anyone who speaks passionately and on many topics will sometimes wander onto shaky ground. This is what he has done, I believe, in his comments on affirmative action and related issues in "Diversity and the Myth of White Privilege."

Jim Webb is a passionate man. Aside from his military experience, his passion for service clearly grows out of his experiences in Southwest Virginia and his Scots-Irish background.

I first visited Southwest Virginia in 1981, and have been back many times,

including during the hotly contested Pittston coal strike of 1989. There are many striking things about the region, aside from its amazing physical beauty. The coal industry has visibly built it up and brought it down. Tiny communities and old traditions still survive back in the hollers. But as an organizer working around the Commonwealth, the first thing I noticed was a society that, despite hard class issues, was tightly knit by longstanding kin and communal connections – and almost undivided by race.

Southwest Virginia is the whitest region of Virginia. This does not mean it is the most prejudiced region. It certainly does not mean that Senator Webb is racially prejudiced, especially given his interracial marriage and his military and public service. But it does mean that his emotional and political starting point is that of white working people who, day to day, do not interact with African-Americans.

Working statewide, and having been a blue-collar worker in Richmond in the 1970s, I can testify that working-class whites in other parts of Virginia do in fact have privileges in relation to African-Americans, whether we are talking about government services, access to jobs, or financing to buy and maintain a home.

Obviously, though, I am not going to make my case with a pissing contest with Senator Webb about who experienced what. But I can make my case by doing what the Senator barely did – focusing on the facts.

Throughout the article, Senator Webb made assertions with no facts to back them up.

The most striking example is his statement that "a plethora of government-enforced diversity policies have marginalized many white workers." He fails to back up what he must consider self-evident. Unfortunately, this statement is simply wrong.

In a 2002 review of available scientific and polling sources, University of Maryland sociologist Fred Pincus highlighted the following facts:

- While half or more of all white males believe that their group experiences discrimination, only 2-13% report personally experiencing it, and only 2 to 5% of all discrimination complaints are filed by whites claiming racial discrimination or by males claiming gender discrimination.
- Of those complaints which make it through the process to disposition, "reverse discrimination" claims are much less likely to be upheld. In one study, one third of these claims were upheld, while 58% of "regular" cases were upheld. In 1994, only 1% of reverse discrimination cases filed with the federal Equal Employment Opportunities Commission were deemed credible.

- Prof. Pincus ultimately suggests that a small number -- less than 5% -- of white males do experience some kind of race or gender based discrimination, and notes that of those, many “could make use of various antidiscrimination policies and laws in order to seek justice.” (Pincus)

In other words, Senator Webb has built his thesis on very shaky ground. “Reverse discrimination,” despite its media glamour, is a very minor phenomenon, and that part of it attributable to government policy must be even smaller.

On the other hand, he minimizes discrimination that does exist, stating that “Those who came to this country in recent decades from Asia, Latin America and Africa did not suffer discrimination from our government..” It is true that immigrants arriving after the 1968 passage of the Fair Housing Act, the final civil rights bill of the Sixties, should not have experienced *de jure* discrimination. But does the Senator really believe that immigrant people of color have not experienced de facto discrimination in services or other government actions? This leaves out, of course, discrimination by private actors, which was the main focus of most of the civil rights laws.

The fact that, if discriminated against by their local merchants, landlords, and employers, a recent immigrant, or a native-born person of color, can come to the government and have an equal right to complain hardly shows equal status with their white neighbors. First, the damage is already done. Second, the government agencies that enforce the laws Senator Webb cites have more than enough to do already. Forget affirmative action. Just try to get action on an out and out case of overt discrimination – the kind that everyone agrees is bad, and that has been illegal for more than 40 years -- and see how long it takes and how disappointing the results can be.

For example, in 2010, about 10,000 people or groups made fair housing complaints to HUD or HUD-equivalent state organizations. This is, of course, only a tiny percentage of all the cases of housing discrimination, as indicated by our continued segregated housing stock. Of those 10,000, almost half of the complaints were unresolved after 100 days. Frankly, who has the time to be involved in this kind of system? Unless you are working with a nonprofit agency or an attorney, who can get to all the hearings, respond to all the filings, and fill out all the forms? After all, the apartment or house you wanted is long gone. The good news is that about 40% of all cases had some kind of real resolution – but at what expense of time and energy? (HUD)

In addition to fair housing, there are issues of unfair treatment of consumers, of neighborhoods, of students in school, and so on. And of course there is the issue that the Senator is quite familiar with – the grotesque overrepresentation of dark-skinned men in our prisons.

So, yes, Senator Webb, there are civil rights laws. But they have not made the problems of discrimination vanish. They have just provided tools – rather clumsy ones – that some people can use some of the time.

Senator Webb does make a solid case that many white groups are as limited in formal education as African-Americans. But he does not even mention wages, incomes, or the most important economic status determinant, family wealth.

My father grew up in rural Georgia. During the Great Depression, his father mortgaged his mules; they were apparently worth more than his acreage. But that 120 or so acres stayed in the family – unlike in many systematically looted African-American families – and my father recently sold his one-sixth share for a substantial amount. With the help of the G.I. bill and FHA lending, both resources much less available to African-Americans and other dark-skinned minorities, my father in the meantime had a professional career, and gave me an "upper middle class" upbringing. In other words, white privilege played a critical role in the southern rural side of my family history.

Wealth matters, and the difference between white and black wealth is large and well-documented.

- The Institute on Assets and Social Policy, in a May 2010 report, found that the dollar savings gap between whites and African-Americans had increased from $20,000 in 1984 to $95,000 in 2007. (Institute on Assets and Social Policy)
- United for a Fair Economy, in its 2012 report, The State of the Dream: The Emerging Majority found the median net worth for African-American families was one-tenth of the median net worth of white families. (United for a Fair Economy)

I believe that Senator Webb's intention, in writing this article, was to make the case that the great economic disparities in this country do not only affect African-Americans, but that many whites in this country receive unfair treatment. This is not only an incontrovertible fact, but has been long recognized, for example by the creation of the Appalachian Regional Commission, an entity that provides (far from adequate) development resources to a predominantly white area that has long been exploited economically. (Appalachian Regional Commission.)

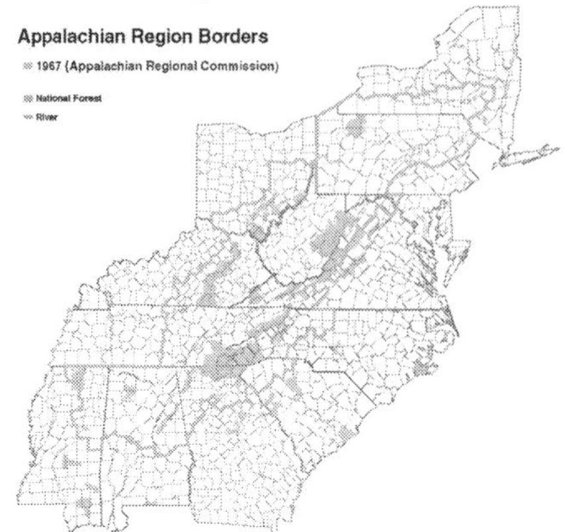

We need justice for every person in the United States who has been denied opportunity, regardless of color or ethnicity or any other extraneous factor. Jim Webb is passionately in pursuit of this goal, as indicated by his recently being given the Andrew Jackson Presidential Award, given to those "who have demonstrated in their civic lives a dedication to the furtherance of our American democracy and to sound governance principles."

But I believe, in common with social justice leaders from the AFL-CIO to the Catholic Church, that continuing to act affirmatively to end racism is not a distraction from, but an essential part of "the furtherance of our American democracy." After all, the southern Freedom Movement, though it was initially seen as anti-white, is now universally understood to have brought economic progress to the South for everyone.

We are a great and complex nation, and we can recognize, and work on, more than one problem at a time. I have confidence that Senator Webb will correct the misstep he made in this article. He will come to understand that he need not deny ongoing racism, or stand in the way of the work against it, in order to advance the legitimate concerns he has about white working class people held back because of their class, region, or other factors.

Mr. Man has a
widescreen tv
Mr. Man's
emails don't
bounce
Mr. Man has a
Blackberry
Provided to
track his
accounts

But Mr. Man
feels no need to
change
His feelings
about who is
strange

Mr. Man likes
church songs
that rock
Mr. Man's wife
has a career
Mr. Man's kids
like hiphop
Mr. Man likes
Mexican beer

But Mr. Man
feels no need to
change
His feelings
about who is
strange

Maybe Mr. Man
doesn't even
remember
His daddy
laughing about
the Klan
The colored guy
disappearing
one December
How it happened
that his grandpa
Bought all that
good land so
cheap
And had that
little store to
keep

Maybe Mr. Man
has forgotten
Making ooga
booga mock
Feeling free
while they
picked cotton
To even thrust
his cock
At married
women who
were grown
But had no
power of their
own

Maybe Mr. Man
no longer knows
He heard Mr.
Thurmond's
rants
Sitting listening
to the radio
About Africans
with no pants
That the white
man raised up
good
At least as far as
they could

Maybe Mr.
Man's not now
aware
Being told he
was superior
That dark skin
and kinky hair
Were a sure sign
of inferior
That those ones
were not his
kind
Because he had a
sharper mind

One thing's sure,
right up to the
hilt
Mr. Man feels no
guilt

One thing's sure,
right up to the
hilt
You can ask him,
he feels no guilt

One thing's sure,
right up to the
hilt
There's no
reason he should
feel any guilt

One thing's sure,
right up to the
hilt
There's no
reason for his
people to feel
guilt

One thing's sure
No no no guilt

Guilt
Never enters his
mind

Even if he
happens to not
avoid in time
The picture of a
lynched Black
man

And he knows
his people, his
kin
Did this kind of
thing

Guilt
Never enters his
mind

There's not room
for guilt
In a mind filled
with excuses
Full of
government
abuses,
Of stories of
those that
refuses
To be of any uses
Because welfare
is what they
chooses
It's not our fault
Not even the
nooses

Guilt is never
allowed
To enter his
mind

Mr. Man has a
widescreen tv
Mr. Man's
emails don't
bounce
Mr. Man has a
Blackberry
Provided to
track his
accounts

And no one
pushes Mr. Man
to change
His contempt for
what to him is
strange

Mr. Man likes
church songs
that rock
Mr. Man's wife
has a career
Mr. Man's kids
like hiphop
Mr. Man likes
Mexican beer

And no one
pushes Mr. Man
to change
His contempt for
what to him is
strange

And then one
day
far away

he hears some
one say
something about
a
Black President

Now Mr. Man
trusts the
President
The man in war
to lead
And he also
knows the
President
Will provide the
subsidies he
needs
To keep his nice
white
neighborhood
Fortified and
guaranteed

Now Mr. Man
and the
President
They've always
been real tight
Cause Mr. Man
is a manly man
Takes care of his
family right
And the only one
he can stand
above him
Is strong, and
mighty white

And then one
day
far away
he hears some
one say
something about
a
Black President

And then it
actually happens

And he feels
mighty uneasy

But it isn't guilt

And he feels
mighty uneasy

But it isn't all
those tales his
daddy told

And he feels
mighty uneasy

But it couldn't be
fear
That the tables
have turned

And he feels
mighty uneasy

So it must be
rage

So it must be
rage

And why he is so
angry?

Since people
want to drink
There are a
thousand kinds
of beer
Since people
want to romance
There's songs
that say I love
you dear
And when
people want to
rage at someone
There will be lots
of lies for them
to hear

Obama is a
socialist
He wasn't born
with us
He got elected by
ACORN
He smells like
asparagus
When people
feel that rage
inside just rise
Someone will
find them
appropriate lies
When that rage
can be pumped
To help a rich
son of a
To get his toxics
dumped
Without a hitch
Keep his taxes
low
So the poor man
pays
To not have to
change
His corporate
ways

When they see
that rage inside
just rise
They will find
and broadcast
the appropriate
lies
They will say
that Klan talk is
modern and
rocks

They will say
what they need
to, clever as a
Fox
Though they
think the Mr.
Mans are just
slobs
They will give
them a
Limbaugh, a
Beck and a
Dobbs

And remember
There is no guilt
involved

As Mr. Man
keeps getting
crazier
Every day he has
a Black
President

No it's all about
facts
We report you
decide
We have the
facts
No one has lied

And a quiet
rational guy
from Hawaii
That went to
Harvard
And married
into a
respectable
Chicago family
Really has
turned into a
Raving socialist
who somehow
Has been
granted the
power
Not even
available to
Nixon or Clinton
or Bush
To take the
country straight
to hell
do not pass go

Why should
there be,
Buried deep
inside the rage
and resentment,
Underneath the
lies upon lies
Any guilt?

Why should 400
years of treating
a people
as subhuman

while
proclaiming the
gospel of Jesus
lead to any
guilt

I resent that
You're insulting
us
The news has
proved
He smells like
asparagus

You do have to
wonder
Isn't it painful
To believe that
your own
country
Has elected an
insane terrorist
from Kenya
Who is imposing
socialism?

Oh it hurts
It hurts all right
It hurts til you
might go blind
But nothing
could hurt Mr.
Man
As much
As looking into
his own mind

But nothing
could hurt Mr.
Man
As much
As looking into
his own mind

Mr. Man has a
widescreen tv
Mr. Man's
emails don't
bounce
Mr. Man has a
Blackberry
Provided to
track his
accounts

But Mr. Man
feels no need to
change
His feelings
about who is
strange

Mr. Man likes
church songs
that rock
Mr. Man's wife
has a career
Mr. Man's kids
like hiphop
Mr. Man likes
Mexican beer

But Mr. Man
feels no need to change
His feelings about who is strange

And nothing could hurt Mr. Man
As much
As looking into his own soul

============

This poem is also on YouTube in video format.

Oregon Hill – A Virginia Neighborhood

Oregon Hill, a Richmond neighborhood, is the first place I bought a home, the place where I began and defined my professional life. A place that is home to people I love, and was the home of people I despised and people I feared. A place where I knew my barber as a friend and neighbor, where I saw children become teenagers, where I enjoyed and lost love, where I headed a civic group, where I crawled under a century old house to repair busted water pipes.

NEW TOWNHOMES OVER THE JAMES IN OREGON HILL

Oregon Hill has been a low-income or working-class and white neighborhood for its entire existence, since the days when houses were built there for immigrant ironworkers from Wales and Cornwall before the Civil War. When it was built, it got its nickname because it was so far west of the main part of Richmond. In modern

Richmond, it is a few blocks from downtown; I walked from the Hill to jobs not far from the Capitol that Jefferson designed. Overlooking the urban whitewater of the James River, next to the decorous Hollywood Cemetery where three Presidents and thousands of Confederate soldiers are buried, it keeps threatening to be a choice spot for what we used to call “yuppies,” but never quite gets there.

When I moved there, in 1974, it was in some ways at its lowest point. I was warned by people who had lived in the Richmond area all their lives that it was a dangerous place. Art students on the nearby campus of Virginia Commonwealth University told me of their fears of walking through Oregon Hill to Hollywood Cemetery. In fact, I found out it was a safe place to live, like a lot of "tough" neighborhoods in those days, as long as you didn't get entangled in the affairs of some of the more violent young men in the neighborhood. But it was an almost unrelievedly poor neighborhood; the majority of its residents were either elderly people, many of them widows, who had come there long before and stayed, or families that could not afford to move to the suburbs, to which most of Richmond's white people had fled.

In Oregon Hill, I was involved in defending the neighborhood from the University's encroachments, in starting and sustaining a natural foods cooperative, in making art, in learning wild plants, and above all in deep friendships and relationships.

Most of us white Americans spend most of our time in a thousand other pursuits besides thinking about race. We raise families, go to work, entertain ourselves, worship, worry, love and hate. But, just as has been true of Oregon Hill, each of us operates within boundaries of possibility that are defined by race. And like most of the people of Oregon Hill, we almost never let ourselves really think about what that means.

VIEW OF DOWNTOWN RICHMOND FROM NEAR OREGON HILL

Today, a very powerful force in the lives of many white people is the vision of better days, when there was less crime, more respect, more religion, or more of whatever we think was good then. While I lived there, in the 1970s and 1980s, many residents of Oregon Hill were caught up in Richmond's past, in "better" days. This was particularly true of neighborhood attitudes towards African-Americans and towards the white power structure of Richmond.

In the past, in Virginia's old hierarchy, white working class people could count on being privileged relative to African-Americans, and they could count on being taken care of by paternalistic members of the white power structure. The system of "classical racism" -- of the old-fashioned form of white supremacy -- worked pretty well for them. There were times when it broke down. During the last days of the Civil War, when Richmond suffered serious economic hardships, residents of Oregon Hill rioted for bread. Rioting was the only recourse they had. The Richmond power structure didn't encourage participation by the lower classes. Virginia for decades has had one of the lowest voting rates -- among whites -- of any state, and had a much less "populist" politics than other Southern states. But the whites of Oregon Hill could count on municipal jobs, skilled craft work, and "overseer" type positions relative to black people. They could count on the really lousy jobs being done by African-Americans. Jobs like those of the railroad workers that were buried in the collapse of a tunnel they were digging a few miles from Oregon Hill. (They still lie there today.)

Oregon Hill benefited enormously from this paternalistic system. St. Paul's Episcopal, the church that Robert E. Lee and other luminaries of the Old Dominion attended, made the improvement of Oregon Hill a special project. A Richmond tobacco heiress, Miss Grace Arents, focused her charity on Oregon Hill. Among the benefits of her attention, during the early decades of the twentieth century, were privately subsidized apartments for some neighborhood residents, a public bath, a free library, and a free private school. No African-American neighborhoods got the same benefits.

By the time I came to live in Oregon Hill, this system had broken down, but many residents of Oregon Hill still lived under its spell. After the Korean War, the Richmond power structure had decided, despite neighborhood protests, to let the neighborhood be eroded by the building of a war memorial, which pretty much destroyed several blocks of Oregon Hill. A highway followed in the early 1970s, cutting a swath through the neighborhood so that commuters from the suburbs could get to downtown, taking another six blocks. I moved to the Hill while the road was still a vast valley of mud, and after most of the houses in its path were gone.

BALD EAGLE ON A SYCAMORE NEAR OREGON HILL

In the late 1970s, Virginia Commonwealth University, whose campus borders Oregon Hill, began to let outsiders in on plans to expand its campus all the way to the James River, in the process wiping out Oregon Hill. In 1978, I attended a meeting where VCU administrators confirmed plans to replace most of what had been cut off by the highway with sports facilities. While my companion drew a picture of the VCU administrator with long teeth and wolf's ears, I took copious notes. My information and other research soon led to a serious battle between VCU and organized residents of Oregon Hill.

While I learned a great deal from Oregon Hill's fight with VCU, especially from a few remarkable leaders, I came to the fight with the anti-authoritarian assumptions of a former Sixties activist. So it surprised me to see that many neighborhood residents, some of them very intelligent and militantly opposed to VCU, believed that if they could only reach the familiar names from Richmond's power structure on the VCU Board, like the wife of the ex-Congressman, they would be protected. They believed in something I sometimes call Whitefare, or classical racism. They believed not because they were naïve, but because that was the system they had grown up with. The members of the Board of Visitors of VCU were the heirs of Robert E. Lee and Miss Grace Arents; they were expected to act in the same protective and supportive way.

Some of Oregon Hill's residents responded to their situation by reviving the worst of the old racism. Klan leaflets have been distributed there more than once. Far worse, an African-American family that had moved into the neighborhood had their home set on fire while they slept, around the corner from where I lived in the late 1970s. (The family woke up in time to escape danger, but lost their home.) On the other hand, the Vietnam vet who sat out all night and guarded the elderly African-American couple that lived next door to the house that was burned was also a lifelong product of the neighborhood. Still, the violence that has flared up, and that is always a presence among certain groups that live in or frequent the neighborhood, has been generally undirected and ineffective in stopping change, though it has undoubtedly made African-Americans (and some whites, including eventually me) unwilling to live in or move to the neighborhood.

After enough organized pressure, the Board members of VCU were forced to take a stand. Despite his un-Richmondlike abrupt demeanor and his Northern accent, the VCU Board, though well-supplied with Old Richmond names and bloodlines, supported its President over the residents of Oregon Hill.

In many ways, the history of the fight then became one of choosing between two courses of action. One was to seek out the only reliable allies -- other low-income and working-class neighborhoods facing similar problems.

All of these other neighborhoods in Richmond were predominantly African-American. The other course of action was to retreat to the old days, and the old ways, and try to regain the old identity. In the meantime, because of its prime downtown location, the slow but steady process of gentrification kept changing the neighborhood, making it more likely that either course of action would be irrelevant.

While I lived in Oregon Hill, I took an excellent class on the sociology of racism (ironically, at VCU). The class gave me an opportunity to come to some conclusions about my experience in Oregon Hill. My conclusion was that for residents of Oregon Hill, the old system of "classical racism" provided real benefits. Modern "neo-racism," however, does much less for them. The power structure now makes its decisions on the basis of institutional needs and patterns of profit, not on the basis of a paternalistic relationship. Instead of bounty from St. Paul's, the only additional goodies now available to poor people are those they can pressure the system to give them.

Most of Oregon Hill's native residents were elderly by then. Their children had moved to the suburbs, where they benefit from segregated suburban comfort. Frequently, the elderly residents were being pressured by their adult children to come out to the wonderful suburban world, where racism still works. The modern system of racism finds it hard to give advantages to whites who do something as strange as stay in a run-down inner city neighborhood. (Though VCU did succeed in taking several blocks where African-Americans lived before it succeeded in demolishing any houses lived in by whites.)

For many of the longtime residents in Oregon Hill, while the old Klan-style racism seems ugly and risky, and the new racism gives them almost nothing, going beyond racism to ally with African-Americans seemed too difficult and risky. Oregon Hill residents were part of a city-wide alliance of neighborhoods called Richmond United Neighborhoods; I became very active in this group. I found that very few Oregon Hill residents would come to the neighborhoods they perceived as "black" to events like Board meetings and even fundraising carnivals. I finally left Oregon Hill after a confrontation, bordering on violence, with a man who had returned to the Hill to reclaim his boyhood neighborhood, and felt that Richmond United Neighborhoods represented outside interference.

Under his leadership, the neighborhood group cut off ties with other neighborhoods, to solve its own problems on its own. Rumors spread throughout the neighborhood that his supporters were willing to use violence; I certainly felt I had been threatened.

Within a year or so, that neighborhood régime had collapsed; but it took longer to put good leadership back together, and by that time a few more blocks had been lost.

I believe that the story of Oregon Hill is pretty much the story of all white Americans. As a people, we got a deal once upon a time. A deal I call Whitefare. It was one Hell of a deal; for a while, we were undeniably the richest and most powerful country in the world. A small power structure got most of the goodies, but there was plenty left over for the average white person. The average white American in most ways had it better than a lot of the kings of ancient times. The racism gravy train kept on rolling, with the benefits growing, generation after generation. Only a few prophetic voices pointed out what we were trading for our benefits.

The world always changes. No empire has lasted forever, but ours may well be one of the shortest-lived. Sometime between the oil crisis of 1973 and the fall of Saigon in 1975, the élite that has been running racism decided to change the deal, just like it was changed for Oregon Hill. Basically, they designed neo-racism. Designed is the key word, because this is Designer racism. It looks, smells, and even feels like the old system that worked for so long, but it actually delivers much less. It turns out it's cheaper to manipulate folks through television than it is to give them the world's highest standard of living.

Racism was always wrong, even though a lot of wonderful people, including my ancestors, participated in it. Now it is doing for all of us what it did for the people of Oregon Hill. It is giving us less. But it is also telling us that the reason we are getting less benefits is because the outsiders are taking them away.

In some ways, racism was always a sucker's game for the average white person. It took away dignity and independence and eventually even faith and self-respect, and that is a very high cost. It undermined our families, our communities, the Bible, the Constitution, and every other traditional source of strength in our culture.

But now racism is really a sucker's game. One percent of Americans now own 34% of all the nation's wealth, and 20 percent own 85% of all the nation's wealth. (Domhoff) They are spending billions to hire foundations, television networks, politicians, and authors to tell us white people that they are just like us. We are all white, and we all want a return back to traditional values.

Guess what. These guys aren't about to go back. These guys are not nostalgic for the old days. They aren't even nostalgic for last week, because they get richer every week. From 1979 to 2008, the wealthiest one percent had a 224% increase in wealth. The least wealthy 20% lost ground, with their net worth falling by 7%. (United for a Fair Economy, Comparing..)

Instead, they are counting on the fact that, no matter how smart we are, how bitterly angry we are at the conditions of our lives, no matter how much we love our children and our communities, we won't give up the racism deal.

And they may be right. It's not an easy deal to give up. It is almost down to our bones. It seems like it is who we are.

I began with Oregon Hill because it is the one place where I found out for myself how strong racism is. How it could distort the lives and the thoughts of good people. But it is also the place where I learned how good those people could be. How brave in fighting for a community. How generous in taking care of their neighbors. How creative in getting through the day. How delightful to talk to and listen to. I learned that racism is not all that any white person is. I learned that people like me -- white Americans -- deserve to break out of this sucker's game. We deserve to begin the process of growing up out of racism, of facing our own real history.

Fraud and Fable Number Eighteen: Virginia Politics Is Exceptionally Clean And Fair, Thanks To Virginia Tradition.

Purpose: This is not stated so much as assumed. Other places like New Jersey or Alabama have bosses and bribery, but Virginia is magically protected. This illusion of purity enables the Virginia Gentlemen to get away with more in the open that most politicians can in the back room.

Virginia has long prided itself on ethical government, but the state's lax oversight rules, weak consumer representation protections, dwindling capitol press corps and coziness between political and economic elites, have all combined to undermine the validity of that self-image. Meanwhile, the few ethics and disclosure requirements that do exist tend to be flawed, limited or fraught with exemptions and qualifications, according to state ethics experts.
And so Virginia ranks a low 47th out of 50 states, with a grade of F and a numerical score of 55 percent from the *State Integrity Investigation*, a collaborative project of the Center for Public Integrity, Global Integrity, and Public Radio International. (LaFay)

Is it optimal to have a system where the lobbyists and Executive branch have tremendous power vis-à-vis the Legislative branch, and where our Delegates and Senators barely have time to

know what they're voting on? Not in my book. Would lengthening the sessions of the Virginia General Assembly help balance this out? Along with restrictions on the activities of lobbyists, I'd argue that it's worth a try. (Feld)

These two comments reveal that Virginia politics looks a bit ugly now and then, underneath the Virginia Gentleman makeup. It's surprising, isn't it? Of course, we know about Virginia elites collaborating with one of the longest-lasting and most autocratic political bosses in U.S. history, disenfranchising almost every one in sight in 1902, and loving Robert E. Lee so much they just couldn't give up segregation even after it was illegal. Aside from the obvious stuff, though, which is just our charming legacy from the past, we all thought Virginia had clean politics.

Well, don't worry your little citizen head. The façade of Virginia Tradition will quickly slip back into place.

You see, other states just have legislatures, made up of normal human beings who do things a certain way because it makes sense, or because someone paid them off, or for some other comprehensible reason.

But Virginia has Virginia Tradition. No one at the General Assembly does anything for any evil or selfish reason; they just trot along in the sacred footsteps of Washington and Jefferson and Lee.

Chico Marx asked, in the Marx Brothers' movie Duck Soup, "Who you gonna believe, me or your own eyes?" Virginia Tradition will tell you what to believe, and it's not your own eyes.

The Virginia General Assembly: It's Farmer Friendly!

A good example is the practice that blogger Lowell Feld mentions in the second comment at the beginning of this article – the Virginia General Assembly's practice of meeting for a short session and then a shorter session, thus being on the job less than in any other state of Virginia's size.

As Feld notes, this practice keeps power in the hands of the "permanent government" of lobbyists, as well as in the hands of the governor, who is in Richmond all year and has serious resources to gather information and make his case on his issues. It is one of the many ways that political power in Virginia is centralized in the hands of a few people.

But no! That's not why Virginia has its short and shorter sessions! Just ask a member of the Virginia General Assembly, or any of the crowd that hangs out on Richmond's Capitol Hill. There's a great explanation.

As he or she responds to texts on her/his iPhone from an African-American colleague about legislation to increase high-tech employment in the formerly tobacco-producing area of Southside Virginia, sitting in an office in the recently totally refurbished General Assembly building before going to a fundraiser where hopefully the health care industry will donate her or him some of the $4.6 million or so it may have to offer, the Richmond insiders will give you this explanation:

"Back in the old days, the Virginia General Assembly only met during the winter, because during the warm months, the members had to go home and work their farms. And, this being Virginia, we just don't like to change the old way of doing things."

Norfolk political blogger Vivian Paige, calling for a full-time Virginia General Assembly in a March 2011 op-ed, refers to this justification for the current situation, writing “Ours is no longer the agrarian society of yesteryear that allows gentlemen legislators to serve between planting seasons. “

Yep. They sure don’t like to change things. That’s why the members of the General Assembly still ride in their traditional oxcarts from their home constituencies to Richmond, and only receive campaign contributions in Confederate money or doubloons while communicating with their home offices with carrier pigeons.

But let’s set aside picturesque Virginia Tradition for a moment, and see what our actual history tells us, as embodied in the various Virginia Constitutions. (We’ve had seven or so, depending on how you count them.) Because that’s where this “agrarian” requirement is – in Virginia’s Constitution, which took effect in the Olde Days in 1971.

But let’s look back to the 1776 Virginia Constitution. Lots of farmers back then, right? Well, here’s what it said about this issue:

> **“The legislative shall be formed of two distinct branches, who, together, shall be a complete Legislature. They shall meet once, or**

> **oftener, every year, and shall be called, The General Assembly of Virginia."**

Hmmm.. Perhaps in the revolutionary fervor of 1776, folks forgot about the farmers' needs. The General Assembly was apparently allowed to meet whenever it wanted, for as long as it wanted, even during harvest season.

Okay, another Virginia Constitution in 1830. Whoops. Same language.

Then another Constitution in 1850. Big changes were made, including white males without property getting the right to vote. But the General Assembly was still allowed to meet whenever they wanted -- even right in the middle of harvest season or spring planting!

Those noble sons of the soil must have been fuming at the inconvenience!

(The 1850 Constitution also affirmed the right of habeas corpus for all Virginians while also recognizing and regulating slavery. Don't try that one at home unless you are a strict contortionist.)

And so it goes. The 1870 Constitution -- still no designated dates for the session.

At last! Though generation after generation of the loyal Virginia peasantry had been plowed under while patiently waiting for this relief, the 1902 constitution finally put in place a constitutional requirement that the General Assembly meet in January for no more than 90 days. And something similar has remained in place ever since.

In other words, this "tradition" began in the 20th century, when Virginia was just starting to see a drop in the number of farmers, and Virginians had access to trains, telegraphs, and motorized machinery.

If one were a suspicious sort, one might say that the current arrangement has nothing to do with farmers at all. One might say that the arrangement is in line with the general intent of the 1902

Constitution – to reduce the power of the average Virginian, especially those of African descent, and to concentrate power in a few hands. One might suspect that the story about being nice to farmers is one that someone made up, while knowing all along the real reason for short sessions – to limit the power of citizens to influence the legislature, and increase the power of lobbyists and the Richmond inner circle of power.

Following the Money

Well, that's not democracy, but it's not corruption, right? We see corruption all the time in those northern states. Bribery, theft, selling votes. But we know that never happens in Virginia. Well, maybe once.

In the summer of 2011, long-serving Delegate Phil Hamilton was convicted in federal court of bribery and extortion. He had tried to get a state university to create a job for him. Afterwards, Governor McDonnell said, "Virginia has long been a state marked by honest, transparent and ethical governing by both parties. Today's judgment is a reminder that no one is above the law." (LaFay)

William and Mary University Professor John McGlennon commented on the State Integrity Investigation, mentioned at the top of this article. "How they can take the case of the one guy who got caught and say it proves that no one does anything wrong is beyond me...Part of the reason we identify those states like Illinois and New Jersey as more corrupt is because they have more rules identifying corrupt behavior." (LaFay)

Virginia has no cap on donations to legislators, and allows corporations to donate to campaigns, a practice that is illegal in federal elections. It also has rather vague requirements for lobbyist disclosure.

Speaking of disclosure, I have been a registered lobbyist under Virginia law a couple of times over the years, while working for the Virginia Housing Coalition and later Virginia Organizing. The latter group spent just over $20,000 in 2009-2010 on lobbying, mostly to pay its lobbyists, and spent nothing for gifts or entertainment. (To put that in perspective, that's 1.5% of what one corporation, Dominion Power, spent on lobbying the Virginia General Assembly in the same time period.) (Virginia Public Access Project)

Information for Citizens

If you want to believe your own eyes, instead of the stories of Virginia Tradition, there are some good resources.

One is www.vpap.org, the website of the Virginia Public Access Project (VPAP). VPAP works with two related organizations to keep Virginians able to find out what their governments (state and local) are up to. It has a great website where you can find out pretty much anything that has been reported by lobbyists, legislators, and candidates in Virginia politics.

The Virginia Coalition for Open Government, one of VPAP's partners, has a board representing "the state's access activists and friends of open government, including Virginia's librarians, genealogists, broadcasters, newspapers and the public at large." Its focus is on the Freedom of Information Act as applied to local and state government in Virginia.

The third group is Richmond Sunlight, "a non-partisan website that aggregates information about the General Assembly." You can learn what the General Assembly is up to, and also what various bloggers, newspapers, and others think it is up to.

I Can See It, But I Can't Fix It

Those three organizations focus on helping Virginians to understand our government. And they can help you rapidly and efficiently get all the information available about what is going on.

But what if you want to change what is going on? What if you just want to change how much you get to know about what is going on?

Well, that's a problem. The traditional "good government" groups don't really operate here. For example, Virginia no longer has a state branch of the watchdog group Common Cause.

So what's going on while there is no public integrity watchdog here in Virginia?

In contrast to relatively penniless public interest groups like Virginia Organizing, the VPAP site shows that the largest eight lobbyists at the Virginia General Assembly in 2010-2011 together spent $1.8 million. All eight represented private industry, if one includes the Koch Brothers-associated group

Americans for Prosperity in that category.

The largest two donors provide an interesting picture of the history of the Virginia Gentleman. The largest was Altria, which is of course tobacco giant Philip Morris's new name; Altria donated almost $329,000 from the industry that is Virginia's oldest producer of wealthy people. Second at just under $312,000 is the Northern Virginia Technology Council, representing Virginia's best shot at Silicon Valley, and a source of new wealth, much of from high-tech contracts from federal agencies.

A small part of Altria's spending -- about as much as the total lobbying budget of Virginia Organizing – was spent to fly Governor McDonnell and two aides to the Republican Governors Association. Presumably that included plenty of time to schmooze in comfortable surroundings thousands of feet in the air above the common folk.

Hard-headed corporate folks felt it was worth putting almost two million bucks into influencing the Virginia General Assembly. We can be sure they were getting something for this.

Were they buying votes? Well, if it matters to you, everybody denies that's happening. You see, that would be contrary to the Virginia Tradition.

In 1980 and 1981, I worked at the Richmond City Jail. While there, I talked to the few white collar criminals there. Every one of them could explain in detail why he was not guilty, and how everyone else did exactly what he had done. I am sure that's the prevailing attitude in Virginia's legislature. They probably all believe they are honest.

And so do we. That belief has be worth a fortune to Virginia's genuinely corrupt legislators. I wish I had some moral X-ray vision that would allow me to see, in dollars and cents, what they are getting away with. I am sure that the carefully cultivated "clean" reputation of the Virginia General Assembly provides cover for millions of dollars worth of activities that could not bear the light of day.

But in the metaphorical shade of the Old Dominion's magnolias, who really knows what is going on?

Stealing in Plain Sight: Power to the Few

Elsewhere in these Notes, I have illuminated the Virginia Gentleman's habit of keeping power in few hands.

In this, as in so much else, the Virginia Gentleman's strengths are those of the con-artist. The con-artist, of course, steals from you in plain sight, smiling the whole time, seeming to include you in the joke, but actually holding you in contempt the whole time.

While I am sure there is plenty of good ole-time stealing going in Virginia's political circles, it may not really be needed. The deck was openly stacked before the game began, and the unfairness was explained to you in such pretty terms that you accepted it, smiling even as you shook your head.

In the 1600s, the deck was stacked in favor of aristocracy. Even then, it wasn't too hard to figure out that the Virginia gentry weren't real gentry. But they had the reins of power, including the cruel penal system and the one sure way of getting wealthy – bringing in a big tobacco crop. And they had the means to dole out favors. By the end of Virginia's first century, they had established the basic system that Virginia Gentlemen have tried to keep in place ever since.

That system appears to fit the social science concept of patrimonialism. Sociologist Julia Adams, a widely recognized authority on this system, contrasts it to the 'machinery' of a modern bureaucratic state:

> **"Patrimonialism is more like a manor house with, one would suppose, particularly extensive grounds. Patrimonial rulers cite "age-old rules and powers" – sacred tradition – as the basis of their political authority. Their power is discretionary, and the line between persons and offices notional."**
> (Adams)

This "P" word is not the total explanation of Virginia's politics. Of course our Commonwealth has elements of rational bureaucracy, of corporate capitalism, and now and then even of populist democracy. But patrimonialism does capture the ideal pretty well– the system the Virginia Gentleman aspires to. Of course, every claim of "sacred tradition" that he has ever appealed to was phony at best. But, you know what? The kings and dukes of medieval Europe, the pharaohs of ancient Egypt, the emperors of Rome -- they were liars and bullies too.

Erroneous Yankee Political Notions Like Democracy

As The Confederacy came into existence, "many conservative southern politicians ... saw 1861 as the moment to reverse ... democratic tendencies." Historian Drew Gilpin Faust, in The Creation of Confederate Nationalism writes that "perhaps the fullest expression of such sentiments appeared in Virginia." A Virginia committee proposed restricting the vote to taxpayers, and proposed "a constitution far less democratic than that which had been in force." The universal male suffrage and increased direct election of officials that western Virginians had pushed for were now characterized as "erroneous Yankee political notions." (Faust)

In 1901, Virginia Gentlemen were again in a position to frame how Virginia worked, after having been forced for thirty years to be at least somewhat accommodating to federal troops, organized African-Americans, national Republican politics, and the Readjuster movement. They began to write a new constitution truly to their liking.

Historian Jeremy Boggs, in his thesis on the convention that wrote this constitution, summarized its purpose well: “the 1902 constitutional convention’s primary motivation was the disenfranchisement of black Virginians and the constitutional reassertion of white racial dominance in Virginia society.” Boggs points out that by making this their explicit goal, the constitutional planners “revealed how unstable their racial world had become,” and that they felt a need to respond to “the increasing presence and assertion of power by black Virginians.” (Boggs)

Those who fought for the 1902 Constitution claimed it would clean up what had become a notoriously corrupt Virginia political system. The logic here was that corruption had been the only way to keep Black voting power in check. If Black voting was eliminated, elections could be conducted honestly.

(Yeah, read that last sentence again.)

Most importantly, the white power structure would no longer get involved in factionalism resulting from the Black vote and Republican power. "Progressive reform," then, meant something very different in Virginia than it did in the Midwestern hotbeds of populism. As Boggs wrote,

> **Progressivism in Virginia included not only a promotion of industrialism and business expansion, it also promoted a paternalistic social reform embodied in 'strong, able-bodied' political and social leaders who made decisions for the good of their constituents. Progressive reform, then, took shape in strong, centralized government and state intervention ..... Exclusively white, these paternalists in Virginia saw themselves as**

> **the champions of the glory of 'Old Virginia' and the guardians of social and cultural morality. Of course, this morality hinged upon the establishment of 'proper' race relations that kept the white population 'pure' through segregation. Virginia's progressives embodied a paternalistic view of race relations, a view that embraced white superiority as the bulwark of civilization.** (Boggs)

In other words, the reforms of the 1902 Constitution were by, for and on behalf of the Virginia Gentleman.

As the twentieth century wore on, the tools that the 1902 Constitution put in place – the poll tax, the grandfather clause, and tests of voters – were eroded away. But this erosion happened slowly over decades, and Virginia's élite made the shifts they needed to stay in power. The Democratic Party managed to integrate liberal ideas – especially inclusion of some African-American and women and even gay leaders – without succumbing to any kind of populism. At the same time, the main elements of the Byrd Organization moved into and took over the Republican Party, re-organizing it as a firm defender of white supremacy, business power, and patriarchal taboos.

Together, these two conservative parties have kept in place a "pro-business" environment in Virginia. Among other things, this means that the 20% of Virginians who have the lowest incomes, with an average income of $11,100, pay 8.9% of their income in state and local taxes. At the other end of the spectrum, according to the Institute for Tax and Economic Policy, the 1% of Virginians with the highest incomes (averaging $1,557,700 annually) pay only 5.2% of their income in state and local taxes. It also means that 11 major corporations that are headquartered in Virginia (including General Dynamics, Altria (formerly Philip Morris), Dominion Resources, Norfolk Southern, and Capital One) all paid 5.4% or less of their profits from 2008 through 2010 in Virginia taxes. (Institute for Tax and Economic Policy)

So that's "clean government" in Virginia. Whether or not anyone is stealing much in the strict sense – and we Virginians really have no way of knowing if they are – there is no question that the Virginia Gentleman has organized his system to protect and increase his wealth and his interests.

Fraud and Fable Number Nineteen: Virginia Is And Always Has Been Fair And Moderate In Punishing Crime

Purpose: Virginia's leaders avoid harsh, violent, or obviously racist rhetoric in talking about crime. But Virginia has been and still is a national leader in cruel and unfair punishment, especially of African-Americans.

First, A Suburban Vision

A little nostalgia for those of you who have lived in the mostly white suburbs here in Virginia – Virginia Beach, Fairfax County, Chesterfield County and the like.

It's a nice Saturday afternoon. The little kids are lumbering up and down the sidewalk in their Big Wheels. A few young teens are practicing skateboard tricks. Homeowners are mowing their lawns. A few outdoor grills are powering up.

Suddenly three black SUVs screech around the corner, and the SWAT team is at the door of the house across the street. In seconds, there's a chopper overhead. And within minutes, three of your neighbors are coming out of the house in handcuffs with the SWAT team's guns trained on them.

Yeah, you must remember that. After all, 1 out of every 270 Virginians is serving time in Virginia's prisons right now; 1 out of every 91 Virginians is in the Department of Corrections system, in prison or on probation or parole. Once you add in all the Virginians in federal prisons, and all those who have already served their time, and those who were arrested and not convicted, the statistics would suggest every Virginia neighborhood of a couple hundred folks must have seen a bust. Right?

Or we could look at it a little differently. According to the 2009 Community Health Status Indicators issued by the US Department of Health and Human Services, there were an estimated 68,294 recent drug users in Fairfax County. Since 54.6% of the people in Fairfax County are non-Hispanic whites, and since drug use is endemic in roughly equal proportions among all racial and ethnic groups, presumably there are around 37,000 recent non-Hispanic white drug users in Fairfax County. Surely a lot of them must be homeowners living on quiet cul de sacs, and they must get arrested, right?

Or not.

We all know the real story -- at least vaguely. But here are the official details. Of Virginia's state prisoners, as reported at the end of 2011, about

18,900, or 61.5%, were African-American, and about 10,900, or 35.7%, were white.

PRISON POPULATION

But only 19.4% of Virginians are African-American, while 68.6% are white.

TOTAL POPULATION

In other words, African-American imprisonment rates are about three times as high as their representation in the population, while whites are imprisoned at about half their representation in the population.

> **"Are the percentages of prisoners evidence of the extent of actual criminal conditions, or of the extent to which such criminals are punished?... the native whites have the administration of the law, the advantage of education and of wealth ... the negro is generally too impecunious to provide for and prepare his defense and to prevent imposition of the jail sentence after conviction by payment of the fine and costs."**(Southern Sociological Congress, 1912)

Punishment in the Old Dominion

Virginia, as the state where the U.S.A.'s system of racism was invented, was a pioneer of our nation's bizarre and bloated modern penal system. The first three and a half centuries of that story was told by Paul Keve, once a professor at Virginia Commonwealth University, in The History of Corrections in

Virginia (University of Virginia Press, 1986).

Keve describes the penal system in the earliest period of European settlement of Virginia as consisting "of severe corporal punishments and hangings." As of 1612, hanging was "the first penalty for nearly half the defined offenses.."

Race-based slavery included an even more brutal system for those designated as hereditary slaves. Even when the Revolution brought various ideas for reforming prisons, these could not be harmonized with the status of "persons who already had no real freedom that could be restricted, ... no real rights that could be abridged." Punishment of slaves could only be "punishment inflicted directly on the person."

In 1692, a special system of local courts was set up to try slaves for capital offenses. Then a 1705 law stated that "owners" who killed a slave while punishing her or him were not guilty of any crime.

FLOWER OF TOXIC "JIMSON" OR "JAMESTOWN" WEED

Any striking back against masters was punished with special cruelty. In 1746, Eve, a woman in Orange County, was burned alive for poisoning her "owner." In 1763, Tom, who shot and killed his "owner," was hanged and had his head affixed on a pole.

The First Reform

The first notable Virginia prison reformer, active during Jefferson's life and an associate of Virginia Founders, was George Keith Taylor, a member of the Virginia House of Delegates from Dinwiddie County. Taylor introduced a comprehensive penal code proposal and saw it passed in 1796. It was based to some extent on the ideas of the Italian reformer Cesare Beccaria. Beccaria was one of the first known advocates of prevention, rather than punishment, in Europe. The Italian thinker also opposed torture and capital punishment.

By accepting Taylor's proposals, Virginia found itself in the company of states like Pennsylvania, where the penitentiary idea was transforming thinking about prisons. Penitentiaries, as the name suggests, were intended to be places where those accused of crimes learned and practiced penitence. In 1800, Virginia opened the State Penitentiary in Richmond, based roughly on this model. However, despite the liberal thinking of Taylor, Jefferson and others, Virginia's penal system soon began to resemble others in the South more than those in the North. (Keve)

The Use of Laborers in Bondage

After the defeat of the Confederacy, convict labor became key to the prison systems of the South. It was a major means of racial control, as well as a way for wealthy whites to obtain cheap labor in lieu of slavery. Virginia was not as committed to this practice as Deep South states were, but in general, "with their vast experience in the use of laborers in bondage, the southern state governments easily applied slave status to the prisoner class…" By 1893, in Virginia 500 African-American men were working as convict labor for a granite quarry and three railroads. In that year one of 667 African-Americans was in prison, but only one out of every 5,000 Virginia whites. Some of the convict workers worked barefoot and sick; beatings were common; and death rates were high. (Keve)

Convict labor practices clearly showed slavery's legacy. Joseph Anderson, who used convict labor in his barrel-making company in the 1880s and 1890s, was the son of the president of the pre-war Tredegar Iron Works, which had rented large numbers of slaves as workers. And one group of convicts was assigned to help build the monument to honor Lost Cause icon Robert E. Lee.

By 1900, convicts were working less often for private firms, while many were working on highway projects out of road camps around the state.

Like the rest of Virginia society, the prison system was racially segregated. Black prisoners outnumbered white prisoners four to one. Beatings and bizarre forms of torture were regularly practiced to punish any unwanted behavior.

Twentieth Century Changes

The early twentieth century saw a lot of modernization of the Virginia prison system. More provisions were made for women in the system, and for the first time children were put in their own institutions separate from the general prison population. (The institutions for African-American boys and girls were established only by the hard work of African-American civic leaders, who raised private money to supplement state funding.)

In the 1940s, change began to come to the Virginia correctional system. Corporal punishment was formally banned, and parole and probation were put into place. Standards were put in place for local jails, which had been really atrocious institutions.

Killing by Virginia

Virginia has had the death penalty, as noted above, from its colonial beginnings. According to the Death Penalty Information Center, the first execution in what is now the United States took place in Virginia in 1608, and since then Virginia has executed more people than any other state – 1,386 at last count. Those receiving Virginia's death penalty have overwhelmingly been Black men. Most of these people went to their deaths with little public attention to their cases. But a little more than a century ago, newly emerging forces among African-Americans, socialists, and liberals began to pay attention to, and to try to influence, Virginia's habit of killing.

In 1895, four African-Americans were charged with participating in the murder of a white neighbor lady in a tiny rural community in Lunenburg County. Two women and a man faced hanging and a third woman a prison term. The newly organized women's movement in Virginia's African-American community, especially in Richmond, came to their defense, along with John Mitchell, publisher of the African-American newspaper, the Richmond Planet. Mitchell hired highly reputable white lawyers, but the funds to pay them came from African-Americans. Suzanne Lebsock, in A Murder in Virginia, notes that "vulnerable themselves, and many of them born in rural places like Lunenburg, Richmond's everyday working women identified profoundly" with the women defendants.

WOMEN TOBACCO WORKERS, RICHMOND 1899

Ultimately, the two women at risk of the death penalty were both found not guilty; the man, who does seem to have some kind of involvement with the crime, was hanged, and the other woman did serve time in prison. Given the times, Lebsock's statement that "Black people, as a people, won this one" is accurate. (Lebsock)

Perhaps the first Virginia death penalty case to draw national attention was that of Odell Waller. In the early 1940s, Waller, an African-American sharecropper killed a white man in a dispute, possibly in self-defense, and almost certainly without premeditation, also in a small rural community, this one in Pittsylvania County. A jury of white men, mostly landlords, quickly convicted him, and he was sentenced to death. This case also drew the attention of various national and statewide groups. African-American, liberal and socialist organizations came to his defense. Despite factional disagreements, they did manage to delay, but ultimately not to prevent, his 1942 execution. Waller's case became nationally known as his elderly mother traveled across the nation talking about it.

> **You take big people as the President, governors, judges, their children will never have**

to suffer. They have plenty money. Born in a mansion, nothing to ever worry about. I am glad some people are that lucky. The penitentiaries all over the United States are full of people who were poor tried to work and have something, couldn't do it, that made them steal and rob. from Odell Waller's dying statement – with some changes to make the language more accessible. (Sherman)

In 1949, seven African-American men in Martinsville raped a white woman. When all seven received the death penalty, their case also drew widespread protests. As with Waller's case, national African-American, liberal and socialist organizations took action.

The Virginia Supreme Court of Appeals today agreed to review the cases of seven Martinsville Negroes sentenced to death for rape. The seven are, left to right, Booker T. Millner, Frank Hairston, Jr., Howard Lee Hairston, Joe Henry Hampton, John Clabon Taylor, Francis DeSales Grayson, and James Luther Hairston.

Nevertheless, all seven were executed in February, 1951.

Rape was a capital crime when African-American men were convicted of it in Virginia and other Southern states. Virginia has executed 122 African-American men for rape and 28 for attempted rape. Only three white men have been executed for rape by the Commonwealth of Virginia -- in 1626, 1775, and 1868. Virginia last executed a Black man solely for the crime of rape in 1961. (Death Penalty Information Center)

Since the Waller case, Virginians have continued to protest state killing. In the 1970s, members of the Prisoner Solidarity Committee regularly protested at the penitentiary, then the scene of executions. In 1991 what is now Virginians for Alternatives to the Death Penalty (VADP) was formed and has been active since. Today, there is widespread belief that the death penalty is racist, ineffective and immoral, and there are vigils at every Virginia execution, some larger and some smaller depending on the particular case.

Nevertheless, Virginia has continued to vigorously apply the death penalty. According to the VADP, since the death penalty was reinstituted in 1976, Virginia has executed more people than any state but Texas. (Texas has about three times the population of Virginia.)

Also, Virginia rushes to judgment, settling death penalty cases in an average of 295 days, more quickly than any other state. And racial disparity, of course, continues; the Virginia Joint Legislative Audit and Review Commission of Capital Punishment found that a person is over three times as likely to be sentenced to death when the victim is white vs. when the victim is black. (Virginians for Alternatives to the Death Penalty)

More Twentieth Century Changes

In 1976, a new kind of facility for Virginia was opened in Mecklenburg County – a rural prison that was not a farm or work camp. In the past, prison planners had felt urban locations were best, both for recruiting qualified staff and for facilitating families visiting prisoners. But "prison planners ... were faced with intense resistance to prisons [in urban areas]... while ... rural communities with depressed economies were interested in acquiring any such institution." (Keve)

The Mecklenburg Correctional Center was designed to provide greater security and control than other facilities, and initially included Virginia's death row. The American Civil Liberties Union filed suit against the facility and forced some changes. However, Mecklenburg's design was an indicator of the direction the prison system would take in the last years of the twentieth century.

As control of Virginia politics moved back to the right, parole was abolished in 1995 in a grandstanding move by Governor George "Macaca" Allen. Judith Greene describes Allen's program in her article "Entrepreneurial Corrections" in the 2002 book Invisible Punishment: The Collateral Consequences of Mass Imprisonment. Allen organized a Commission on Parole Abolition and Sentencing Reform, which held town meetings across Virginia, "taking emotion-charged testimony from victims of violent crime." Allen estimated that his actions to lengthen sentences would require 8,100 new prison beds, and six new prisons were built with about that many cells. (Chesney-Lind)

In 1998 and 1999, two of these especially cruel "supermax" prisons Red Onion and Wallens Ridge, were opened in far Southwest Virginia. Red Onion was built on land donated by the Pittston Coal Company. Wallens Ridge "was financed by ... bonds issued by the Big Stone Gap Housing and Redevelopment Authority." These prisons were clearly endorsed by the powers that be in that region.

> **I was leg-shackled, cuffed from behind and "escorted" by a mob of guards to the D-3 housing unit. Every cell in the unit was empty. I was put into D-301, one of only two cells in the block with a steel box approximately 8" x 12" x 18" with a Plexiglas cover, welded to the outside of a cell door and around the opening in the door through which food and other items are passed and handcuffs applied and removed. I was made to kneel to have the leg shackles removed, and to put my hands outside the slot into the box where the handcuffs were removed. I then removed my hands from the box and a steel plate was slid in place across the door opening, closing off access to the box. (Johnson)**

It turned out the Allen administration's guesses about increased prison cell needs were wrong by about half. The decision was made to "rent" prison space to other states, and by the end of 1999, more than 3,000 out of state prisoners were in Virginia prisons.

Solidly documented bases of abuse have happened to out of state prisoners, especially at Wallens Ridge. Greene describes both Wyoming and the Virgin Islands sending "ill-behaved prisoners" to Virginia, suggesting that Virginia's abusive prison system is seen as "the convenient solution to management problems" by other states. (Chesney-Lind)

Virginia's jails, which are locally controlled institutions, generally for prisoners serving less than one year, have also jumped on this trend, especially by housing federal prisoners for a fee. In fiscal year 2009, 10.6 percent of all Virginia jail inmates were federal prisoners, according to a 2010 report from the Department of Criminal Justice Services. Many, if not most, are undocumented immigrants; frequently, they were picked up for minor offenses that would not have led to jail time except for their immigration status. (Virginia Department of Criminal Justice Services)

Profiling: The Entry Point

Some people in prison are there because they were "caught in the act." Many others caught the unwelcome attention of a law enforcement officer when they weren't engaged in any significant law-breaking, often because of their apparent race or ethnic or religious background, or because they live in a neighborhood with such a background.

Discretionary stops, like those for traffic offenses, are those made according to the judgment of an officer. Legally, there must be a minor crime of sorts taking place, or some sign that there is, but in the case of a minor crime, the officer has discretion to act or not.

This is unlike the situation where the officer sees a burglary or assault taking place and must intervene. These discretionary actions are the point at which many people enter the criminal justice system.

In some cases, someone happens to live in a neighborhood that is targeted by law enforcement, and gets caught in a chain of events that leads to prison. It's common in Black and Latino neighborhoods for there to be mass drug arrests. In the nature of things, some people picked up are serious drug dealers, while others are minor players, or just users. But once you are charged in one of these busts, usually with a conspiracy charge along with other charges, the process plays out according to rules that have nothing to do with who actually did what.

Because it's pretty typical for sentences of twenty or thirty years or more to result from these cases, there is a lot of pressure to inform on others arrested with you. This is true whether or not you actually have any information. Within hours after the bust, the horse-trading begins. The last one to offer information the officers involved want loses and gets the longest prison term.

Either way, human biases ensure that , from this very first step in the criminal justice process, unfairness creeps in.

I have often heard law enforcement officers express confidence in their judgment and fairness, and I am sure there are some who are exceedingly wise. But most Virginia officers are pretty typical Virginians – and typical of the United States in general. And as the New York Times noted in 1999 "Cops .... [are] not the only ones who profile. Civilians profile all the time--when they buy a house, or pick a school district, or walk down the street." (Goldberg) Law enforcement officers are as likely as anyone else to tend to believe that people in a certain neighborhood or of a certain color are drug users, even though research has established this as false. And of course, it's a lot easier and more acceptable to arrest and convict dark-skinned or poor drug users.

Nor are prosecutors, judges, and even defense attorneys free of bias. It only takes a certain bias at each step to achieve the results cited above, the massive over-representation of African-American men in Virginia's prisons.

From 2004 to 2010, while working for what is now Virginia Organizing, I staffed a campaign against racial profiling and talked to numerous officers about the issue. I heard everything from a realistic view that profiling is happening to total denial – sometimes from the same department. I also found out that the leadership of the Commonwealth of Virginia is just as ambivalent on this issue – and just as unwilling to take any serious action.

Profiling, of course, has a long history in Virginia. A 1785 statute, passed during the administration of Governor "Give me liberty or give me death" Patrick Henry, included this language, establishing racial profiling as a vital local function:

> **"...the commanding officer of the militia in every county, shall from time to time, as he shall deem it necessary, appoint an officer, and so**

> **many men of the militia as to him shall appear necessary, not exceeding four, once in every month, or oftener, if thereto required by such officer, to patrole and visit all negro quarters and other places suspected of entertaining unlawful assemblies of slaves, servants, or other disorderly persons, as aforesaid, unlawfully assembled, or any others strolling about from one plantation to another, without a pass from his or her master, mistress, or owner, and carry them before the next justice of the peace..”** (Virginia General Assembly 1785)

Some African-Americans still refer to the police as “paddy-rollers” or “rollers,” from the old terms for “patrol.” Of course, in that day, profiling was not only approved of, but required. If the patrol happened to profile a free African-American, or a white person of suspiciously African appearance, the burden was on them to prove they were not slaves. Race was evidence of guilt of being where you were not supposed to be, unless you could prove otherwise.

Like other race-based practices, the aggressive patrolling of “negro quarters and other places," and the detention of persons of colors "strolling about" without the sanction of a white person, have not disappeared over the years, just changed in tone and method. Plenty of studies across the nation have shown that people of color are treated differently by law enforcement in discretionary situations. However, there are no such studies in Virginia, because the Virginia Gentleman has shown he has no interest in knowing the facts.

The first official step against racial profiling in Virginia was taken by the General Assembly's Joint Subcommittee Studying the Status and Needs of African-American Males in Virginia, established in 1996. A statewide symposium by the Subcommittee led in 1999 to legislation creating "a joint committee to study traffic stops of minority drivers and certain other police practices." (Virginia Advisory Committee) Unfortunately, this only led to a survey of "the chief law enforcement officer of each locality" by the Virginia State Police. (Massengill) The people who are actually profiled – people of color -- were not surveyed. Unsurprisingly, the survey's result was, according to the Associated Press, "that bias was not seen by local officials as a significant problem, but most of those officials agreed that state guidelines would help correct the perception that significant problems did exist." (Buettner)

Governor Mark Warner came into office in 2002 on a campaign pledge to "...put an end to racial profiling. First, he [would] order a continuing review of the frequency of racial profiling." (Mark Warner 2001) This has been done in other states by asking officers to record the race of people they stop. Studies based on reporting of traffic stops by officers have proved to be a useful tool in other states, not only to demonstrate profiling exists but to better understand how and when it happens. For example, in many cases, people of color are not stopped more often, but once they are stopped are more likely to have their cars searched. Where this is known, action can be taken to remedy the problem.

Neither Warner nor his successors have "ordered" any such study, though it seems clear that the Governor could order the State Police to do this, and might be able to persuade at least some larger localities to do the same.

But what Warner got instead were "draft model training guidelines," and eventually a 2004 study, Bias-Based Policing. (Center for Government and Public Affairs)

This study provides some very valuable, and sometimes surprising, information. The information comes from telephone surveys with almost 400 Virginia residents and almost 1600 law enforcement officers in more than 30 departments, as well as from focus groups of both ordinary Virginia residents and law enforcement officers. For example, 61.9% of Virginians surveyed answered "Yes" to the question -- "Do you think the police should collect information pertaining to bias-based policing?" This is precisely what no Virginia law enforcement official, nor any statewide elected official, has been willing to call for.

In addition,"42.8% of respondents felt that bias-based policing is presently practiced in Virginia police departments." Not only that, but about one of five officers interviewed were found to "believe officers in their department currently practice bias-based policing."

Unfortunately, the so-called "conclusions" of the report bear little relation to the findings of the surveys, and read as if they were dictated to fit a law enforcement agenda before the facts were gathered. In unpublished comments on the report I did for Virginia Organizing, I noted that the conclusions section suggests "that data collection on traffic stops is not a useful tool for preventing biased policing, that data collection is just a 'politically correct' idea, and that 'interest groups and the media' are undermining efforts to deal with constructively with biased policing." Not one of these claims was based on data that was collected.

And as for the media fanning the flames, I got some experience with this in 2007. A collection of raw numbers from the State Police came out which everyone agreed really didn't prove anything, but sparked a discussion. So what were the "inflammatory" headlines from the not "constructive" media? The same article by reporter Mark Bowers ran in several Virginia papers. The Daily Progress from liberal Charlottesville ran it under the headline "Racial profiling on Virginia's highways – real or perceived." The more conservative Richmond Times Dispatch ran it under "Racial Profiling: Real or Not?" (Bowes)

In other words, white Virginia media and politicians have not advanced beyond questioning whether racial profiling even exists.

The Commission on Accreditation for Law Enforcement Agencies (CALEA) is an international body that offers law enforcement agencies the opportunity to become more professional by being accredited. It was formed in 1979 by four major law enforcement bodies, including the International Association of Chiefs of Police and the National Sheriffs' Association. It has an extensive list of standards that must be met for accreditation, numbered from 1.1.1 to 91.4.1. Number 1.2.9 speaks to "biased policing," the term most law enforcement folks use for racial and religious profiling. To meet this standard, a law enforcement agency must do four things, one of which is training all its staff on the issue, and one of which is conducting "a documented annual administrative review of agency practices including citizen concerns." This does not suggest that CALEA believes "biased policing" is a nonexistent problem, but rather that it is a problem that needs annual attention and effort. (Commission on Accreditation for Law Enforcement Agencies)

More importantly, the organizations that represent the people who are profiled are clear that racial profiling exists. In a December 2011 statement, the national NAACP stated "In light of the overwhelming evidence that racial profiling continues to be employed today," it was endorsing the End Racial Profiling Act, legislation currently before Congress.(NAACP)

Another small but strong force for the End Racial Profiling Act is a national organization that I really respect – largely because it has a strong commitment to grassroots organizing. The Rights Working Group is headquartered in DC, but is connected to people working in African-American, Latino, South Asian, Muslim and other communities of color to oppose racial profiling. Among its fifty national members, organizations that clearly see fighting racial profiling as a priority, are the ACLU, Amnesty International, the Council on American-Islamic Relations, the Japanese American Citizens League, and the National Council of La Raza. (Rights Working Group)

Not only are these organizations reputable representatives of millions of U.S. citizens, they are organizations that don't have the time or energy to take on imaginary issues.

I call myself a skeptic, but I don't classify the resistance of the Virginia Gentleman to the existence of racial profiling as real skepticism. Rather, their denial reflects the power balance in Virginia. Whites in power feel no need to respect facts that people of color experience as real every day.

Since the 2007 kerfuffle, there has been no significant action at the state level on this issue. Governor Kaine was urged to at least require the State Police to collect data on traffic stops, but he never did so.

Virginia local law enforcement agencies are required by the Department of Criminal Justice Services to train their officers not to carry out racial profiling, and some take this more seriously than others. Some agencies have integrated the CALEA standards into their operations, implicitly accepting the reality of racial profiling, but none to my knowledge collects data to evaluate the problem.

As some white Virginians have become increasingly uptight about the unprecedented Hispanic population in the Commonwealth, police bias towards this group has become a bigger issue in Virginia.

Some localities in the Shenandoah Valley were quick to ally with Bush Administration officials to set up processes to arrest and deport immigrants. The police departments of most urban localities at first resisted targeting immigrants, recognizing this would lead not only to racial profiling but to an inability to get police cooperation from the immigrant population.

Under the Obama Administration, with the expansion of the Secure Communities program, marketed as milder than prior immigration enforcement, this situation deteriorated. As a result of the October 2009 "Memorandum Of Agreement Between U.S. Department of Homeland Security, Immigration And Customs Enforcement And Virginia State Police Criminal Justice Information Services," all law enforcement in Virginia is connected into the immigrant enforcement process. (Turner) Arlington County attempted to opt out of the process, and was told they could not legally do so. (Stout)

When today's "paddy rollers" approach a group of dark-skinned people in Virginia and start making arrests, those people aren't going back to a plantation. But they are often going into what Michele Alexander has described as The New Jim Crow of her book of that name. (Alexander, Michele) Some of them may end up in for-profit prisons. Some may end up in hundreds of miles from home behind the walls of Red Onion or Wallens Ridge. And some of the immigrants will essentially vanish, their families knowing only that they are gone but having no contact with them, while they wait in indefinite detention to be "sent back" to a country that often is no longer home.

It angers me to see another generation of young people of color assigned to our massive prison system. But I also feel pain for their parents and grandparents, some of whom I know well. I am thinking of people I have come to know who were born in a time of open and unembarrassed segregation, and who have struggled up from that time to respectability and even professional status, only to see their children fall into another pit that looks just as deep. Each time their children or grandchildren leave home, they never know if one officer's "discretion" will take that child away for years to come.

Michele Alexander's The New Jim Crow, mentioned above, not only diagnoses our terrible national practice of mass incarceration, but lays out the necessity of a movement to oppose it. Other steps, like the mobilization around the End Racial Profiling Act, are also signs of hope. But we have a long way back up from this pit.

Changes in Hell

Virginia is on the cutting edge of the new era of the prison-industrial complex, the "New Jim Crow" of drug war incarceration, and the horrors of supermax solitary confinement, as well as a leader in the merciless use of the death penalty. From the point of view of nations with modern humane standards, including all members of the European Community, Virginia is comparable to Iran or China in its penal practices, and not much ahead of where it was in 1612.

Almost every prisoner has a family that is suffering with that prisoner. Virginia's prison policies have made family contact harder, by putting prisoners much farther from population centers. Not only families, but communities, feel the absence of people who were not only "criminals," but also friends, employees, and consumers. And this impact is, of course, far from evenly shared in different communities and populations across the Commonwealth.

Virginia is also one of the four least welcoming states for the ex-felon – the person who has paid the dues society and the judge required. In Maine and Vermont, a felony conviction has no impact on citizen rights, and in 38 states, those rights are restored automatically on completion of their sentences, according to the National Conference of State Legislatures.

Virginia, though, is far more vindictive. As Marc Mauer writes in another article in Invisible Punishment, "an eighteen-year-old convicted of a one-time drug sale in Virginia who successfully completes a court-ordered treatment program and is never arrested again has permanently lost his voting [and other] rights" unless that person gets a statement restoring those rights from Virginia's Governor. In one two year period, out of more than 200,000 Virginia ex-felons, 404 had their rights restored. (Chesney-Lind)

Over the last four centuries, Virginia's system of legal punishment has gone through several changes of theory and of style. Consistently, though, Virginia prisons have played a key part in the race-based system of domination initiated here more than three centuries ago. Whether embodied in the legal burning to death of a woman or the terrifying living conditions of a man in a Supermax, the message is clear. There is a special Hell on earth that is reserved for Virginia's African-Americans who are singled out for the "justice" of the Commonwealth. And every African-American family must consider the possibility that one of its members may be among those singled out.

Fraud and Fable Number Twenty: Virginia Owes No Reparations For Its Past.

Purpose: The Virginia Gentleman takes credit for the good things from the past – the Revolution, culture, natural beauty – but refuses to be accountable for the past crimes that have enriched him.

Is it not a principle of common sense ... that the victor in a civil war, as well as in an international conflict, has a right to protect himself against immediate and prospective danger?

Is it not the very height of insanity to say that the Government of the United States has no right to provide for the future security of the Republic, because the defeated Rebels regain all their rights at the moment of their failure, and by the very fact of their defeat? (Schurz)

No more auction block for me
No more, no more.
No more auction block for me
Many thousand gone.
African-American postwar song.

In April, 1944, a Free French speaker, broadcasting from London, warned the French people who had collaborated with Nazis, "You are known, catalogued, labeled.." When you face justice, he continued, "You'll turn green, sweat will pour from your forehead and down your back; you'll be taken away and, a few days

> **after that, you'll be nothing more than a small heap of garbage.... "** (Lottman)

Were the crimes of more than two centuries of slavery less than those of four years of Nazi occupation of France? Did it make sense to unconditionally forgive those who led the conspiracy to keep slavery known as the "government" of the Confederacy?

Why Reparations Hasn't Happened Yet

From the moment the "Confederate" rebellion was crushed, the slave owners were on the path to regaining most of their power. The former slaves had to fight to save any of the freedom they had won. White Northerners still saw white Southerners, even the most overt and obvious traitors, as more "American" than African-Americans. There can be little question that, for example, people who were serving in the U.S. Army and then took up arms against it, like Robert Lee, could have been tried and executed by courts martial. But the political will to take such steps was just not there. Reconciling with Southern whites as quickly as possible was the highest value for Northern whites. The federal troops that were intended to hold off the restoration of a racial system that had been in place for more than two centuries were withdrawn after a dozen years.

When Jim Crow was defeated, the situation was somewhat similar. By the time of the last civil rights law of the period, the 1968 Fair Housing Act, whites North and South were backing away from Black liberation. Punishing Harry Byrd and James J. Kilpatrick and Mills Godwin for their open conspiracy against the law of the land was not on the table.

White solidarity again was the reason. Massive Resistance was clearly an illegal activity. Byrd and his allies were no fools; they knew that they were conspiring to undermine orders by the Supreme Court and other federal courts. They could not have been more obviously in contempt of court. But as with Robert E. Lee and Jeff Davis, Harry Byrd had been an insider for many years before he was, briefly, a defeated outsider.

Frederick Douglass and Martin Luther King Jr., though they met with Presidents and will be remembered long after the criminals are forgotten, were never insiders. They were never white.

However, after each of the previous defeats of the Virginia Gentleman and his allies, the power of the African-American community has grown. After the first Appomattox, African Americans had a new, if very limited, ability to control their collective development. After 1968, African Americans gained a position in the system, even as very junior partners.

Why Reparations Are Logical

For many years, I have belonged to a tiny organization of white folks, Caucasians United for Reparations and Emancipation (CURE). Its main principles are, first, that we support reparations for the descendants of enslaved people of African Descent, and second, that we have no specific plan or proposal for reparations. It is not my job to decide what reparations should look like, any more than I should decide the date of the Nebraska State Fair. Reparations must meet the needs of African-Americans, not my needs.

One of the most important things CURE has done is to publish a book, The Debtors, for which I wrote a chapter. In that chapter, I wrote:

> **Unless a system of reparations is imposed overnight by aliens from another planet, it will, like every other major social change, be the result of a political and historical process over time and with the involvement of millions of people. Reparations will never happen unless, at a minimum, they have massive support in the African-American population -- and at least some support among other groups. This means that any real-life reparations program must make sense and seem fair to a lot of people.** (Yates, 2005)

Sure, sometimes policies have been forced on society. Virginia Gentlemen happen to know how that works.

Virginia Gentlemen decided in 1902 not to let Virginians vote on the constitution they had just come up with. Instead, the convention just declared it in effect, though they had no authority to do so. Apparently, the Gents felt that the tens of thousands who would lose the right to vote under that Constitution might get all upset and vote against it. People get that way sometimes when you are taking away a constitutional right with trickery. (Disfranchisement, Encyclopedia Virginia)

In the 1950s, Virginia Gentlemen again failed to consult, or even heed, Virginians before deciding to defy the law of the land on school integration. The Byrd Machine governor in place when Brown vs. Board of Education set up a commission to figure out Virginia's response. There were no African-Americans, no educators, and no moderate whites on the commission, and it only held one public hearing. The panel developed a "local option" plan that would have allowed some Virginia communities to integrate their schools, while supporting segregation in those communites where those in power wanted that. A statewide referendum on part of this plan passed by two-to-one. But then Byrd and his coterie overruled even that plan, and committed Virginia to the Massive Resistance strategy, with no local option. (Heinemann)

But African-Americans have never had the kind of autocratic power that Virginia Gentlemen have had. African-Americans have won their fights the hard way, openly, democratically, and courageously. That is how they will win the fight for reparations.

An Honest Look at the Past Calls For Reparations

We tend to think of history as automatic progress from the old dark days to the bright modern era. Thus, we see the anti-slavery movement in England and North America as a modern reaction to slavery, and Virginia's slavery as a barbaric relic of the past.

This actually reverses and distorts history.

Those who think of Virginia-style slavery as a normal practice in its day, or a continuation of traditional slavery, are simply mistaken. Profit-driven mass slavery was an innovation of the 1600s in the Americas.

It was not normal in Africa, where enslaved captives had families and were integrated into the enslaving society, as they were in native North American societies. It was unknown in Europe, and for that matter in China, India and elsewhere in Eurasia. In those places there were peasants tied to the land, and there were household servants, but they all had certain rights with a larger feudal system.

Slave-owners made much of the fact that slavery was mentioned uncritically in the Bible. For example, William Smith, in his 1856 defense of slavery, wrote “not a word is known to have escaped [Jesus], either in public or in private, declaring the relation of master and slave to be sinful!” (Smith, William A.)

It’s quite true Jesus never condemned the practice, for example, of separating a child from its mother in order to make a profit. He also failed to condemn chopping up one’s grandmother and using her for fish bait. Both crimes would have been equally unimaginable to those he taught.

The slaves of Jesus’ day lived with their families. They were subjugated people, but they were not items in an account book subject to sale to buyers hundreds of miles away. They did not work in huge labor gangs. And there was no doctrine declaring them to be morally and mentally inferior to the “race” of their masters.

Chattel slavery as developed in Virginia was a new system, made possible by the transatlantic trading and financial system. Never before had millions of people been transported across an ocean into slavery. Never before had an entire group of people been assigned to a sub-human role.

Only in the European colonies in the Americas was for-profit mass agricultural production carried out by people who were considered to be no more than business equipment or cattle.

The General Court of Rhode Island set a penalty of 40 pounds to block the practice of "buy[ing] negroes, to that end that they may have them for service or slaves for ever" in 1652. (Earle) Not long after the Rhode Islanders, Quakers and Mennonites condemned slavery as it was practiced in the North American colonies. This was before Virginia and Maryland had even established the legal structure for lifetime hereditary slavery for all Africans.

The Methodists and Baptists also opposed Virginia-style chattel slavery within a few decades of the establishment of the slavery system. These were Christian organizations, organizations we would call fundamentalist by today's standards. Their opposition to Virginia's and the South's slavery system was based on traditional Biblical values, not on modern liberalism.

Nor were those whites of the late 17th and early 18th centuries fighting slavery as a generic idea. They were fighting the specific system that emerged here in

Virginia and around the Chesapeake Bay.

This Christian-based opposition to Virginia-style slavery became less and less popular in the South in the decades leading up to the Civil War. But it was still on many people's minds – even the minds of slave-holders. In 1832, a Virginia slave-owner wrote:

> **"This, Sir, is a Christian community. Southerners read in their Bibles, 'Do unto all men as you would have them do unto you'; and this golden rule and slavery are hard to reconcile."** (Oakes)

Pro-slavery writer, William A. Smith, in his lectures glorifying the institution published in 1856, admitted:

> **"We are told that all men *believe* slavery to be wrong in principle; that is, wrong in itself! ... The ... doctrine is not without advocates at the South; whilst many more, as we have before stated, who may not be said to believe it, are nevertheless often the subjects of painful misgivings. They *fear* it may be true."** (Smith, William)

Slavery was the subject of intense political conflict, ultimately leading to war. It was important to the slavocrat leadership to give an appearance of Southern unanimity. It was important to keep thoughts like these out of the public conversation:

> **"'Always I felt the moral guilt of it,' a Louisiana mistress admitted, 'felt how impossible it must be for an owner of slaves to win his way to heaven.'"** (Oakes)

The slave system developed in Virginia and its neighbor states was powerful. It brought comfort, ease and massive wealth to some slave-owners. But it was never right, even in the minds of many slave-owners, and certainly not in the minds of most of its contemporaries. We do our ancestors no favors by assuming that, while we recognize the profoundly immorality of that slave system, they couldn't see it when it was right in front of them.

Reparations is the Final Step in The Abolitionist Campaign

Let us look at the lives of those who were brought to Virginia as captives from Africa in the hard years of the early 1700s.

These people had an experience comparable to those of slave laborers under the Nazis or in the worst of the Soviet gulag. Many of them were worked to death before they could have children. Most lived in barracks and worked in the fields; few were given any opportunity to worship, and almost none could read, at least in English. (Berlin) (Every generation kidnapped from Africa has included people literate in Arabic, as well as highly sophisticated scholars and priests from various African cultures.)

When twentieth century nations adopted massive forced labor schemes, faith groups and concerned people called for international action to end them. People of good will sought to expose and end gulags, Jim Crow, Nazism, apartheid, and slavery-like exploitation of indigenous people in places like King Leopold's Congo and 1980s Guatemala.

That is exactly what happened in the eighteenth century.

The response to the slave trade and to Virginia-style slavery was not as rapid as the response to, say, the Nazis. But the British government of the early 1800s was not able to respond as rapidly and powerfully as the governments of the twentieth century.

As for the United States government, in the case of both the Nazis and the Confederates, it sadly only acted against these vicious regimes when they actually became a military threat.

The Virginia system of slavery, of course, never took hold in most of the United States. All major U.S. Protestant denominations opposed it, separating from Southern white congregations who would not give it up. And, though so many ignore the fact, it was opposed by those who had the most at stake – those whose labor and lives were abused by it. It's more than insensitive to talk about the opinion of Americans towards slavery and discount the opinions of the Americans who were enslaved.

This modern profit-driven slavery was ended within two centuries, despite the fact it was immensely profitable and was well integrated into the global economy. This could not have happened without widespread action from both the enslaved themselves and from free sympathetizers.

Yet the Virginia Gentleman has again scammed us so well that we often hear "that's how people thought in those days." Yeah, some people.

If we believe in abolitionism, we need to complete the process, not mock it by believing the slave-owners' propaganda that they represented majority opinion.

Judge Yesterday by Yesterday's Standards

Let us simply be as fair and charitable as the average person in the early 1700s was, and be horrified by the Virginia Gentlemen's actions. Let us do what the average contemporary would like to have done, and undo the legacy of the Virginia Gentleman, to the extent we can.

We often hear that we can't judge the practices of "those days" by the standards of today. I agree. Let's judge them by human standards that made sense then and make sense now. Let's not judge them by the standards of the worst and most self-interested people in the past.

Why should we see Virginia's slavery – and the system of white supremacy that it has metastasized into – only from the point of the slave-owner? Are we comfortable with seeing a child only from the point of view of a pedophile, or a gay person or Jew or Gypsy only from the point of view of a Nazi?

Some of those who oppose reparations or who defend the Confederacy urge us to take a more balanced view of slavery. I agree. I am eager to "balance" the views of the majority of people, which ranged from bitterly opposed to slavery to uneasy about it, against the views of the tiny minority who "owned" large numbers of human beings, and the even tinier minority that actually felt comfortable doing so.

Why We Minimize Slavery

Why do we find ways to dismiss or minimize the horror and immorality of the slavery institution?

We (and I especially mean we white folks) do this because the Virginia Gentleman and his cronies have, in every generation, normalized the slave-owner perspective. Over and over, they have given us updated versions of the idealized slave-owners, while minimizing everyone else.

They have tried to make us forget there was anyone alive in the South in 1863 but Robert E. Lee and the other guys in his buddy movie of gallant warfare. We are not supposed to remember tens of thousands of white people who had left the South in disgust, or the few who stayed and helped keep the Underground Railroad going.

The Virginia Gentlemen have blurred the individual lives of the slaves, already obscured by enslavement, while dwelling endlessly on every human element of the personality of white slave-owners, especially the few positive ones.

Yes, Robert E. Lee was a real person. He may even have been, in his limited sphere, as noble as we are so often told. But is there any reason to think that there were not hundreds of people in the South who were just as noble, and who lived and died in slavery, who escaped slavery, who hated slavery?

I don't ask that Lee be singled out for hatred. I ask only that you do not give that one Virginian, who has already had the benefit of a massive "personality cult" lasting far longer than Stalin's, any more respect or attention than those other human beings. Just because you know the name of his wife, his horse, his church, does not mean he was, in his day, any more real than those other humans whose lives you know nothing about, but who we know breathed and loved and suffered.

This has nothing to do with guilt, or shame, though those may come up in you. It has to do with simple honesty. In 1862 or 1682, it was just as true as it is today that slavery was ugly and that most people wished it had never happened.

Oh, and for those who say "It was a long time ago, let's let it be in the past." Fine. As soon as you agree to forget the American Revolution. (And, of course, you must forget the Confederacy. Mosby and Stuart were a long time ago too.) If you genuinely believe that we begin today brand new, with no historical baggage, then give up your claim to the good baggage too. In fact, give up your claim to be human, because all humans are rooted in history.

We have been hustled by con-artists for centuries on this race thing. Sometimes we white folks con ourselves. Let's try to live in the real world. Let's pay our debts, so we actually can move on.

In 2001, The Debt: What America Owes to Blacks, written by a son of Richmond, Virginia, was published. The title of our CURE book was chosen to complement that book, and I want to close this section with words from Randall Robinson.

Robinson grew up in Richmond's African-American community. He went on to found Transafrica, an organization providing a voice in the United States for the needs of people of African descent all over the world. In particular, he was a key leader in work in this country against the South African apartheid system. But his work in support of overseas struggles was not separated in his mind from that fact that he "grew up in a profoundly segregated Richmond, Virginia ... [and[never had a sustained exchange with a white American until he had graduated from his historically black university, Virginia State University." (Spector)

In The Debt's Introduction, Robinson writes:

> **At long last, let America contemplate the scope of its enduring human-rights wrong against the whole of a people. Let the vision of blacks not become so blighted from a sunless eternity that we fail to *see* the staggering breadth of America's crime against us. Solutions must be tailored to the scope of the crime in a way that would make the victim whole. In this case, the psychic and economic injury is enormous,**

multidimensional and long-running. Thus must be America's restitution to blacks for the damage done. (Robinson, 2001)

These are words that need to be said – and need to be heeded by all of us who are part of the United States of America, including Virginia.

But as I was writing this book, I came across another book by Randall Robinson. I have not followed his career carefully, but I have admired him for a long time. I actually did meet him once, in a way that probably mystified him.

I was walking in Washington, DC, and passed a hotel entrance. I saw a tall handsome African-American man who I was pretty sure was Randall Robinson. I went up to him, and asked him if he was Robinson; he confirmed it. I thanked him for his good work. He looked at me, puzzled, and said "Do I know you?" I told him he didn't, told him to take care, and headed off into the night.

So naturally, when I saw a book by him at a thrift store, I bought it. It was in some ways quite a painful read. It's called Quitting America, and it is about his new life in exile, in the island nation St. Kitts. He seems to have made a good decision for himself; St. Kitts is his wife's birthplace, and they are raising a daughter there. But in some ways this book cuts deeper than The Debt – and makes clear how deep the debt runs to this man and the other daughters and sons of Virginia living under slavery's legacy.

> **In America, I do not exist..., not even fully to myself. This has nothing to do with money or prominence or social station. Those are the facile exterior conditions of a black person's unimportant fortune. They are relative like garments we put on and take off. It is the important fortune, the interior defining condition, the ageless unfed black self that cannot flourish within the culturally intolerant space of self-absorbed white America.** (Robinson, 2005)

Fraud and Fable Number Twenty-One: A Radical Scalawag Like Larry Yates Might Be Amusing, But He's Not Objective, and Has Nothing Of Value To Say About Virginia

Purpose: The Virginia Gentleman must find some disreputable category to put any serious critic in. Maybe they will come up with a "birther" theory, once they find out I was born in North Carolina and didn't leave until I was 4 years old.

Autobiographical Note

who is this guy,
making trouble and making poems?

who is this guy,
a European talking about Africa,
claiming kinship with goddess-driven
dark-skinned trader priests?
what is this obsession with
bird song, the wind, and
the tales of poor old women?
what is his crazy quilt story?

check the reports.
he's been seen before.

after he was told he'd have to apprentice
for twenty years to a fortuneteller in
Athens,
he disappeared, and came back
babbling about Ethiopian mysteries,
starting this whole philosophy thing.
(he said he didn't start anything,
said old black guys with hardly any clothes
on
had told him all this stuff and a lot more...)

he was part of the bunch
that thought the monasteries
should collect less taxes and
spend time with lepers and addicts,
even if it did cut into their drinking time.
he ended up, they say,
with the Anabaptists or the Quakers,

or maybe the Rosicrucians.
(he may have been part of that
wacky occult
"the earth revolves around the sun"
gang
or maybe mixed up with the Witches
or the Cathars
that we had to wipe out)
middle-aged ex-student pamphleteer
pretty well describes him
(or Tom Paine, or Pythagoras,
or George Orwell, or Francis of Assisi,
or any of that crowd)

complaining at every progressive step
as if the old broken houses of the poor
were gem-studded palaces
as if an old man begging in the street
was administering the sacraments
and should be praised instead of shut away

we seem to keep producing them somehow
despite the opportunities for advancement
we have created
all over the known world.

guys like him, with a good education,
and all kinds of advantages,
but just not wanting to fit in,
not willing to wait it out for a good
position,
kind of allergic to going along with the
system,
they get caught up in some crazy dream or
other.

we know all about them.

check the reports.
he's been seen before;
we know he's been around

for quite a while

More About Larry

As a child, I was an American in Bangkok, Thailand. I attended a school whose students came from countries across Asia, Europe, North America and Oceania. My favorite teacher -- the best I ever had, and one who inspired devotion from many of her students that remained fervent at her death a few years ago -- was Thai. My closest friends were Chinese, German and British, and others were from Pakistan, Denmark, Canada, and Australia. In addition, my father worked closely with Thai colleagues, and clearly conveyed to me his attitude of respect towards them.

Respect for those who are defined as different became a fundamental value in my life, not a matter of choice or of good manners. To me, respect is the essential value.

This sense of respect has led me to commit my adult life to organizing for social justice. As a result, I have come to know amazing people who are almost invisible to their own communities -- like the elderly barber who spent 15 years as an NAACP leader in Virginia when that was seriously dangerous, or the intelligent and committed young Mexican immigrant now putting herself at risk of deportation as she fights for the American Dream.

Thanks to amazing colleagues and mentors, I have learned strategies and techniques from the civil rights, feminist and community organizing movements that help people from any community to define their goals and then to achieve those goals. The high point of my career so far has been assisting a network of hundreds of intelligent, committed low income tenants working to save their homes from budget cuts and rapacious landlords.

My respect for all humans has also led me to think differently about religion and history than most folks around me do. I find it impossible to be a secular humanist, because I cannot disrespect thousands of years of humanity's belief in a spirit world; for the same reason, I cannot be a conventional Christian and follow a faith that was spread mostly by conquest and colonialism. I also cannot approach race in the half-nonchalant, half-guilty way that most white people do; I have to take it on, talk about it.

We have a hard task ahead, creating a global order that works for us all. We can't really imagine what that world will look like, but we can be sure that it will not be the world we know today.

I believe that each of us are, by virtue of our humanity, engaged in the process of seeking justice and democracy, just as we are engaged with language, family and other forms of being human together. I have spent a lot of time thinking about, discussing and being consciously involved in this process. Most of that time has been in Virginia.

When I returned to the USA in 1964, we lived in Fairfax County. Since then I have lived in Fairfax County, the City of Richmond, Arlington County, Shenandoah County, and now the City of Winchester. For work, play and organizing, I have spent time in every region of Virginia, from Chincoteague to Jonesville.

I know of only a few dozen Virginians who have been as fortunate as I to experience so much of our social justice spectrum. That's why I dare to think this book may be useful.

Jesus is a favorite figure for almost all Virginians, including those of us who are not Christians. Jesus called on us to focus our energy on giving to the poor, the prisoner, the hungry and above all the children. I believe he did so not because those people are better than the rest of us – though they certainly are no worse. I believe their condition is the sign of how well we are doing our inherent human task. I believe we can do better in Virginia.

My Virginia History

Organizations in Virginia in which I have been active (several of which no longer exist) include:

- *Action Coordinating Committee to End Segregation in the Suburbs*
- *Appalantic Federation of Cooperatives*
- *Arlington Village Housing Cooperative*
- *Chidiock Amorphous (arts/culture/??)*
- *Cornucopia Trading Company (natural foods cooperative)*
- *CONVERT (opposing militarization of Northern Virginia)*
- *Fifth Fret (coffeehouse)*
- *Ishmael Amorphous (student organizing)*
- *Justice Coalition (mass incarceration)*
- *Northern Virginia Fair Housing*
- *Northern Virginians for Peace and Justice*
- *Oregon Hill Civic Association*
- *Richmond Alternative Energy Coalition*
- *Richmond Artists Workshop*

- *Richmond United Neighborhoods*
- *Save Oregon Hill Organization*
- *The Newspaper*
- *Virginia Association of Neighborhoods*
- *Virginia Coalition For Cooperatives*
- *Virginia Housing Coalition*
- *Virginia Organizing Project (now Virginia Organizing)*

Obviously, none of these groups, nor any individual but me, is responsible for my opinions; but all of them, and many more, have helped to shape me, providing the experiences on which they are ultimately based.

A Challenge

As the Scalawag Scholar, I will take on any historian, political figure, or anyone else living in Virginia in debate about these Notes.

for the new year: meditation by the north fork of the Shenandoah

when many rivers and streams
finally overwhelm
a mountain
they lose their names

we call that "the ocean"

when many voices
speak truth to power
when many hands raised
in joint action
fundamentally change
a social condition
a condition that many believed was eternal

then those who come after
see only the lightly ruffled surface
extending blue into the distance

"Wasn't that always there?"

meanwhile
high on a slope
of another mountain
a first spring finds its way
through the stones
works its way
through the hard-packed earth

BIBLIOGRAPHY
THE SCALAWAG SCHOLAR'S NOTES ON VIRGINIA 2012

Note: I have put the notation FAV!! next to the books that are real favorites of mine. This does not mean that I don't really like a lot of the other books.

700 Club, "Bob McDonnell: A Politician Full of Faith," https://www.cbn.com/700club/Guests/Bios/Bob_McDonnell052506.aspx

Adams, Julia, "The Rule of the Father: Patriarchy and Patrimonialism in Early Modern Europe," www.russellsage.org.

Alexander, Ann Field, Race Man: The Rise and Fall of the 'Fighting Editor' John Mitchell Jr., University of Virginia Press, 2002.

Alexander, Michele, The New Jim Crow: Mass Incarceration in the Age of Colorblindness, New Press, 2010. FAV!!

Allen, Theodore W., Summary of the Argument of The Invention of the White Race" (http://clogic.eserver.org/1-2/allen2.html).

Anderson, Virginia Creatures of Empire, Oxford University Press, 2001.

Andrews, Charles W. *Memoir of Mrs. Anne R. Page* (Philadelphia, 1844). The quotation here is at http://www.librarycompany.org/women/portraits_religion/page.htm.

Anonymous, The History of the Order of the Sons of Temperance, 1848.

Appalachian Regional Commission, About ARC, http://www.arc.gov/about/index.asp.

Aptheker, Herbert, American Negro Slave Revolts, International Publishers, 1943. FAV!!

Ayers, Edward, The Promise of the New South, Oxford University Press, 2007.

Baker, Judge Richard, Circuit Court of Norfolk County, Comments on sentencing Margaret Douglas to one month in jail for teaching African-American children to read the Bible, January 10, 1854. http://www.pbs.org/wgbh/aia/part4/4h2945t.html.

Barden, Thomas, ed., Virginia Folk Legends, Publications of the American Folklore Society, 1991.

Barnett, Donald L. and Karari Njama, Mau Mau from Within: An Analysis of Kenya's Peasant Revolt, Monthly Review Press, 1968.

Bartholomew, Dave, email message, as reprinted in various locations, including "Va. GOP Chair Compares Black People to Dogs on Welfare," by Boyce Watkins, Ph.D., at http://www.bvblackspin.com/2010/10/20/va-gop-chair-compares-black-people-to-dogs-on-welfare/.

Berkeley, Edmund, Jr., editor, The Diary, Correspondence and Papers of Robert "King" Carter of Virginia, 1701-1732, University of Virginia, http://carter.lib.virginia.edu/.

Berlin, Ira, Many Thousands Gone: The First Two Centuries of Slavery in North America, Harvard University Press, 2000. FAV!!

Bible, King James Version.

Blackwell, Morton C., "The Real Nature Of Politics," Leadership Institute, http://www.leadershipinstitute.org/resources/Writings.cfm.

Blume, Michele, Psy. D., Understanding and Working Through Shame in Therapy, December 30, 2011, http://drmicheleblume.com/blog/unde

rstanding-and-working-through-shame-in-therapy/#more-29

Boggs, Jeremy, We the “White” People: Race, Culture, and the Virginia Constitution of 1902, Virginia Polytechnic Institute and State University Department of History, Virginia Polytechnic Institute and State University Department of History, 2003. Available on Virginia Tech website.

Bonis, Ray, “100th Anniversary of the founding of the Equal Suffrage League of Virginia,” Virginia Commonwealth University Libraries, Spring 1998, http://www.library.vcu.edu/jbc/speccoll/exhibit/crenshaw.html.

Bond, Julian, “Interview With Oliver W. Hill,” Virginia Quarterly Review, Winter 2004, http://www.vqronline.org/articles/2004/winter/bond-interview-oliver/

Bowes, Mark, “Racial profiling on Virginia's highways: Real or perceived, Daily Progress, Charlottesville, Sept. 6, 2007.

Bragg, Susan, "Martinsville Seven (1949-1951)" , http://www.blackpast.org/?q=aah/martinsville-seven-1949-1951.

Breen, Patrick, "Abstract: The Female Antislavery Petition Campaign of 1831–32," Virginia Magazine of History and Biography, Volume 110 / Number 3, http://www.vahistorical.org/publications/abstract_breen.htm.

Bradley, Arthur Granville, Other Days, Recollections Of Rural England And Old Virginia, 1860-1880, Constable And Company Ltd, 1913.

Brickwedde, Dick, "Interstate Garbage: The Carbone Case and the Commerce Clause," 2011, http://brickwedde.com/publications/8-interstate-garbage-the-carbone-case-and-the-commerce-clause.html

Brown, John, speech at his trial, 1859, quoted in The Anti-Slavery History Of The John-Brown Year; Being The Twenty-Seventh Annual Report Of The American Anti-Slavery Society. American Anti-Slavery Society, 1861.

Brown, John, Letter to a minister, 1859, in American Anti-Slavery Society.

Brown, Kathleen, Good Wives, Nasty Wenches, and Anxious Patriarchs, Omohundro Institute, 1996.

Brown, William Wells, "Nat Turner" in The Black Man, His Antecedents, His Genius, and His Achievements, 1863, published electronically at http://docsouth.unc.edu/neh/brownww/brown.html#brown59.

Bruce, Philip Alexander, The Virginia Plutarch, University of North Carolina, 1929.

Bruce, Philip Alexander, The Social Life of Virginia in the Seventeenth Century, 1907.

Buchanan, Patrick, Decline of the West, Saint Martin's Press, 2002.

Buettner, Michael, "Governor Announces Moves To Prevent Racial Bias Among Virginia Police," Associated Press, January 2003.

Bullard, Robert, Dumping in Dixie: Race, Class, and Environmental Quality, Westview Press, 1990.

Cabell, James Branch, Let Me Lie, His Commentaries on the Commonwealth of Virginia, Farrar & Straus, 1947. FAV!!

Cable, George Washington, "The Freedman's Case in Equity," Century Magazine, 1885, published online by the University of Virginia, http://etext.virginia.edu/railton/huckfinn/hfequity.html.

Cabral, Amilcar, Revolution in Guinea, Monthly Review Press, 1969. FAV!!

Calhoun, Arthur W. The American Family in the Colonial Period, Dover, 2004.

Carwile, Howard W., Speaking From Byrdland, L. Stuart, 1960.

Cathedral Basilica of St. Augustine. "History," http://thefirstparish.org/History.html.

Charles City County Community Website, "Attractions," http://www.charlescity.org/attractions.shtml.

Center for Government and Public Affairs, Auburn University Montgomery, Bias-Based Policing, August 2004 (available online from the Virginia Department of Criminal Justice Services.)

Chesney-Lind, Meda, and Marc Mauer, Invisible Punishment: The Collateral

Consequences of Mass Imprisonment, 2002.

Citizens for Safe Water Around Badger and other groups, "Communities Seek Accountability for Military Pollution," March 26, 2009, http://www.dmzhawaii.org/?p=2038.

City of Virginia Beach website.

Coleson, Edward, "Our Heritage," The Wesleyan Church website, http://www.wesleyan.org/heritage.

Commission on Accreditation for Law Enforcement Agencies, "Law Enforcement Program: The Standards," http://www.calea.org/content/law-enforcement-program-standards

Council of Colonial Virginia, Executive Journals, as cited in the Encyclopedia Virginia.

Cousins, Norman, In God We Trust: The Religious Beliefs and Ideas of the American Founding Fathers, 1958.

Crooks, Elizabeth Willits, The Life of Adam Crooks, Wesleyan Methodist Publishing House, 1875, http://docsouth.unc.edu/nc/crooks/crooks.html.

Crum, Mason, The Negro in the Methodist Church, Methodist Church Board of Missions and Church Extension, 1951.

Counseil for Virginia, A True and Sincere Declaration of the Purpose and Ends of the Plantation Begun in Virginia, 1610.

Custalow, Dr. Linwood "Little Bear" and Angela L. Daniel "Silver Star", The True Story of Pocahontas: The Other Side of History, Fulcrum Press, 2007.

Dabbs, James McBride, Who Speaks for the South?, Funk & Wagnalls, 1964.

d'Angerville, Count, editor, "Pat Robertson's Bloodline, from Living Descendants of Blood Royal (in America),"World Nobility and Peerage, London and Paris, 1964, reproduced at http://www.patrobertson.com/Family/Bloodline.asp.

Daniel, Sadie Iola, Women Builders, 1931, Associated Publishers.

Death Penalty Information Center, "Executions in the U.S. 1608-2002: The Espy File," http://www.deathpenaltyinfo.org/executions-us-1608-2002-espy-file.

Degler, Carl, The Other South: Southern Dissenters in the Nineteenth Century, Harper and Row Publishers, 1974.

Delany, Martin, "To the National Board of Commissioners," printed in the Provincial Freeman, Ontario, Canada, October 13, 1855. http://research.udmercy.edu/find/special_collections/digital/baa/item.php?record_id=1608&collectionCode=baa.

Disney, Walt, Pocahontas, Grolier Enterprises, 1995.

Domhoff, G. William, "Wealth, Income and Power," Who Rules America (website linked with book of same title), http://www2.ucsc.edu/whorulesamerica/power/wealth.html.

Drayton, Michael, "To the Virginian Voyage," poem, 1619.

DuBois, W.E.B., John Brown, G.W. Jacobs & Company, 1909. FAV!!

DuBois, W.E.B., The Suppression of the African Slave Trade to the United States of America, Harvard University, 1896.

Dutty, Boukman, "Boukman's Prayer," spoken at Bois Caiman in 1791. Cited in many places, including http://altreligion.about.com/od/history/a/bois-caiman.htm

Earle, Thomas, editor, The Life, Travels and Opinions of Benjamin Lundy, first published in 1847, republished in 1971 by Augustus M. Kelley Publishers, New York. (Lundy was the main abolitionist activist in the U.S. in the 1820s and 1830s; the Rhode Island reference in this book is from the February 1832 issue of the Genius of Universal Emancipation, his newsletter.)

Early, Jubal, The Heritage of the South: A History Of The Introduction Of Slavery, Its Establishment From Colonial Times, And Final Effect Upon The Politics Of The United States, published by R.H. Early, 1915. http://www.archive.org/stream/heritageofsouthh00earl#page/n7/mode/2up

Ebony Magazine, "The White Problem," August, 1965.

Edmunds, Pocahontas Wight, Virginians Out Front, Whittet & Shepperson, 1972.

Eggleston, George Cary, The History of the Confederate War, Sturgis and Walton, 1910, New York.

Encyclopedia Virginia, www.encyclopediavirginia.org.

Faust, Drew Gilpin, The Creation of Confederate Nationalism, Louisiana State University Press, 1990.

Fayette Area Historical Initiative and the Virginia Foundation for the Humanities, Fayette Street, A Hundred-Year History of African-American Life in Martinsville, Virginia, 2006.

Feld, Lowell, "Virginia Legislative Session Length: An Issue That Keeps Coming Up," Blue Virginia blog (http://www.bluevirginia.us/user/lowkell).

Fiske, John, Old Virginia and Her Neighbors , Houghton & Mifflin, 1897.

Fiske, Walter, "The Black-and-White World of Walter Ashby Plecker," Norfolk Virginian-Pilot, August 18, 2004.

Freehling, William, The Reintegration of American History, Oxford University Press, 1994.

Freehling, William W., The Road to Disunion, Volume I, Secessionists at Bay, Oxford University Press, 1990.

Friddell, Guy, The Virginia Way, Burda Gmbh, 1973.

Foner, Eric, Reconstruction: America's Unfinished Revolution 1863-1877, Harper & Row, 1988.

Foner, Eric, The Voice of Black America, Major Speeches by Negroes in the United States, New York City, New York: Simon and Schuster, 1972. FAV!!

Gallagher, Gary, and Alan T. Nolan, eds., The Myth of the Lost Cause and Civil War History, Indiana University Press, 2010.

Garnet, Rev. Henry Highland, "Address to the Slaves of the United States of America," delivered to the National Convention of Negro Citizens in 1843.

Goldberg, Jeffrey, "The Color of Suspicion," New York Times, June 20, 1999

Gordon, Lesley "Let the People See the Old Life As It Was": LaSalle Corbell Pickett and the Myth of the Lost Cause," in Gallagher, Gary, and Alan T. Nolan, eds., The Myth of the Lost Cause and Civil War History, Indiana University Press, 2010.

Grant, Joanne, editor, Black Protest: History, Documents and Analyses, Fawcett, 1968.

Grant, Joanne, Ella Baker: Freedom Bound, John Wiley and Sons, 1998. The Virginia schedule excerpt from the chapter "Putting People in Motion: The NAACP Years" is online at http://www.evergreenreview.com/102/print/ella.txt.

Green, Elna C., This Business of Relief: Confronting Poverty in a Southern City, 1740-1940, University of Georgia Press, 2003.

Hampton University website, www.hamptonu.edu.

Harding, Vincent, "Do Not Grow Weary or Lose Heart," Sojourners Magazine, March 2012.

Harding, Vincent, There is a River: The Black Struggle for Freedom in America, Houghton Mifflin Harcourt, 1993. FAV!!

Harper, Chancellor, and Governor Hammond, Dr. Simms, And Professor Dew. The Pro-Slavery Argument; As Maintained By The Most Distinguished Writers Of The Southern States. Charleston: Walker, Richards & Co., 1852. Online at http://name.umdl.umich.edu/ABT7488.0001.001

Harper, Scott, "Navy reaches Superfund milestone at Norfolk base," Norfolk Virginian-Pilot, November 2, 2010.

Harrison, Nathaniel, Will executed December 15, 1726 in Surry County, currently available on the Web at http://freepages.history.rootsweb.ancestry.com/~pistoleros/wills.html.

Heinemann, Ronald, Harry Byrd of Virginia, University of Virginia Press, 2006.

Hendericks, Garret, and others, "These are the reasons why we are against the traffik of men-body..," Germantown Pennsylvania meeting, February 1688.

Herrnstein, Richard, and Charles Murray, The Bell Curve, Free Press, 1994.

Higginson, Thomas Wentworth, "Negro Spirituals," Atlantic Monthly, 1867.

Holladay, Waller, & James M. Bell, letter to Gov. Wilson Cary Nicholas re. the conspiracy of George Boxley to start an insurrection in Spotsylvania, Louisa, & Orange (1816 March 1).

hooks, bell, Killing Rage: Ending Racism, Holt Paperbacks, 1996.

Howard University School of Law, "Charles Hamilton Houston Biography," http://www.law.howard.edu/1397.

HUD (U.S. Department of Housing and Urban Development), Live Free: Annual Report on Fair Housing Fiscal Year 2010, portal.hud.gov/hudportal/documents/huddoc?id=ANNUALREPORT2010.PDF.

Hundley, Daniel Social Relations in the Southern States, Henry B. Price, 1860.

Ignatiev, Noel, and John Garvey, Race Traitor, Routledge 1996. FAV!!

Institute for Tax and Economic Policy, "Who Pays? A Distributional Analysis of the Tax Systems in All 50 States," November 2009.

Institute on Assets and Social Policy, The Racial Wealth Gap Increases Fourfold, May 2010 report.

Irwin, Helen, "A Pioneer of the Arts: Miss Adele Clark, Distinguished Artist and WPA Head," Richmond Times-Dispatch, March 14, 1935, published on the web at http://richmondthenandnow.com/Newspaper-Articles/Adele-Clark.html.

Isaac, Rhys, The Transformation of Virginia 1740-1790, University of North Carolina Press, 1999.

Jackson, Mary Anna Life and Letters of General Thomas J. Jackson (Stonewall Jackson), Harper & Brothers, 1892: Diary entry, Friday, December 2, 1859 (John Brown's death) http://hd.housedivided.dickinson.edu/node/2044.

Jefferson, Thomas, Autobiography, http://libertyonline.hypermall.com/Jefferson/Autobiography.html.

Jefferson, Thomas, Letter to Henry Lee, May 8, 1825, http://www.ashbrook.org/constitution/henry_lee.html.

Jefferson, Thomas, Notes on the State of Virginia, 1781.

Jefferson, Thomas, Virginia Statute of Religious Freedom.

Johnson, Kevin "Rashid", From "Bad to Worse: Transferred from Red Onion to Wallens Ridge State Prison," http://sketchythoughts.blogspot.com/2012/01/from-bad-to-worse-transferred-from-red.html
See also
http://sparcva.wordpress.com/.

Johnston, James Hugo, Race Relations in Virginia and Miscegenation in the South 1776-1860, University of Massachusetts Press, 1970.

Jones, Jacqueline, "Black and White Hands in a Slaveholders' Republic" from American Work, Norton, 1998.

Jones, John William, Life and Letters of Robert E. Lee Soldier and Man, Neale Publishing, 1906.

Kagi, John, Letter to his father, from Lawrence, Kansas, September 1858. From A Virtual Repository of Kansas Territorial History (http://www.territorialkansasonline.org/~imlskto/cgi-bin/index.php).

Kate Waller Barrett Chapter, National Society Daughters of the American Revolution, "Dr. Kate Waller Barrett: Humanitarian, Philanthropist, Social Activist" http://katewallerbarrettdar.org/kwb.html.

Katz, William Loren, Black Indians: A Hidden Heritage, Atheneum, 1986, New York. FAV!!

Katz, William Loren, The Black West, Doubleday, 1973.

Kennedy, John Pendleton, **Swallow Barn, excerpted in Southern Literature From**

1579-1895, By Louise Manly, B. F. Johnson Publishing Company**, 1900.**

Kenny, J.F., Barber, N.L., Hutson, S.S., Linsey, K.S., Lovelace, J.K., and Maupin, M.A., 2009, Estimated use of water in the United States in 2005: U.S. Geological Survey Circular 1344.

Kensey, Paul, "Remembered Not For Their Greatness But For Their Flaws, American Civil War Round Table Of Australia," (New South Wales Chapter), June 2005 http://www.docstoc.com/docs/28271672/Remembered-Not-For-Their-Greatness-But-For-Their-Flaws.

Keve, Paul, The History of Corrections in Virginia, University of Virginia Press, 1986.

King, Mary, Freedom Song, William Morrow, 1988.

Kumar, Anugrah, " Pat Robertson: Mitt Romney an 'Outstanding Christian,'" Christian Post, October 2, 2011, http://www.christianpost.com/news/pat-robertson-mitt-romney-an-outstanding-christian-57017/#Lv2fSAevQMoFtFhj.99.

LaFay, Laura, "Virginia: The Story Behind The Score," article on www.stateintegrity.org.

Lebsock, Susan, **A Murder in Virginia: Southern Justice on Trial,** W. W. Norton, 2003.

Lee, Robert Edward, (son) Recollections and Letters of General Robert E. Lee, Doubleday, 1904, now published free on Kindle and other sources.

Lester, J.C. and D.L. Wilson, Ku Klux Klan: Its Origin, Growth And Disbandment, undated, 1884 apparently the original publication date, no publisher listed. Reproduced on the World Wide Web at http://www.gutenberg.org/files/31819/31819-h/31819-h.htm

Lewis, Bob, "Akin rape remark haunts GOP in Virginia," Winchester Star, August 27, 2012.

Lewis, Diane, "Anthropology and Colonialism," Current Anthropology, December 1973.

Library of Congress, Born in Slavery: Slave Narratives from the Federal Writers' Project, 1936-1938, http://memory.loc.gov/ammem/snhtm

l/snhome.html

Lincoln, Abraham, The Gettysburg Address, November 19, 1863.

Litwack, Leon, Trouble in Mind: Black Southerners in the Age of Jim Crow, Vintage, 1999. FAV!!

Logomasini, Angela "Trashing The Poor: The Interstate Garbage Dispute," (cei.org/pdf/1659.pdf).

Lottman, Herbert, The People's Anger: Justice and Revenge in Post-Liberation France, Morrow, 1986.

Lower Norfolk County Order Book 1637-1646, quoted in Billings, Warren, The Old Dominion in the Seventeenth Century: A Documentary History of Virginia, 1608-1689, University of North Carolina Press, 1975.

Lusane, Clarence, Pipe Dream Blues: Racism and the War on Drugs, South End Press, 1991.

Magill's First Book of Virginia History by Mary Magill, J.P. Bell, 1908.

Mahon, Michael, Winchester Divided, Stackpole Books, 2002.

MarkWarner2001.org/issues , Nov 6, 2001, as reproduced on

http://www.ontheissues.org/Domestic/Mark_Warner_Civil_Rights.htm

Marschak, Beth and Alex Lorch, Lesbian and Gay Richmond, Arcadia Publishing, 2008.

Massengill, Colonel W. Gerald, Virginia State Police, Racial Profiling In Virginia: An Analysis Of State And Local Law Enforcement Practices: A Report to the Militia and Police Committee, January 2002

McConnell, John Preston, Negroes And Their Treatment In Virginia From 1865 To 1867, B.D. Smith & Bros.,1910.

Mckelway, Bill, "Retired Henrico officer is convicted in nearly fatal DUI," Richmond Times-Dispatch, May 28, 2011.

Miller, John Chester, The Wolf By the Ears: Thomas Jefferson and Slavery, University Press of Virginia, 1991.

Minnigerode, Charles Frederick Ernest, "He That Believeth Shall Not Make Haste." A Sermon Preached on the First of January, 1865,
in St. Paul's Church, Richmond: Electronic Edition at http://docsouth.unc.edu/imls/minnigerode/minnigerode.html.

Moeser, John and Rutledge Dennis, The Politics of Annexation: Oligarchic Power in a Southern City, Schenkman Books, 1982. FAV!!

Monk, K. Steven, "Confederate American Pride's Humor Page," http://www.confederateamericanpride.com/index.html

Morris, Aldon, The Origins of the Civil Rights Movement, Free Press, 1986. FAV!!

Mount Zion Baptist Church, Arlington, Virginia, website. http://www.mountzionbaptist.com/content.cfm?id=2002.

Muse, William T., editor, Proceedings of the Sixty-fifth Annual Meeting of the Virginia State Bar Association, Richmond Press, 1955.

NAACP, "NAACP Strongly Supports "End Racial Profiling Act of 2011, http://www.naacp.org/press/entry/naacp-strongly-supports-end-racial-profiling-act-of-2011

National Conference of State Legislatures, "Felon Voting Rights," updated March 2012, http://www.ncsl.org/legislatures-elections/elections/felon-voting-rights.aspx.

Neely, Caroline Elizabeth, "'Dat's one chile of mine you ain't never gonna sell': Gynecological Resistance within the Plantation Community," Master's Thesis, Virginia Polytechnic Institute and State University, 2000, Blacksburg Virginia, http://scholar.lib.vt.edu/theses/available/etd-05262000-09340014/.

New York Times, obituary of James E. Jackson Jr., Sept. 7, 2007, http://www.nytimes.com/2007/09/07/nyregion/07jackson.html.

Norfolk Virginian-Pilot, Editorial, "Reservoir fight ends on Peninsula," September 26, 2009, http://hamptonroads.com/2009/09/reservoir-fight-ends-peninsula.

Norton, Mary Beth, and Herbert Gutman and Ira Berlin, "The Afro-American Family in the Age of Revolution," in Slavery and Freedom in the Age of the American Revolution, Ira Berlin and Ronald Hoffman, editors, University Press of Virginia, 1983.

Oakes, James The Ruling Race: A History of American Slaveholders, W. W. Norton & Company, 1998.

Osborne, Charles, Jubal, Algonquin Books of Chapel Hill, 1992.

Oxford Universal Dictionary, 1955.

Vivian Paige, "Let's shift to a full-time legislature," March 2011 op-ed in the Virginian-Pilot, also on Ms. Paige's blog at http://blog.vivianpaige.com/2011/03/10/lets-shift-to-a-full-time-legislature/

Paquette, Robert, "Slave Rebellion of 1811," Encyclopedia of Louisiana, http://knowla.org/entry.php?rec=756 [Another resource on the 1811 Rebellion is "To Kill Whites: The 1811 Louisiana Slave Insurrection," by Nathan Guman, a detailed thesis on the event; http://etd.lsu.edu/docs/available/etd-07112008-110053/]

Page, Thomas Nelson, 'Marse Chan,' from In Ole Virginia, Charles Scribner's Sons, 1895.

Painter, George, "The Sensibilities of Our Forefathers: The History of Sodomy Laws in the United States," Gay and Lesbian Archives of the Pacific Northwest, http://www.glapn.org/sodomylaws/sensibilities/virginia.htm

Peeples, Ed, "Richmond Journal, thirty years in black and white" in Ignatiev,

Noel, and John Garvey, Race Traitor, Routledge 1996.

Phillips, Ulrich, Life and Labor in the Old South, Little Brown & Company, 1929.

Pincus, Fred, "The Social Construction of Reverse Discrimination: The Impact of Affirmative Action on Whites," published in the Journal of Intergroup Relations, Volume XXXVIII, No. 4 Winter 2001/2002, available on the web at http://adversity.net/Pro_AA/pincus_main_frame.htm

Piven, Frances and Richard Cloward, The New Class War, Random House, 1995. FAV!!

Poe, Edgar Allen, "The Fall of the House of Usher," first published 1839.

Poland, Charles P., Jr., From Frontier to Suburbia, Walsworth Pub. Co., 1976, as cited in Scheel, Eugene, "History Affects 1860 Presidential Election Vote in Loudoun County and Northern Virginia," The History of Loudoun County website, Balch Library, http://www.loudounhistory.org/history/loudoun-1860-vote.htm

Pope-Hennessy, James, Sins of the Fathers: The Atlantic Slave Traders

1441-1807, Phoenix Press, London, 2000.

Project Censored, 2003, http://www.projectcensored.org/top-stories/articles/15-us-militarys-war-on-the-earth/

Quarles, Garland R., Occupied Winchester 1861-1865, Winchester-Frederick County Historical Society, 1976.

Raboteau, Albert J., "The Slave Church in the Era of the American Revolution," in Slavery and Freedom in the Age of the American Revolution, Ira Berlin and Ronald Hoffman, editors, University Press of Virginia, 1983.

Rachleff, Peter, Black Labor in Richmond, 1865-1890, University of Illinois Press, 1989. FAV!!

Raflo, Frank, Within the Iron Gates: Loudoun: Stories Remembered, Loudoun Times-Mirror, 1988.

Randolph, John, Speech in the U.S. House of Representatives on war, December 9, 1811. Large portions included in Randolph of Roanoke A Study in Conservative Thought, Russell Kirk, The University of Chicago Press, 1951. Published at http://www.archive.org/stream/randol

phofroanok008621mbp/randolphofroa nok008621mbp_djvu.txt

Randolph, Thomas Jefferson, January 1832 debate of the Virginia General Assembly on slavery, quoted in Slavery Agitation in Virginia 1829-1832, Johns Hopkins Press, 1930, re-published 1969 by Negro Universities Press.

Ransby, Barbara, Ella Baker and the Black Freedom Movement: A Radical Democratic Vision, University of North Carolina Press, 2003. FAV!!

Richmond Afro-American Newspaper, March 1977, celebrating the Black majority on City Council.

Richmond Sunlight, website.

Rights Working Group, "Our Members," http://www.rightsworkinggroup.org/members

Robertson, Pat, Comments on The 700 Club on January 13, 2010.

Robertson, Pat, The New Millennium, Word, 1991.

Robinson, Randall, Quitting America: The Departure of a Black Man From His Native Land, Penguin Plume, 2005. FAV!!

Robinson, Randall, The Debt: What America Owes to Blacks, Penguin Plume, 2001.

Roediger, David, editor, Black on White: Black Writers on What it Means to be White, Schocken, 1999. FAV!!

Rollins, Avon W., "Progress Report, Danville, Virginia," Early 1964. Published in Black Protest: History, Documents and Analyses, edited by Joanne Grant, Fawcett, 1968.

Rountree, Helen, Pocahontas, Powhatan, Opechancanough: Three Indian Lives Changed by Jamestown , University of Virginia Press, 2006. FAV!!

Ruffin, Edmund, Southern Quarterly Review, July 1848.

Schurz, Carl, speech, printed in The Philadelphia Inquirer, September 10, 1866.

Schuyler, George, "Our White Folks," 1927 essay, reprinted in Roediger.

Scotchie, Joe, "Richard M. Weaver: Philosopher From Dixie: Review of Ideas Have Consequences," http://www.knowsouthernhistory.net/Articles/People/richard_weaver.html

Scott, Representative Robert C. "Bobby", "Maggie Lena Walker," Extension of Remarks in the U.S. House of Representatives, March 30, 2001.

Scott, W.W., A History Of Orange County, Virginia, Richmond, Va. Everett Waddey Co., 1907.

Seligman, Herbert, "The Conquest of Haïti, The Nation, 1920.

Seneca Falls Women's Rights Convention, Declaration of Sentiments, 1848.

Sheridan County Historical Society, unknown author, A Man with a Price on His Head, The Life and Times of George Boxley, Sheridan, Indiana, 1925, as quoted at http://www.iupui.edu/~kcganth/Historical%20Narrative.html

Sherman, Richard B., The Case of Odell Waller and Virginia Justice 1940-1942, University of Tennessee Press, 1997. FAV!!

Shirley Plantation website, http://www.shirleyplantation.com/shirley%27s_history.html

Sledd, Robert Newton, "A Sermon Delivered in the Market Street M. E.

Church, Petersburg, Va. Before the Confederate Cadets, on the Occasion of their Departure for the Seat of War," Sunday, Sept. 22d, 1861: published at http://docsouth.unc.edu/imls/sledd/sledd.html

Smith, Bob, They Closed Their Schools, M.E. Forrester Council of Women, 1996.

Smith, John, 1580--1631. The Generall Historie of Virginia, New England & The Summer Isles Together with The True Travels, Adventures and Observations, and A Sea Grammar, Printed by I.D. and I.H. for Michael Sparkes. 1624. http://memory.loc.gov/cgi-bin/query/r?ammem/lhbcb:@field%28DOCID+@lit%28lhbcb0262a%29%29:

Smith, William A., Lectures on the Philosophy and Practice of Slavery, as Exhibited in the Institution of Domestic Slavery in the United States: with the Duties of Masters to Slaves, Nashville, Tenn
Stevenson and Evans, 1856, published online at http://docsouth.unc.edu/church/smith/smith.html

Sobel, Mechal, The World They Made Together, Princeton University Press , 1989.

Southern Regional Committee of the Communist Party U.S.A., "The Southern People's Common Program for Democracy, Prosperity and Peace," 1953, reprinted in Highlights of a Fighting History: 60 Years of the Communist Party U.S.A., Philip Bart, Chief Editor, International Publishers, 1979.

Southern Sociological Congress, The Call of the New South, 1912.

Southern Baptist Convention, "Resolution On Racial Reconciliation On The 150th Anniversary Of The Southern Baptist Convention," June 1995.

Spector, J. Brooks, "Randall Robinson and the legacy of Transafrica," Daily Maverick, May 1, 2012, http://dailymaverick.co.za/article/2012-05-01-randall-robinson-and-the-legacy-of-transafrica

Sterling, Dorothy, editor, We Are Your Sisters: Black Women in the Nineteen Century, W. W. Norton, 1984.

Still, William, The Underground Railroad, originally published 1871, republished by Johnson Publishing, Chicago, 1970. FAV!!

Stout, Brian, Federal Liaison for Arlington County, "Arlington and Secure Communities Program" website, http://www.arlingtonva.us/departments/CountyManager/page81216.aspx

Stowe, Harriet Beecher, Uncle Tom's Cabin, John Jewett & Co., 1852.

Strachey, William, A true reportory of the wracke, and redemption of Sir Thomas Gates Knight, as quoted in the Encyclopedia Virginia

Strong, Augusta, "Southern Youth's Proud Heritage," Freedomways Magazine, 1964, Vol. 4, No. 1, reprinted in Highlights of a Fighting History: 60 Years of the Communist Party U.S.A., Philip Bart, Chief Editor, International Publishers, 1979.

Stuckey, Sterling "Slavery and White America," in Critical Lessons in Slavery and the Slavetrade, edited by John Henrik Clarke, Native Sun Publishers, Inc., 1997.

Tarter, Brent , "Making History in Virginia," Virginia Magazine of History and Biography, 2007.

Tarter, Brent, "Mary Berkeley Minor Blackford (1802–1896)," on the Virginia Memory website of the Library of Virginia, http://www.virginiamemory.com/online_classroom/union_or_secession/people/mary_blackford

Taylor, William R., Cavalier and Yankee, Harper, 1961.

Thomas, Emory M., The Confederate Nation 1861-1865, Harper, 1979.

Thompson, Robert, "Robert E. Lee, The Human Being," May 2, 2009, http://bobcivilwarhistory.blogspot.com/2009/05/robert-e-lee-human-being.html

Thompson, Leonard, The Political Mythology of Apartheid, Yale University Press, 1986.

Thurmond, Strom, Southern Manifesto.

Ticknor, Francis Orrery, "Virginians of the Valley," in numerous anthologies.

Tourgée, Albion, A Fool's Errand, Belknap Press, 1961. FAV!!

Townsend, George Fyler, translator, Aesop's Fables, 1887, available online at http://www.gutenberg.org/files/21/21-h/21-h.htm

Tragle, Henry, The Southampton Slave Revolt of 1831, Vintage Books, 1973.

Tucker, Nathaniel Beverley, The Partisan Leader, 1836.

Turner, Captain Thomas W., Criminal Justice Information Services Division, Memorandum Of Agreement Between U.S. Department of Homeland Security, Immigration And Customs Enforcement And Virginia State Police Criminal Justice Information Services, October 2009, http://www.ice.gov/doclib/foia/secure_communities-moa/r_virginia_10-1-09.pdf

United for a Fair Economy, "Comparing the Growth of U.S. Family Incomes," http://faireconomy.org/node/1713

United for a Fair Economy, The State of the Dream: The Emerging Majority, 2012, http://faireconomy.org/issues/racial_wealth_divide/state_of_the_dream_reports FAV!!

University of Virginia Library, "A Guide to the Papers of Alice Jackson Stuart, 1913-2001," http://ead.lib.virginia.edu/vivaxtf/view?docId=uva-sc/viu03705.xml

Unknown author, "Economic Aspects of Tobacco during the Colonial Period 1612-1776," Tobacco.org, http://archive.tobacco.org/History/colonialtobacco.html

U.S.History.com, "Abolitionism," http://www.u-s-history.com/pages/h477.html

U.S. Census Bureau, Census of Population and Housing 1860 Census, http://www.census.gov/prod/www/abs/decennial/1860.html

U.S. Census Bureau, State and County Quick Facts: Charles City County, http://quickfacts.census.gov/qfd/states/51/51036.html

U.S. Census Bureau, Farms, Land in Farms, Value of Land and Buildings, and Land Use: 2007 and 2002, http://www.agcensus.usda.gov/Publications/2007/Full_Report/Volume_1,_Chapter_2_US_State_Level/, Table 8

US Department of Health and Human Services, 2009 Community Health Status Indicators, http://communityhealth.hhs.gov/homepage.aspx?j=1

U.S. Environmental Protection Agency, "Mid-Atlantic Superfund, Virginia Superfund Sites," http://www.epa.gov/reg3hwmd/super/va.htm

Virginia Advisory Committee to the United States Commission on Civil Rights, Unequal Justice: African Americans in the Virginia Criminal Justice System, 2000.

Virginia Coalition for Open Government, website.

Virginia, Constitution of, 1776.

Virginia, Constitution of, 1830.

Virginia, Constitution of, 1850.

Virginia, Constitution of, 1870.

Virginia, Constitution of, 1902.

Virginia, Constitution of, 1971.

Virginia Department of Corrections, various materials from website.

Virginia Department of Criminal Justice Services, Virginia's Peculiar System of Local and Regional Jails,

Spring 2010, linked from http://www.dcjs.virginia.gov/publications/list.cfm?#V

Virginia Department of Environmental Quality, Solid Waste Managed in Virginia During Calendar Year 2010.

Virginia Department of Historic Resources, "Women's Suffrage in Virginia, Early Efforts," http://www.dhr.virginia.gov/SlideShows/CrenshawHouse/CrenshawSlide4.html

Virginians for Alternatives to the Death Penalty, website, http://www.vadp.org/

Virginia General Assembly, "An act to repeale a former law makeing Indians and others ffree," 1682, http://www.vagenweb.net/hening/vol02-24.htm

Virginia General Assembly, "An Act concerning Servants and Slaves," October 1705.

Virginia General Assembly, "An act to amend and reduce into one act the several laws for regulating and disciplining the militia and guarding against invasions and insurrections," October 1785.

Virginia Historical Society, "The Civil Rights Movement in Virginia: Danville," Online Exhibit, http://www.vahistorical.org/civilrights/danville.htm

Virginia Historical Society, "Old Virginia: The Pursuit of a Pastoral Ideal," Online Exhibit, http://www.vahistorical.org/ov/resurgence.htm

Virginia Joint Legislative Audit and Review Commission, Review of Virginia's System of Capital Punishment, December 10, 2001.

Virginia Public Access Project, website, http://www.vpap.org

Virginia State Board of Education, Virginia School Laws: Codified for the Use of School Officers by Order of the State Board of Education, Superintendent Public Printing, Richmond, 1915.

Virginia Women's Cultural History Project, A Share of Honour":Virginia Women 1600-1945, Virginia State Library, 1984. FAV!!

Washington, Booker T., Up From Slavery, A.L. Burt Publishing, 1900.

Watson, Justin, The Christian Coalition, Palgrave Macmillan, 1997.

Weatherford, Jack, Native Roots: How the Indians Enriched America, Ballantine Books, 1992.

Weaver, Richard M., The Southern Tradition At Bay: A History of Postbellum Thought, 1968, Republished by Regner Gateway, 1989, 1989 edition edited by George Core and M.E. Bradford.

Webb, Senator Jim, "Diversity and the Myth of White Privilege," Wall Street Journal, July 2010.

Webber, Thomas L., Deep Like the Rivers: Education in the Slave Quarter Community, 1831-1865, WW Norton, 1978.

Wesley, John, Thoughts Upon Slavery, 1774.

White, Deborah Gray, Ar'n't I a Woman? Female Slaves in the Plantation South, W.W. Norton, 1999 Revised Edition.

White, Henry Alexander, Robert E. Lee And The Southern Confederacy 1807-1870, G.P. Putnam's Sons, 1897.

Whitehead, A .C., Two Great Southerners: Jefferson Davis and Robert E. Lee, American Book Co., 1912.

Whitfield, Theodore, Slavery Agitation in Virginia 1829-1832, The Johns Hopkins University Press, 1930, re-published 1969 by Negro Universities Press..

Whitlock, Rosemary Clark The Monacan Indian Nation of Virginia: The Drums of Life, University of Alabama Press, 2008.

Whittier, John Greenleaf, "War Time," poem, 1861.

Wills, Garry, Negro President: Jefferson and the Slave Power, Houghton Mifflin, 2003.

Wilson, Joan Hoff, "The Illusion of Change: Women and the American Revolution," in The American Revolution: Explorations in the History of American Radicalism, Alfred Young, editor, Northern Illinois University Press, 1976.

Wilson, William J., "What Shall We Do With the White People?," published in 1860 in Anglo-African Magazine.

Winchester Star, "Out of the Past... from the archives of the Winchester Star," March 12, 2012.

Wood, Karenne and Diane Shields, The Monacan Indians: Our Story, Monacan Indian Nation, 1999. FAV!!

Woolman, John, Journal, 1772. FAV!!

Yates, Larry, "On Webb's 'Diversity and the Myth of White Privilege'", Alt.Daily, Norfolk, Virginia, July 27, 2010, http://www.altdaily.com/features/news/opinion-news/on-webbs-%E2%80%9Cdiversity-and-the-myth-of-white-privilege%E2%80%9D.html

Yates, Larry, "A Response to David Horowitz' 'Ten Reasons Why Reparations for Blacks is a Bad Idea for Blacks - and Racist Too,'" in The Debtors, edited by Ida Hakim, Caucasians United for Reparations and Emancipation, 2005.

Zigler, J. Hiram, The Virginia Farm Bureau Story, Virginia Farm Bureau Services, 1982.

15473666R00330

Made in the USA
Charleston, SC
05 November 2012